Rethinking Existentialism

Rethinking Existentialism

Jonathan Webber

OXFORD
UNIVERSITY PRESS

Great Clarendon Street, Oxford, OX2 6DP,
United Kingdom

Oxford University Press is a department of the University of Oxford.
It furthers the University's objective of excellence in research, scholarship,
and education by publishing worldwide. Oxford is a registered trade mark of
Oxford University Press in the UK and in certain other countries

© Jonathan Webber 2018

The moral rights of the author have been asserted

First Edition published in 2018

All rights reserved. No part of this publication may be reproduced, stored in
a retrieval system, or transmitted, in any form or by any means, without the
prior permission in writing of Oxford University Press, or as expressly permitted
by law, by licence or under terms agreed with the appropriate reprographics
rights organization. Enquiries concerning reproduction outside the scope of the
above should be sent to the Rights Department, Oxford University Press, at the
address above

You must not circulate this work in any other form
and you must impose this same condition on any acquirer

Published in the United States of America by Oxford University Press
198 Madison Avenue, New York, NY 10016, United States of America

British Library Cataloguing in Publication Data
Data available

Library of Congress Control Number: 2018932578

ISBN 978-0-19-873590-8

Links to third party websites are provided by Oxford in good faith and
for information only. Oxford disclaims any responsibility for the materials
contained in any third party website referenced in this work.

To Suzi, Tilly, and Lettie

Preface

This book argues for a new conception of existentialism through comparative analyses of the works of Simone de Beauvoir, Albert Camus, Frantz Fanon, Maurice Merleau-Ponty, and Jean-Paul Sartre published between 1942 and 1952. The term was first given a definition by Beauvoir and Sartre in autumn 1945, when they appropriated it as a brand name for their shared philosophy. It has since been applied very widely, naming an extensive and loosely associated assortment of thinkers and artists. By returning to the original definition and analysing closely the works that it describes, as well as some related works published by their friends and colleagues, we can articulate a precise understanding of existentialism that allows us to identify new contributions it can make to philosophy, psychology, and psychotherapy.

The first chapter presents the book's overall argument. The second advances a new analysis of *The Outsider* as premised on a conception of human nature that shows Camus to already be opposed to existentialism in this novel. The third argues that Merleau-Ponty's argument against Sartre's theory of freedom fails, in part because he does not identify his target precisely enough. The fourth argues that Beauvoir's novel *She Came To Stay* dramatizes her disagreement with Sartre over the metaphysical structure of human freedom. Beauvoir considers freedom to require that projects gather inertia as they are pursued, whereas Sartre considers it to require that projects never have inertia of their own. The fifth develops this disagreement through reconsidering Freud's influence on the development of existentialism and the distinction between Beauvoir's form of existential psychoanalysis in *The Second Sex* and Sartre's in *Being and Nothingness*. The sixth argues for a new interpretation of Sartre's play *Huis Clos*, arguing that it dramatizes Sartre's view that it is bad faith, the commitment to a specific mistaken view of human existence, that condemns interpersonal relations to being fundamentally conflictual.

At this point, the book turns from the theory of human being at the core of existentialism to its cultural and ethical aspects. The seventh chapter argues that Sartre's first attempt to ground a cultural theory in his existentialism fails because it inevitably relies on an entirely unexplainable coincidence. For this reason, the chapter argues, Sartre abandoned his initial theory of freedom in favour of accepting Beauvoir's theory, first detailing his revised form of existentialism in *Saint Genet* in 1952. The eighth chapter argues that Fanon's *Black Skin, White Masks*, published in the same year, is fundamentally a work of existentialism that rests on the sedimentation of projects. The ninth outlines Fanon's and Sartre's eudaimonist ethical arguments for the existentialist virtue of authenticity, which is the recognition of and respect for the true structure of human existence. The tenth argues that Beauvoir has presented an important argument for a categorical imperative of authenticity.

These details and intricate interrelations of these central texts of twentieth-century European thought have been obscured by the loose classification of a much broader range of thinkers and artists as existentialists. Uncovering these details allows us to pinpoint more precisely the philosophical theories that Beauvoir and Sartre indicated as defining existentialism in 1945, the differences between them, and the reason why Sartre had adopted Beauvoir's within a few years. The theory that they both settled upon and that Fanon also articulated in 1952, therefore, should be considered definitive of existentialism. The final chapter sketches some contributions that existentialism so understood can make to our understanding of the functioning of the mind, the development of personal character and cultural identity, the grounding of ethical and moral values, and the purposes and practice of psychotherapy.

Contents

Acknowledgements   xiii

1. What Is Existentialism?   1
   1.1 Existence Precedes Essence   2
   1.2 Freedom and Sedimentation   4
   1.3 Existentialism and the Mind   7
   1.4 The Influence of Other People   9
   1.5 Existentialism Is A Humanism   11
   1.6 Existentialism and Existential Philosophy   14
   1.7 Rethinking Existentialism   16

2. Why Meursault is an Outsider   20
   2.1 Meursault's Emotional Strangeness   21
   2.2 Meursault as a Hero of Absurdity   24
   2.3 Meursault's Progress   26
   2.4 The Origin of Meursault's Estrangement   29
   2.5 A Literary Moral Cogito   32
   2.6 Why Camus is not an Existentialist   33
   2.7 Human Nature and Political Violence   35

3. Freedom and the Origins of Reasons   39
   3.1 Freedom, Reasons, and Projects   40
   3.2 The Field of Meaning   42
   3.3 The Field of Reasons   45
   3.4 The Phenomenology of Reasons   47
   3.5 Freedom Without Reasons   50
   3.6 Projects as Commitments   52
   3.7 Sartre's Progress   54

4. Why Xavière is a Threat to Françoise   57
   4.1 A Metaphysical Novel   58
   4.2 The Sedimentation of Projects   60
   4.3 Why Xavière is a Threat to Françoise   63
   4.4 Beauvoir's Critique of Sartre   65
   4.5 The Weight of Situation   67
   4.6 Why Beauvoir is an Existentialist   70
   4.7 The Ambiguity of Influence   73

5. Psychoanalysis and the Existentialist Mind   76
   5.1 The Puzzles of Repression and Resistance   77
   5.2 In the Shadow of Descartes   79

5.3	Sartre's Critique of Freud	82
5.4	Bad Faith in a Unified Mind	84
5.5	A Psychoanalysis of Radical Freedom	87
5.6	Sedimentation and the Origins of Gender	89
5.7	A Psychoanalysis of Sedimented Projects	91

6. Why Inez is not in Hell — 95
   6.1 A Metaphysical Play — 96
   6.2 An Ambiguous Situation — 98
   6.3 Why Inez is an Insider — 100
   6.4 Garcin's Progress — 103
   6.5 Why Garcin is in Hell — 105
   6.6 The Sins of Garcin and Estelle — 107
   6.7 Bad Faith and Other People — 109

7. Sedimentation and the Grounds of Cultural Values — 113
   7.1 Two Varieties of Existentialism — 114
   7.2 Cultural Values Without Sedimentation — 116
   7.3 Bad Faith as the Ground of Cultural Values — 118
   7.4 The Project of Bad Faith — 121
   7.5 An Unexplainable Coincidence — 123
   7.6 Sedimentation in the Formation of Saint Genet — 125
   7.7 Existence Precedes Sedimentation — 128

8. Black Skin, White Masks — 131
   8.1 Eclecticism and Theoretical Unity — 132
   8.2 The Dilemma of White Masks — 134
   8.3 The Strategy of Negritude — 137
   8.4 The Inferiority Complex — 139
   8.5 Black Skin and the Dilemma of White Masks — 142
   8.6 Why Fanon is an Existentialist — 145
   8.7 An Existentialist Eclecticism — 148

9. From Absurdity to Authenticity — 151
   9.1 The Origins of Absurdity — 152
   9.2 Why Irony is not the Answer — 154
   9.3 Eudaimonism and the Renunciation of Racial Essence — 156
   9.4 Eudaimonism and the Threat of Despair — 159
   9.5 Eudaimonism and the Trouble with Other People — 161
   9.6 Why Eudaimonism is not the Answer — 163
   9.7 From Eudaimonism to Existentialist Humanism — 166

10. The Imperative of Authenticity — 169
    10.1 A Kantian Moral Cogito — 170
    10.2 From Subjective Ends to Objective Value — 173
    10.3 A Reconstruction of Beauvoir's Argument — 175
    10.4 The Commitments of Beauvoir's Argument — 178

10.5 The Value of a Potential Means	181
10.6 Why the Argument could not be Shorter	183
10.7 An Existentialist Kantian Ethics	185
11. The Future of Existentialism	**188**
11.1 Authenticity and Social Conditioning	189
11.2 Sedimentation as Character Formation	192
11.3 Empirical Psychology and the Philosophy of Mind	194
11.4 Stereotypes and Implicit Bias	197
11.5 Existentialist Psychotherapy	199
11.6 Refining Existentialism	202
11.7 Existentialist Reading and Writing	205
Bibliography	209
Index	223

Acknowledgements

This book was drafted during a period of research leave funded by Cardiff University's School of English, Communication, and Philosophy and by an AHRC Research Leadership award (AH/M008614/1). Much of the work was completed in the libraries of the University of Bristol, thanks to a Visiting Fellowship, and in two nearby cultural institutes, Boston Tea Party and Little Victories. I am grateful to all these organizations for facilitating this project.

The book's arguments were developed through a Beauvoir workshop, a Fanon workshop, and a psychotherapy conference all funded by the AHRC award in 2015–16, work-in-progress seminars at Bristol and Cardiff in 2015, and a talk given at the Oxford Post-Kantian Philosophy Seminar, University of Wolverhampton Royal Institute of Philosophy lecture series, and Freedom Through Materiality conference at Radboud University in 2017. These ideas were first formulated and later refined through the undergraduate French Existentialism module at Cardiff University in 2013 and 2016. I am grateful to the participants of these for insightful discussions and searching questions.

I am especially grateful to Sarah Bakewell, Marc Bevan, Joanna Burch-Brown, Darshan Cowles, Matt Eshleman, Anthony Everett, Lewis Gordon, Christina Howells, Kathleen Lennon, Rafe McGregor, Seiriol Morgan, Katherine Morris, Sebastian Nye, Richard Pearce, Stephanie Rennick, Simon Robertson, Stella Sandford, Alison Stone, and Alessandra Tanesini for responses to chapter drafts, to two anonymous reviewers for Oxford University Press for detailed comments on the whole draft, and to Peter Momtchiloff for his patience and sound judgment.

I hope to have put all of this to good use. After all, as Sartre pointed out, what is important is not what people make of us, but what we ourselves make of what they have made of us.

1
What Is Existentialism?

When the term 'existentialism' became popular across the arts and culture of the Western world in the aftermath of the Second World War, it was defined by its most prominent exponents as a substantive philosophical position. But articles and books on existentialism written in English ever since have eschewed precise philosophical definition, instead identifying it loosely as a movement of thinkers concerned with certain questions and to some extent providing similar answers. These works disagree over which questions and which thinkers to include, which makes it difficult to see why there is thought to be any genuine movement here at all. Categorizing diverse thinkers together in this way, moreover, has distorted the reception of their ideas by foregrounding superficial similarities at the expense of deeper disagreements and features that do not easily fit this classification. This is why scholars specializing in a particular thinker who is regularly classified as existentialist often reject that classification, as indeed have some of those thinkers themselves.

Although there are good historical reasons for this divergence of writings about existentialism from the substantive philosophical definition set out at its inception, these reasons do not provide any theoretical justification for preserving this divergence. In this book, we will recover and delineate a sharper and more fruitful understanding of existentialism by returning to that original definition and using it to analyse the works it describes. This allows us to identify a range of new contributions that classical existentialism can make to the theoretical models currently being developed and deployed in social psychology, philosophy of mind, moral philosophy, cultural theory, and psychotherapy, and conversely to release the potential for each of these areas of inquiry to enrich one another by refining this existentialist perspective.

As originally defined by Simone de Beauvoir and Jean-Paul Sartre, existentialism is the ethical theory that we ought to treat the freedom at

2 WHAT IS EXISTENTIALISM?

the core of human existence as intrinsically valuable and the foundation of all other values. It is grounded in a theory of what it is to be human that Sartre summarized in the slogan 'existence precedes essence'. One central aim of this book is to argue that Beauvoir and Sartre did not agree on the details of this theory when they first defined existentialism in 1945 and that by 1952 Sartre had found good reason to adopt Beauvoir's position. This agreed theory of freedom is therefore the canonical existentialist understanding of human existence. A second central aim is to argue that the ethical theory built on this theory of human being holds there to be both a moral imperative and strong eudaimonist reasons to respect human freedom. This conception of existentialism will be sketched in more detail across the first five sections of this chapter, before we return to its relation to the loose category usually found in articles and books on existentialism and the advantages of this sharper conception of existentialism.

1.1 Existence Precedes Essence

Beauvoir and Sartre gave the term 'existentialism' its first clear definition in autumn 1945, during a sustained campaign of public talks, interviews, and articles designed to promote their shared philosophy and influence the new cultural and political shape of post-war France, a campaign Beauvoir later described as 'the existentialist offensive' (FC: 46).[1] Sartre gave his version of this definition in his public lecture 'Existentialism Is A Humanism', subsequently published as a book. Beauvoir gave hers in 'Existentialism and Popular Wisdom', an article in the third issue of the journal *Les Temps Modernes*, of which they were both founding editors. Sartre's lecture was delivered off the cuff in a chaotic situation, which is perhaps why he manages to confuse his core message with the apparently incoherent set of claims that there are Christian existentialists, existentialism is a form of atheism, and it does not matter for existentialists whether God exists (EH: 20, 27–30, 53–4). Beauvoir's article is more

---

[1] Works by Beauvoir, Camus, Fanon, Freud, Heidegger, Merleau-Ponty, and Sartre are indicated by title abbreviations rather than dates, to avoid confusion between first publication and edition used. Full details are given in the Bibliography by surname and abbreviation, listed for each author in order of first publication. All other works are cited in the usual way, by publication date of edition used.

carefully considered and composed. But it was overshadowed by Sartre's lecture, partly because Sartre was already a major literary and philosophical figure by the time it was delivered whereas Beauvoir was not yet.

Sartre's use of a series of memorable images and phrases is perhaps also why his lecture had the greater impact. His slogan 'existence precedes essence' is intended to convey the idea that a human being has no inbuilt essence, no innate or fixed personality, but instead creates their essence, or their character and outlook, through the values and projects they choose to adopt (EH: 22). Beauvoir, by contrast, presents the same claim without any handy soundbite to summarize it (EPW: 211–13). Sartre's slogan, however, can seem paradoxical. For if this is indeed the defining feature of human being, then it might seem to be an essence that already defines any person prior to their adopting any values or projects. It seems contradictory, moreover, to claim that any qualities of a person resulting from their own undertakings could be essential to that person, given that the person is thereby claimed to have existed without those qualities.

These difficulties can be dispelled by distinguishing different senses of the term 'essence'. In one sense of the term, the essence of a kind of thing is the set of properties necessary for an item to be that kind of thing. One might argue, for example, that a specific chemical composition is essential to water, so that nothing could be a sample of water unless it had that chemical composition. In a closely related sense, the essence of a particular item is the set of properties without which that item could not exist. It has been argued, for example, that it is essential to a particular person that they are the product of a specific act of conception, such that the very same person could not have been conceived by different parents or on a different occasion (Kripke 1980: 112–13). But neither of these senses captures the inherently teleological conception that Aristotle originally developed under the name 'to ti ên einai', a phrase so obscure that his Roman translators invented the word 'essentia' for it to have a Latin equivalent.

In this teleological sense, an essence is the relational property of having a set of parts ordered in such a way as to collectively perform some activity (Witt 2013). A house is essentially a shelter for living in, in this sense, which is why it has walls and a roof for keeping out wind and rain, doors for entrance and exit, windows for light, and so on. Likewise, the eye is essentially an organ for seeing, which is why it has a retina, a lens, an optic nerve, and so on, arranged in a specific way. Sartre is applying this sense of 'essence' to human individuals. His claim is that a person does not have an inbuilt set of values that they are inherently structured to pursue. Rather, the values that shape a person's behaviour result from the choices they have made. A person's essence is formed of their chosen values. Moreover, this sense of 'essence' does not entail that the properties it identifies are necessary features of their bearer. The qualities that explain a particular person's behaviour need not be necessary aspects of that person, so could have been adopted by that individual and could later change.

Sartre makes it clear that his view that people do not have inbuilt essences, in this sense of the term, entails that there is no such thing as human nature, no inbuilt essence common among people. Humans are neither inherently selfish nor inherently altruistic, for example. This contrasts sharply with the view of human existence that Albert Camus develops in his philosophical and literary writings. Camus is often classified as an existentialist despite explicitly refusing the label in a newspaper interview during the existentialist offensive, declaring that 'Sartre and I hold nothing in common and refuse to be held responsible for one another's debts' (IJD: 345). 'The whole effort of German thought has been to substitute for the notion of human nature that of human situation', he wrote in his notebooks soon afterwards, and 'existentialism carries that effort even further', whereas 'like the Greeks I believe in nature' (CN: 136). Indeed, as we will see in Chapter 2, he was already developing a theory of human nature and its grounding of ethical value profoundly opposed to existentialism before he even met Sartre and Beauvoir and well before the existentialist offensive.

1.2 Freedom and Sedimentation

Despite their apparent agreement during the existentialist offensive, however, Sartre and Beauvoir disagreed profoundly about the structure of human agency and freedom at this stage of their careers. Sartre's version of the view that existence precedes essence was that an individual's outlook, the reasons for action that they encounter and respond to in the world, depend on the values at the heart of their projects, which have no weight or inertia of their own but are sustained only by the agent's continuing tacit or explicit endorsement of them. This is his conception of 'radical freedom', as we will see in more detail in Chapter 3. If an agent chooses to abandon a project, then that project will offer no resistance to the agent overcoming it. Projects are interwoven into a holistic complex, however, which means that the cost of abandoning a project may be that one needs to abandon or significantly modify many other aspects of one's value system. But one retains absolute freedom, according to Sartre's initial conception of existentialism, to do this.

Beauvoir, by contrast, understands the repeated endorsement of a project to increase both that project's own inertia and the influence it exerts over the individual's cognition. This sedimentation of projects is central to her theory of the social conditioning of gender in *The Second Sex*, published a few years after the existentialist offensive. As we will see in Chapter 4, it is also central to the plot of her debut novel *She Came To Stay*, published in the same year as Sartre's *Being and Nothingness*, two years before the existentialist offensive. Indeed, the plot of that novel dramatizes her disagreement with Sartre over the nature of freedom: the contrast between her theory of sedimentation and his view that a project has no inertia of its own is reflected in the attitudes of the novel's two central characters to their shared life project. Beauvoir holds that freedom consists in the ability to commit to projects that shape one's outlook and that sedimentation is essential to such commitment. She recognizes that projects can become so embedded that they can be difficult to overcome, but her position does entail the ongoing freedom to alter or reject any project through the sedimentation of new values.

The concept of sedimentation is also central to the philosophy of Maurice Merleau-Ponty, who had been friends with Beauvoir and Sartre since they were students together in the late 1920s (Bakewell 2016: 109–14). Their philosophical influences and interests were so closely aligned during the subsequent two decades that they are aptly described as 'a phenomenological trio' developing their ideas through collective critical discussion (Howells 2011: 24). Merleau-Ponty's primary focus, however, is on the individual's understanding of the world, the knowledge that allows us to navigate and manipulate our surroundings. Beauvoir and Sartre focus primarily on an individual's motivations, the values we endorse and the reasons for action that we encounter as a result. Merleau-Ponty's central conception of sedimentation is the process by which our knowledge of our spatial environment, our social context, and our bodily abilities becomes embedded in the intuitive understanding that we rely on for action. This contrasts with Beauvoir's emphasis on the sedimentation of the values that motivate us through shaping the reasons for action that we experience in our environment.

Merleau-Ponty does mention, briefly and tentatively, a kind of sedimentation of motivation. This is towards the end of his critique of Sartre's theory of freedom in the closing chapter of his *Phenomenology of Perception*, published in 1945. This critique, however, does not properly address Sartre's theory, as we will see in Chapter 3, partly because Merleau-Ponty does not recognize the distinction between our experience of the meanings of items in our environment and our experience of the reasons for action that our environment presents. The sign that tells us to keep off the grass, to borrow one of Sartre's famous examples, has a linguistic meaning and in some cultural contexts may imply some sanction if it is disobeyed. But whether it is a reason to keep off the grass, according to Sartre, depends on one's own values. If you value defying authority for its own sake, you may well experience the sign as a reason to stride across the lawn. It is perhaps Merleau-Ponty's own focus on the sedimentation of knowledge that leads him to mistakenly read Sartre as holding that the meanings we encounter, rather than the reasons, are dependent on our projects.

Since existentialism is defined by the idea that existence precedes essence, the idea that we have freedom over the values that organize our experience and so shape our behaviour, Merleau-Ponty's rejection of this theory of freedom means that he is not an existentialist, despite his commitment to the philosophical methodology of phenomenology that drives both Beauvoir's and Sartre's forms of existentialism. This is not to say that his analyses of the phenomenology of experience have nothing to offer existentialism. To the extent to which they are consistent with the idea of freedom over the values that shape the reasons we encounter, existentialism could be enriched by integrating them into its conception of the human individual. But his refusal of any metaphysical conception of freedom as the individual's ability to shape their own essence, as this was defined in the previous section, classifies his overall conception of agency as standing in opposition to existentialism, just as the idea of human nature that Camus endorses excludes his theory of human existence from the existentialist camp.[2]

---

[2] Throughout this book, I use the term 'metaphysical' interchangeably with 'ontological' to describe anything pertaining to the structures of being. Thus, metaphysical freedom is

1.3 Existentialism and the Mind

One of the interests that Beauvoir and Sartre share with Merleau-Ponty is in the foundations of psychology. All three aim to identify the essential structures of the mind through their phenomenological analyses. Indeed, this is the central aim of Sartre's philosophical publications prior to *Being and Nothingness* and motivates the development of the philosophical methodology he then deploys to develop his existentialism (Webber forthcoming). This central aspect of existentialism is obscured by the common practice of classifying Martin Heidegger's *Being and Time* as a paradigmatic existentialist work, despite Heidegger's rejection of the label. For his concern in that book is ultimately with the nature of being, which he approaches through the analysis of human being (which he calls *Dasein*) that almost fills the whole work. Heidegger argues that this investigation of human being is distinct from any empirical study of psychology and must proceed without presuppositions grounded in psychological vocabulary (B&T: §§ 9–10). If we see this as a paradigmatic work of existentialism, then we are likely to conclude that existentialist concern with the structures of human being eschews any psychological ambition.

However, once we have understood what Sartre means by the claim that 'existence precedes essence' it becomes clear that his analysis of the structures of human being requires some theory of the essential structures of the mind. Sartre does tend to avoid using the term 'mind', which carries connotations of an inner realm distinct from the world (see e.g. IPPI: 5–7). But the structures of consciousness, perception, imagination, affectivity, deliberation, and rational motivation are central to his analysis of human being. Beauvoir's publications of the 1940s are likewise replete with theories of desire, emotion, perception, and motivation. Since a person's 'essence', in Sartre's famous slogan, is the overall structural property that explains their behaviour, it must organize the experience of the world that motivates that behaviour. Moreover, since this

---

the freedom that existentialists consider human agents to have over their own being, their ability to shape their own essence. This is despite the distinction that Sartre draws towards the end of *Being and Nothingness* between 'ontology' as the analysis of the structures of being and 'metaphysics' as the study of the aetiology of those ontological structures, a study which he declares that he has not undertaken (B&N: 639). So far as I know, Sartre's definition of 'metaphysics' here is entirely idiosyncratic. My use in this book is normal in contemporary anglophone philosophy.

essence consists in the person's projects, which have values at their core, the claimed freedom over this essence must consist in their ability to alter the values that structure their experience of the world. The central ontological claim of existentialism therefore requires a model of psychological functioning, with the difference between Beauvoir's and Sartre's versions of that claim requiring different versions of this model.

The reason Heidegger gave for rejecting the label 'existentialist' was that the terms '*existentia*' and '*essentia*' carry metaphysical connotations that derail any serious attempt to think clearly about the ontology of human being or about being in general, so the slogan 'existence precedes essence' must be rejected (LH: 157–8). This does not reflect the outlook of *Being and Time*, however, which was written two decades earlier. In that book, Heidegger does proclaim 'the priority of "*existentia*" over "*essentia*"' (B&T: § 9). The resemblance between this phrase and Sartre's slogan is part of the reason why Heidegger is often classified as an existentialist. But this resemblance is merely superficial. Heidegger is not using '*essentia*' here in the Aristotelian sense that Sartre uses 'essence'. Rather, he means the properties necessary for something to be a member of a specific kind: to be the kind of thing that we are is to have a specific kind of existence, which he then describes as structured by concern about one's own existence. Heidegger's phrase, therefore, is not a claim about the motivations behind an individual's behaviour and so does not commit him to a model of psychological functioning.

It is because their shared theory of the ontological structure of human being does entail a model of psychological functioning that both Sartre and Beauvoir develop detailed critiques of Sigmund Freud's psychoanalysis. Both want to retain some of his central insights into human development and motivation while rejecting his theoretical framework as mistakenly mechanistic. Their forms of psychoanalysis are not merely applied spin-offs from a purely ontological existentialism. Rather, they explicitly develop their varieties of existentialism as theories standing in the Freudian psychoanalytic tradition, as we will see in Chapter 5. This is usually obscured in analyses of existentialism. This is partly because Sartre places his argument against Freud's theory of the unconscious much earlier in *Being and Nothingness* than his more nuanced and more positive engagement with Freud's work more broadly. It is also partly because Beauvoir's work has often been read as applying existentialist theory rather than as central to the development of that philosophy itself.

But this relation between existentialism and Freudian psychoanalysis has also been obscured by the tendency of French philosophers from the 1950s onwards to endorse the broad Freudian tradition while exaggerating the distance between their own positions and existentialism (Crowell 2012: 11–13). Together with the absence of Freud from lists of existentialist thinkers, this has led to existentialism being understood as an entirely separate intellectual tradition that provides an alternative to psychoanalysis. Beauvoir and Sartre in fact both preserve much that they find valuable in Freud's work. Their objection is only to his theories of the structure of the mind, which they argue are incoherent and fail to explain the phenomena they are designed to explain. Their own analyses of psychological functioning are designed in part, as we will see in Chapter 5, to explain these phenomena properly, while giving substance to the claim that existence precedes essence.

1.4 The Influence of Other People

The disagreement between Beauvoir and Sartre over the nature of human freedom becomes clearer and more significant when we consider the role of other people in the formation of an individual's essence. Beauvoir's theory of the sedimentation of projects affords her sophisticated account of the role that other people's expectations, encouragements, and admonishments play in the development of gender, as we will see in Chapter 5. A child is effectively directed to adopting projects that are built on the required values for their gender and that incorporate the required understanding of gender roles. As these projects are continually reaffirmed throughout childhood, the values and social knowledge they enshrine become more deeply sedimented. This accounts, according to the theory of *The Second Sex*, for the differences in values and outlook found between men and women, for the widespread acceptance of gender norms, and indeed for their perpetuation by those in whom they have become sedimented. Each individual is able to subject this conditioning to critical appraisal and to reject it, but its social prevalence mitigates against this. The influence this conditioning has over a person's cognition cannot be removed except through another process of sedimentation.

Sartre's initial form of existentialism precludes this account of other people's influence over an individual's essence. Instead, according to this version of existentialism, what matters is how one responds to the views that other people have of oneself. There are three possible responses. One is to affirm one's fundamental freedom, thereby resisting the idea that another person has correctly identified some fixed personality trait that one has. Sartre considers this response of authenticity to be rare. The other two responses are more common, he claims, and are both forms of bad faith. One is to accept the other person's view of oneself as correctly identifying some fixed personality trait that one has. But this is not satisfactory if the other person's view of oneself conflicts with one's own. The other is to deny that one possesses this trait by instead affirming some contrary fixed personality trait. But this leads to a conflict between one's self-image and the image of oneself that other people express. It is this view that the project of denying one's freedom over one's essence ineluctably produces conflict that Sartre summarizes in his famous line that 'Hell is... other people!' (HC: 223), as we will see in Chapter 6.

Beauvoir's theory of sedimentation provides a clear explanation of how specific values can become prevalent among an identifiable cultural group, such as women or men. Sartre's theory, however, cannot provide such an explanation. This failure is demonstrated, as we will see in Chapter 7, in his attempt to explain the origins of Jewish culture through this theory in his book *Anti-Semite and Jew*, written at the time of the existentialist offensive. The central values of Jewish culture, he argues in that book, are a response to a climate of anti-Semitic hostility. This hostility takes the form of a thoroughly negative image of a fixed Jewish personality. The authentic response of affirming one's own freedom is rare, argues Sartre, though he does not say why. The usual response, he thinks, is to affirm fixed personality traits that are contrary to the anti-Semite's image of Jewishness. This is a form of bad faith, since it asserts a fixed personality. The values common among Jewish people, argues Sartre, are those endorsed as though they were a fixed Jewish nature, the values that are directly contrary to the anti-Semite's image of Jewish people.

Much has been written about the shortcomings of this as a theory of the origins of Jewish culture, or indeed of any culture. One central failure of the theory is indicative of a deep problem with Sartre's initial form of existentialism. This is the failure to explain why authenticity is rare and bad faith is widespread. After all, if this is true then it too is a cultural phenomenon that stands in need of explanation and Sartre's theory has no resources to explain it. Sartre's initial form of existentialism can ground a cultural theory, therefore, only on the basis of this unexplainable coincidence. It seems to be for this reason, as we will see in Chapter 7, that Sartre soon abandoned his initial form of existentialism and adopted Beauvoir's theory of the sedimentation of projects. By the time he wrote *Saint Genet*, first published in 1952, he had accepted her view that projects increase in inertia and influence as they continue to be endorsed. This is the theory he employs to explain the formation of Genet's character and aesthetic taste.

In the same year, Frantz Fanon published his *Black Skin, White Masks*, which argues that racial identity is formed through the sedimentation of projects, that there are no genuinely fixed personality traits of individuals, and that the problems of racism can be overcome only by gradually overcoming those sedimented projects and removing the social structures conducive to them. This is, as we will see in Chapter 8, a profoundly existentialist work. Fanon's theory of racialization has much in common with Beauvoir's theory of gender. Fanon does not seem to have read Beauvoir, but does develop his theory through critical analysis of Sartre's initial form of existentialism, alongside many other influences. We should accept, therefore, that this theory common to Beauvoir, Sartre, and Fanon in 1952, according to which an individual's Aristotelian essence is formed through the sedimentation of their projects chosen in their specific social environment, is the canonical form of the theory that existence precedes essence.

1.5 Existentialism Is A Humanism

Existentialism is more than that metaphysical and psychological theory, however. Existentialism is the ethical theory that we ought to treat this structure of human existence as intrinsically valuable and as the foundation of all other values. This is what Sartre means by calling existentialism a form of humanism (EH: 51–3). The virtue of authenticity is this respect for the structure of human agency. The existentialist claim that the reasons we experience in the world are dependent on values we endorse and could replace has often been taken to preclude any objective ethics. After all, what objective reason could there be to adopt some specific value if all reasons are grounded in values that are already endorsed? But this thought is too quick. There are two potential answers that can be drawn from the history of moral philosophy. One is the Aristotelian eudaimonist answer that some evaluative outlooks are conducive to one's own flourishing whereas others are not. The other is the Kantian answer that the very structure of human agency as pursuing values endorsed by the agent entails the imperative to respect that structure of agency as objectively intrinsically valuable. Varieties of both answers can be found in the works of Sartre, Beauvoir, and Fanon during the existentialist heyday.

One kind of existentialist eudaimonist argument for authenticity concerns the significance of one's own projects. If there are no objective values, then the values that we build our lives around, the ones at the core of our projects, are not genuinely valuable at all. Although this thought might seem to lead to the nihilist view that nothing really matters at all, the existentialist conception of human being entails that nihilism cannot really be accepted. For our existence just is one of pursuing projects with values at their core. What the lack of objective value would ground, according to existentialism, is absurdity: the inescapable pursuit of some set of values that do not really matter. Anxiety is the recognition that the commitments that I have built my life around have their significance for me only because I endorse them. In one form, argues Sartre, this sense of the absurdity of our projects can lead to a debilitating despair. From the perspective of authenticity, however, my projects are genuinely valuable as expressions of the structure of human existence, so long as they are consistent with respecting that structure as objectively valuable. Authenticity, therefore, precludes this absurdity, anxiety, and despair.

A second kind of existentialist eudaimonist argument for authenticity concerns the effects of bad faith on one's self-image and relations with other people. Fanon's analysis of the alienation caused by racialization suggests an argument of this kind. The idea that some groups of people are naturally superior and others naturally inferior requires that people have fixed personalities, or natures. Internalizing the idea of natural superiority and inferiority causes not only the public problems of racial discrimination, but also the more private problems of self-loathing that are central to Fanon's analysis. Authenticity therefore precludes these problematic ideas of race. Sartre argues for the similar, though more general, conclusion that the assumption that people have fixed personalities necessarily poisons our relations with one another, as we are inevitably threatened by any dissonance between our self-image and the image of ourselves that other people express. But this is threatening only if we see these images as competing accounts of our fixed personality structures, he argues, so authenticity removes this structure of conflict from our interpersonal relations.

These eudaimonist arguments, as we will see in Chapter 9, are insufficient to establish that we all ought to adopt the virtue of authenticity. Their considerations in favour of authenticity are not overriding, but may be outweighed by competing considerations grounded in an agent's existing projects. Anxiety, despair, alienation, or interpersonal conflict may simply be prices worth paying, according to a particular agent's overall value system, for outcomes that would have to be forgone were they to embrace authenticity. Moreover, these eudaimonist arguments seem only to support the conclusion that we should recognize that existence precedes essence. Not one of them seems to support the further conclusion that we should respect this structure of human existence. Indeed, we might be all the more effective at oppressing other people if we have a better understanding of them. These are ethical arguments in the broad sense of 'ethical', therefore, which labels the concern with how best to live our lives. But they do not support the claim that we are morally required to accept that existence precedes essence. Still less do they place any moral restrictions on behaviour beyond accepting this.

Beauvoir does argue for the strictly moral imperative to recognize and respect the structure of human existence irrespective of our prior commitments across her short book *Pyrrhus and Cineas*, published in 1944. Her argument aims to derive this imperative from the structure of human existence itself. In this regard, it resembles Immanuel Kant's argument across his *Groundwork for the Metaphysics of Morals* that the structure of human agency entails the imperative to treat human agency itself as objectively valuable. Beauvoir's argument, however, does not rely on the conception of rationality or the related metaphysical system that Kant's argument relies on. Instead, her argument aims to derive the imperative of authenticity from an opening premise which, according to the theory that existence precedes essence, everyone must accept. This is the premise that some ends are valuable. Beauvoir's sophisticated argument cannot be summarized easily. But, as we will see in Chapter 10, it deserves serious consideration in contemporary moral philosophy. That it has not been identified before is perhaps partly due to the tendency to read thinkers classified as 'existentialist' focusing on their perceived shared interests and ideas while Kant is not included in that classification.

1.6 Existentialism and Existential Philosophy

Classical existentialism, therefore, is the theory that existence precedes essence and that we ought to treat this structure of human being as intrinsically valuable and the foundation of other values. In its canonical form, the claim that existence precedes essence is the view that an individual's behaviour is to be explained through the set of projects that they have pursued and that have become sedimented. The requirement to treat this as intrinsically valuable and the foundation of other values could be grounded in eudaimonist ethical considerations or in a categorical moral imperative, which are not mutually exclusive grounds. The canonical works of existentialism are therefore Beauvoir's works up to the early 1950s, Sartre's position in *Saint Genet*, and Fanon's *Black Skin, White Masks*, though Sartre's earlier works should also be classified as a variety of existentialism. Other theories of human behaviour should be classified as forms of existentialism only if, or only to the extent that, they agree with this ethical theory or either version of the ontology of human existence that it is grounded in. This is true of later works by Beauvoir, Sartre, and Fanon, as well as works by other authors or by artists.

As we have already seen, this requires excluding Heidegger and Camus from the category of existentialist thinkers. Since these two are almost always included in that category despite their protestations, this might seem unacceptably revisionary. We should first consider, however, exactly why they were included in the loosely identified category of existentialism in the first place. It seems that there were two pressures that led to existentialism being defined in that way. One is that Beauvoir and Sartre began the trend of classifying other thinkers as existentialists despite those other thinkers never having identified themselves as such. Beauvoir and Sartre did this, moreover, in the very works in which they defined existentialism during the existentialist offensive. Beauvoir cites Camus approvingly, for example, though stops short of explicitly calling him an existentialist (EPW: 209; see also P&C: 92–3). Sartre does explicitly classify Heidegger as an existentialist (EH: 20).

The other pressure was the general hostility to European thought in post-war anglophone philosophy (Barrett 1958: ch. 1). At the same time, existentialism enjoyed huge cultural popularity (McBride 2012). In this climate, categorizing diverse European thinkers together in courses entitled 'existentialism' was an important strategy for getting their works analysed and applied at all. Two anthologies set the curriculum for such courses. Walter Kaufman's introduction to his anthology described existentialism as 'not a philosophy but a label for a set of widely differing revolts against philosophy' and 'not a school of thought nor reducible to any set of tenets' (1956: 11). Robert Solomon ended the introduction to his anthology by claiming that 'nothing could be further from the existential attitude than attempts to define existentialism, except perhaps a discussion *about* the attempts to define existentialism' (1974: xix). These comments might appear to disavow any unity to each anthology, but they only strictly deny any shared substantive claims or theoretical methods.[3]

What these anthologies gather together are works with a certain set of philosophical interests, ones that were being sidelined by anglophone philosophy in those decades. The same set of philosophical interests justifies Beauvoir and Sartre in identifying various thinkers as fellow travellers, despite those thinkers not subscribing to the theory that existence precedes essence. This set of interests, moreover, is aptly described collectively as existential inquiry. This is an interest in analysing the structures of the specific kind of existence that humans enjoy,

---

[3] The anthologies cement an already existing tendency, which had been begun by Beauvoir and Sartre in referring to other thinkers in their descriptions of existentialism (see e.g. Blackham 1952). Their editors' comments are then echoed in the ideas that existentialism is defined by 'opposition to the philosophical tradition' (Dreyfus 2006: 137), cannot be clearly and objectively defined because it is opposed to the traditional philosophical aim of providing such definitions (Macquarrie 1972: 13; Earnshaw 2006: 1–2), comprises no substantive tenets but only a set of interactions between thinkers addressing certain concerns (Grimsley 1960: 1–11; Reynolds 2006: 2–3), and can be understood only as a 'family resemblance' category (Warnock 1967: 1–2; Macquarrie 1972: 14–18; Flynn 2006: 8; Joseph et al. 2011: 3–4). David E. Cooper offers a rare substantive definition of existentialism as those philosophical views of Heidegger and Sartre found regularly among the existentialist family (1990: 6–10; 2012: 28–30). All these characterizations result in some way from attempting to discern common ideas of thinkers already identified as existentialists. If the arguments of this book are right, there is now much to be gained by distinguishing the broad existential inquiry in which these thinkers are all engaged from the substantive theory that provided the original definition of existentialism.

which is taken to differ from the kind of existence had by other natural objects and by artefacts. Indeed, it was Heidegger more than anyone else who had made this a central philosophical inquiry in European thought by the time of the existentialist offensive. In identifying this philosophical focus, he reserved the term 'existence' (*existenz*) for the kind of being had by humans and coined the term 'existentialia' (*Existenziale*) as a collective term for the structures of this kind of being (B&T: § 9). These structures include embodiment, location in a material environment, position in a social realm, the sense of one's own mortality, and inherent temporality.[4]

It was Heidegger's 'existential analytic of *Dasein*' developed across *Being and Time* that brought the idea of existential philosophy, the analysis of the various existentialia and the relations between them, into the centre of European thought in the first half of the twentieth century. But this is not to say that existential thought had been invented at this time. Careful attention has been paid to the structures of human life by secular and religious thinkers, and occasionally movements, at various times and places in the history of Western thought. Writers identified by Beauvoir and Sartre as fellow travellers and those anthologized by Kaufman and Solomon have been existential thinkers in this sense. If all that is required to count as an existential thinker is that one's work analyses some dimension of human being, then there have been a great many existential thinkers. If we use the term more narrowly to describe thinkers aiming to produce systematic philosophical understandings of human existence, then far fewer thinkers qualify. Either way, Kierkegaard and Heidegger are landmark figures.

1.7 Rethinking Existentialism

It is very unfortunate, therefore, that the terms 'existentialist' and 'existential' are so often used interchangeably. Existentialism is an ethical theory that rests on a substantive and sophisticated existential philosophy.

---

[4] Heidegger did not invent this restricted concept of existence. Søren Kierkegaard had used the Danish word '*existenz*' in this way almost a century earlier. Karl Jaspers had used the term in a related way, to label the kind of being that he recommends that we adopt, a few years before Heidegger published *Being and Time*. But neither Kierkegaard nor Jaspers was particularly influential on European thought until after Heidegger had established the idea of existential philosophy.

It is a theory of how best to live that rests on a specific analysis of the distinctive structures of human existence. The pressures that led to the conflation of these two terms no longer apply. The philosophies of Beauvoir and Sartre are now sufficiently articulated and substantiated that there is no need to rely on their occasional agreements with other existential theories to explain or argue for them. The anthologies edited by Kaufman and Solomon enabled the growth of anglophone scholarship of European philosophy, which has developed to the point where it no longer has anything to gain from the loose categorization established by those anthologies. To continue to categorize that set of thinkers together as existentialists can now only distort our understanding of them, masking deep differences behind superficial similarities and occluding each thinker's specific influences and ambitions.[5]

We should instead rethink existentialism by returning to its original definition, the one that Beauvoir and Sartre offered during the existentialist offensive. This facilitates a sharper focus on the philosophical theories that defined the term. It brings into perspective a range of psychological aspects of the existentialism of Beauvoir and Sartre that are at least rare in the field of existential philosophy. It affords, for example, a clearer view of Freud's influence on the development of existentialism, an influence generally occluded by the standard practice of contrasting Freudian psychoanalysis with existential theory.[6] And

[5] Jeff Malpas (2012: 293) also argues that we should distinguish between 'existential' and 'existentialist'. But he assumes that 'existential' should be used in its ordinary English sense, which pertains to anything at all that there is, instead of identifying the specific meaning with which it is used by Kierkegaard and Heidegger. As a result, he uses 'existentialist' to refer to the concern with the structures of human existence, leaving him with no term for the substantive ethical theory that Beauvoir and Sartre articulated as the original definition of 'existentialism'.

[6] Two further influences on this aspect of existentialism that have been occluded by the focus on the loose category of existential thought are ancient Stoicism and seventeenth-century French philosophy. Beauvoir and Sartre both cite Stoic philosophers regularly. In a magazine portrait of Sartre published as part of the existentialist offensive, Beauvoir compares his philosophy to that of 'the Stoics of old whose ethics he loves' (JPS: 231). Yet this influence on existentialism has received only scant critical attention. The influence of early modern French thought on Sartre and Beauvoir has recently been highlighted by Kate Kirkpatrick (2017: 48–73) and Susan James (2003) respectively. Kirkpatrick's close attention to Sartre's student curriculum grounds her innovative analysis of the French theological influences on his existentialism. Further use of Kirkpatrick's approach could well draw out a significant degree of influence of the central interests and conceptual repertoire of modern French philosophy and literature on the development of existentialism more generally.

it brings into clear relief the difference between Beauvoir's and Sartre's versions of existentialism at the time of the existentialist offensive and the reasons for Sartre's eventual adoption of Beauvoir's version. This in turn allows us to identify the underlying theoretical unity of Fanon's *Black Skin, White Masks*, which has previously seemed to vacillate between existential philosophy, psychoanalysis, and cultural theory. Once we have a clear view of the unity of these forms of inquiry within the existentialism that Beauvoir and Sartre agree upon by 1952, that is, we can see that Fanon's book published that year is also a work of existentialism.

This rethinking also brings into clearer view the status of existentialism as an ethical theory. For ethics is not an essential aspect of existential philosophy itself. Iris Murdoch's comment that Sartre's biography of Genet is a work of ethics in 'paradoxical guise' is instructive (1957: 676). For this is paradoxical only if we expect ethics to provide moral constraints and prescriptions. We would then be at least surprised to find a work on ethics detailing the life of a professional thief. But as the broader concern with how best to live, ethics necessarily involves clarification of how people develop the commitments, preferences, tastes, and other characteristics that shape their lives. The development of existentialist psychoanalysis is therefore integral to the ethical programme of existentialism. But this does not mean that existentialism eschews the idea of morality. Focusing on the works of Beauvoir and Sartre of this era as equally expressive of existentialism allows us to see that Sartre's comments in *Existentialism Is A Humanism* endorsing an imperative of authenticity that does not reflect any of his own works are best understood as referring to the Kantian moral argument of Beauvoir's *Pyrrhus and Cineas*, published the previous year.

The advantages of abandoning the old loose category of existential thinkers in favour of a clear focus on the works that first defined existentialism are not limited, however, to sharpening our understanding of those works and their development. For the aspects of these works that have been obscured by this broader categorization contain insightful analyses that can make useful contributions to current theoretical debates. A wide range of research in empirical psychology is currently converging on the idea that evaluative attitudes, individual goals, and ways of classifying individuals become gradually more firmly embedded in a person's cognitive system as they are repeatedly used, increasing their influence over that person's thought and behaviour. The central existentialist idea of sedimentation establishes a useful perspective on this process, its role in the development of personal character, and the problems caused by unendorsed biases and stereotypes. Together with the existentialist arguments for the virtue of authenticity, this theory of human being can ground sophisticated contributions to social psychology, philosophy of mind, moral philosophy, cultural theory, and psychotherapy, as we will see in Chapter 11.

For this reason, the analysis of existentialism across this book is resolutely philosophical rather than historical or biographical. It is concerned with identifying and assessing the philosophical arguments published across a ten-year period, 1942–52. These analyses will show why Camus and Merleau-Ponty are not existentialists, though they are both existential thinkers, and will thereby clarify existentialism itself and identify the deep reasons for the bitter political disputes that famously ended each of their friendships with Beauvoir and Sartre. These chapters will clarify the Freudian influence on existentialism, the reasons why Sartre abandoned his initial version of existentialism in favour of Beauvoir's, and the underlying existentialist unity of Fanon's analysis of racialization. They will identify existentialism's central eudaimonist arguments for the virtue of authenticity and their limitations before detailing Beauvoir's argument for a categorical moral imperative of authenticity. These analyses have all already been sketched in this chapter. But their details are essential if they are to make significant contributions to current debates about ethics and the mind. So they are articulated more precisely across the next nine chapters, before a final chapter indicates some potential contributions they could make to current thought.

2

Why Meursault is an Outsider

There was always an air of ambivalence about the relationship between Camus and Sartre, long before it exploded into the famous row in the pages of *Les Temps Modernes*, after which the two never spoke to one another again. They had become friends in 1943. A year earlier, Sartre had written a highly praising review of *The Outsider*, though Camus had been irked by its occasional critical remarks. A few years before that, Camus had written glowing, though not uncritical, reviews of Sartre's novel *Nausea* and collection of short stories *The Wall*. They recognized one another as kindred spirits, though their literary styles were very different. This engendered a rivalry that was perhaps exacerbated by Sartre being older than Camus and having achieved a higher academic distinction at a more prestigious university. For many years, there was a competitive flavour to their regular socializing together. They both endorsed violent resistance to the Nazi occupation, but Sartre was simultaneously more keenly in favour of it and less engaged in it than his younger rival.

How deeply did their differences run? The development of their personal and political disagreements has been very well charted (Aronson 2004; Martin 2012). But these chronological treatments leave unclear whether the thinkers grew apart as a cumulative effect of myriad disagreements over daily political developments, or whether those disagreements had been driven all along by a deeper contrast between their philosophical outlooks. This chapter will argue that even before Camus had met Sartre and Beauvoir, he already disagreed with the idea that they were soon to identify as the fundamental tenet of their existentialism. When he denied in an interview in 1945 that he was an existentialist, this was not merely an attempt to assert his independence as a literary figure. He was reporting, entirely correctly, that he did not share their view of human existence at all.

It is this disagreement that grounds their political differences right from the start. The ferocity of the public dispute in 1952 reflects not only years of growing antagonism since the war, but also a mutual incomprehension. Perhaps being too eager to view Camus as one of them, Beauvoir and Sartre had failed to notice the deep contradiction between the outlook expressed in his published works and their existential philosophy. This explains why they viewed his political development as a betrayal and why he was bemused that they took his political thought so personally. To see this, we need to turn first to the novel that Camus published in the year before he met Sartre and Beauvoir. For in *The Outsider* he already commits himself to views that are incompatible with the central claim of their existentialism.

2.1 Meursault's Emotional Strangeness

It is easy to overlook just how strange Meursault, hero of *The Outsider*, really is. The emphasis in the second part of the novel on his resistance to the demands of his society can give the impression that he is an outsider only in the sense that he does not conform to the prevailing local social norms. But he is more deeply estranged than that. For he seems to depart not merely from arbitrary social conventions, like the expected forms of dress or speech on a particular occasion. What stands out most about him, particularly in the first part of the novel, is his lack of the kind of inner emotional life that seems to run deeper than mere convention. He even lacks any understanding of why people find this odd. Not only does he seem happy and carefree the day after his mother has died, for example, but he finds it puzzling that his girlfriend Marie is surprised by this. Not only is he entirely emotionless at his mother's funeral, which is not merely a matter of contravening a social expectation, but he does not understand why people find this lack of emotion on this occasion strange.

His strangeness is not limited to this kind of awkward social interaction. He is generally quite passive, often responding to events wholly reactively, without any independent motivation of his own. He agrees to marry Marie only because she asks him to, for example, and says that he would have accepted the same invitation from any other woman. He becomes Raymond's friend and even agrees to commit perjury to defend him, explaining this only by saying that he had no reason not to. This passivity is not, however, a pervasive feature of his character. At the first fateful encounter on the beach, it is Meursault who suggests to Raymond a plan to fight their opponents. In the second part of the novel, Meursault actively resists the demands that his society makes of him through the legal process and through the prison chaplain.

In a preface written in 1955, Camus emphasizes this resistance to social pressure, saying that Meursault is condemned because 'he refuses to lie'. How can this be correct, given that Meursault readily commits perjury? 'To lie', Camus continues, is 'above all to say more than is true, and, as far as the human heart is concerned, to express more than one feels' (PS: 336). Meursault does indeed refuse to pretend to have feelings that he doesn't have. Even when his lawyer makes it clear that he could save his life by saying that he controlled his feelings at the funeral, Meursault replies: 'No, because it isn't true' (TO: 69). But this refusal to lie about his feelings does not fully account for his strangeness. If the trial jury could have understood his lack of tears in the context of his particular relationship with his mother, then why did Meursault not explain the context? Is it that Meursault does not understand other people sufficiently well to make his lack of tears at the funeral comprehensible to them? Or does his relationship with his mother not explain that lack of tears? When we consider his feelings more generally, it becomes clear that both of these suggestions are correct.

For his indifference to his mother's death is matched by his indifference to the death of the man he murdered. It is echoed in various places in the story, including his attitudes to the sadness of his mother's friends at the wake and to Marie's feelings when she asks whether he loves her and will marry her. These are not instances of an overall lack of feelings. Meursault enjoys the pleasures of sea, sun, and sex, and is pained by boredom, effort, and the demands that people make of him. Neither is he unable to perceive other people's feelings. He tells us that Marie was annoyed, Perez cried tears of frustration and anguish, Raymond was pleased, Salamano was angry with his dog, the journalist betrayed no discernible emotion, the prosecutor was furious, and the judge passed sentence bearing an expression of respect. What is strange about Meursault is that other people's feelings do not register with him as reasons for his own actions. The callous tenor of his narration across the novel is due to a lack of emotional engagement with the feelings of other people.

This same lack explains why his experience is so superficial. This is not, as has been suggested, because he lives without reflecting on his experiences and reasons for action (Solomon 2006: 15–17; Sherman 2009: 64–76). He does reflect, often giving poetic phenomenological descriptions of his experience. He tells us, for example, that as soon as he had committed the murder, 'I realized that I had destroyed the natural balance of the day, the exceptional silence of a beach where I had once been happy' (TO: 63).[1] Indeed, his whole account of the scene leading up to the murder is replete with his reflective thoughts at the time on his experience and his reasoning about what to do. Throughout the novel, he reflectively reports his feelings of being judged by the various people he deals with (King 1964: 61). When he says earlier that he does not think anything of Raymond beating up a prostitute except that it is interesting, he is reporting the findings of his reflection: that he has no emotional response to the obvious distress of the victim. When he responds to Marie's question of whether he loves her by saying that he does not think so and anyway it does not mean anything, this is because love essentially involves an affective concern for the other person's happiness and well-being. Reflecting on his feelings, Meursault does not find anything distinctive about the ones he has towards Marie. Indeed, his total lack of emotional engagement with the feelings of other people means that he cannot even understand what it would be to love someone.

Meursault's failure to understand why people are surprised by his apparent indifference to his mother's death is also the result of this lack of genuinely other-directed emotion. He cannot empathize with their perception of his behaviour because their perception is shaped by their pervasive experience of a kind of emotional response that he has

---

[1] Quotations are from the recent translation by Sandra Smith, because this is the first single edition available across the English-speaking world. This translation, however, has sacrificed some of the lyrical fluidity of Meursault's reflective descriptions that was best rendered into English by Joseph Laredo in his edition now out of print. The murder scene ends, for example, with Meursault telling us that *'c'était comme quatre coups brefs que je frappais sur la porte du malheur'*, which Smith renders as 'it was as if I had rapped sharply, four times, on the fatal door of destiny' (TO: 64), where Laredo has 'it was like giving four sharp knocks at the door of unhappiness'. Perhaps more importantly, Smith's translation implies that Meursault has been attacked before he fires the shots: 'All I could feel was the sun crashing like cymbals against my forehead, and the knife, a burning sword hovering above me. Its red-hot blade tore through my eyelashes to pierce my aching eyes' (TO: 63). The original is clear that the 'burning sword' (*épée brûlante*) here is not the knife itself, but the light reflected by the knife, *'le glaive éclatant jaillie du couteau toujours en face de moi'*, 'the dazzling spear still leaping off the knife in front of me' as Laredo puts it. Meursault is dazzled by light, not knifed in the eyes.

never had. This is evident in his response to his lawyer's question of whether he grieved at the death of his mother: 'I replied that I'd rather lost the habit of analysing my emotions' (TO: 69). This contrasts sharply with his response to the chaplain soon afterwards that he knows without having to reflect on it that he does not believe in God. In the case of his emotions towards his mother, he seems unaware that he is expected simply to know whether he felt grief, not to find out by analysing himself. He seems equally unaware that his audience have a good intuitive understanding, grounded in their own experience of emotions that he lacks, of what it is to love someone. This failure of empathy extends to his narration of the novel itself. Camus has succeeded in writing a story told by someone who does not empathize with the reader. This is at the heart of why Meursault seems so strange. He does not see that the reasons he is giving for his behaviour are not ones that his audience can empathize with. Why has Camus done this?

2.2 Meursault as a Hero of Absurdity

One of the rhetorical purposes of *The Outsider* is to present an extended example of a hero of absurdity, giving a richer case study than is possible within the confines on the philosophical essay on absurdity, *The Myth of Sisyphus*, that Camus published very soon after the novel and intended to be read alongside it. When he introduces his 'heroes of absurdity' in that essay, Camus tells us that 'an example is not necessarily an example to be followed', and so these 'illustrations are not, therefore, models' (MS: 66). It is each character's affirmation of absurdity itself that Camus means to extol, rather than the particular way that they each make this affirmation. Meursault's particular affirmation of absurdity is bound up with his strange lack of emotional concern for other people, but this lack of concern is not itself explained by his role as a hero of absurdity. To see this, we need first to consider exactly what Camus meant by claiming that life is absurd.

For it is misleading to claim simply that for Camus 'the absurd arises because the world fails to meet our demands for meaning' (Nagel 1971: 721). That would leave open the option of escaping absurdity by ceasing to make those demands. There would be two ways of doing this. One would be to accept that everything is meaningless. The other would be to seek the meaning of our lives within our lives themselves, rather than out there in the world. Camus does not recommend either of these ways of trying to escape absurdity. Rather, he argues that they are both equally futile because he considers absurdity to be an inescapable structure of the human condition (MS: 34).

The problem of absurdity arises, according to Camus, because we have a fundamental 'appetite for the absolute and for unity' that could be satisfied only by reducing the world, indeed the whole universe, to 'a rational and reasonable principle' that would make it fully intelligible (MS: 51). It is the mismatch between this fundamental appetite and the meaninglessness of the world that generates the problem; 'what is absurd is the confrontation of the irrational and the wild longing for clarity whose call echoes in the human heart' (MS: 26). This absurdity 'lies in neither of the elements compared; it is born of their confrontation' (MS: 33). Camus does not consider this problem to concern only our relation with the world. The same problem, he argues, is found when we turn our attention towards ourselves. My own mind and motivations fail to meet my expectations of rational intelligibility, with the effect that I cannot understand myself any more than I can understand the rest of the universe. 'This very heart which is mine will forever remain indefinable to me'; I will always remain 'a stranger to myself' (MS: 24).

Should we read this instance of 'stranger' (*étranger*), echoing the title of the novel, as alluding to the underlying principle of Meursault's character? The failure to understand oneself, Camus has claimed here, is an essential aspect of the human condition. So it cannot itself be what sets Meursault apart, what makes him an outsider. But it is consistent with this that what marks Meursault out is that he has understood that one can never really make sense to oneself, that one's own mind and motivations will evade any search for rational order within them, and so has relinquished the aim of making sense of himself. We have seen that it is not exactly right to say that he does not reflect on his experiences and motivations. But his reflections do have a strangely detached flavour, as though the experiences and motivations he is describing are not really his own or even all those of one person. Might this be explained by his acceptance that the search for order and meaning here, as in the world at large, will be fruitless?

Since he is intended as a hero of absurdity rather than as an illustration of one of the futile strategies for evading absurdity, Meursault cannot have given up on the search for rational meaning. In order to affirm the absurd, he must affirm the longing for intelligibility as well as the ineluctable frustration of that longing. He must be understood as living 'without appeal' to anything that would resolve this problem (MS: 53). Camus describes Don Juan as a hero of absurdity, for example, because he understands the rituals of love as expressing a basic human desire for a particular kind of stable order that can never be satisfied and affirms both the desire and its disappointment. This is why, according to Camus, Don Juan loves each woman that he loves 'with the same passion and with his whole self' even though he loves countless women and his love never lasts long (MS: 67). How, then, does Meursault affirm the demand for rational intelligibility in himself and in the world? What is his distinctive way of combining this with affirming that neither the world nor one's own mind can meet that demand?

2.3 Meursault's Progress

The answer to this question can be approached through a puzzle that arises at the end of the novel. It is clear that Meursault has learned something through the trial and his preparation for execution, but it is difficult to see exactly what he has learned. He tells us in the final few pages that 'I'd been right, I was still right, I had always been right' to think that 'nothing mattered' and yet he also tells us that 'standing before this symbolic night bursting with stars, I opened myself for the first time to the tender indifference of the world' (TO: 127, 129). How can he be accepting 'the tender indifference of the world' for the first time if he has always, or at least for many years, correctly maintained that nothing matters? One way to read this is to see his final acceptance of the indifference of the world as his relinquishing the search for intelligible meaning that has animated the novel up to this point. That search was manifested in a form of nihilism, his insistence against the preferences of his society and at considerable cost to himself that nothing really matters.

For this insistence is not the only possible response to the lack of objective meaning. Another response would be to conclude that it simply does not matter what anyone thinks of the meaning of the world or the meaning of their own minds. Meursault could have affirmed the objective lack of rational order by going along with the expectations and beliefs of his society, whatever they happen to be. He could simply acquiesce in other people's conceptions of order, indifferent to whether those conceptions are correct. After all, someone in his position might reason, it does not matter whether or not one goes along with social expectations. But to take this option would have been to deny his own drive for intelligible meaning in favour of simply accepting whatever meanings his society provides. So this is not an affirmation of absurdity, but one of the strategies for evading absurdity. Rather than take this option, Meursault affirms his drive for order by insisting that the lack of objective order should be recognized and accepted. It is not his nihilism itself, but his insistence on it in defiance of social norms, that expresses his drive for order. He is a hero of absurdity precisely because he resists the social pressure to act as though there is some rational intelligibility to life, even as he accepts that there is no objective meaning that would require him to resist this.

This allows us to make sense of Meursault as a hero of absurdity across the novel up to the final few pages, but nevertheless it does not seem quite right. One difficulty is that on this reading the tale culminates in Meursault giving up his insistence on nihilism, relinquishing his role as a hero of absurdity rather than maintaining it to the bitter end. If he is going to relinquish this role, then why does not he not attempt to do so in a way that would save his life? A second difficulty is that it is unclear just why Meursault should relinquish this role at this point. Clearly, he has had some sort of epiphany. But just what is it that he has come to realize and why? It cannot be some revelation of a deep truth about human existence if it leads only to his abandoning his truthful insistence that nothing really matters. A third difficulty is that this reading leaves Meursault's lack of emotional engagement with the feelings of others entirely incidental to his role as a hero of absurdity, whereas the centrality of this lack to the structure of his character and to the development of the narrative suggest that it is integral to the theme of absurdity and its resolution in his final thoughts.

We can solve these problems by refining this reading of the novel in a way that integrates Meursault's emotional strangeness into his way of being a hero of absurdity. For the first part of the novel, Meursault affirms his drive for intelligibility by insisting on nihilism. His honesty about his own feelings is part of his affirmation of the lack of objective order in the world and in his own mind, including the order his society expect to find in him, while his general dishonesty is part of the nihilism that he sees as part of that lack of objective order. What he learns across the second part of the novel, however, is that there is a source of ethical value despite the lack of intelligibility that confronts our demands for meaning. Ethical value has its source, he comes to realize, in the emotional concern for other people that arises naturally for everyone else, but which he lacks.

His first glimpse of this comes after the director and caretaker of the home where his mother died have testified at the trial about his lack of emotion on the day of the funeral. He tells us that he could feel the indignation and hatred felt towards him by the jury and other people in the courtroom and 'for the first time, I realized I was guilty' (TO: 94). But at this point, he does not yet understand what his guilt amounts to. He tells us that he agreed with every word of the prosecutor's summary of the case against him, which essentially set out Meursault's emotional strangeness, but that 'I didn't understand how the qualities of an ordinary man could be turned into overwhelming proof of his guilt' (TO: 105). It is only through his confrontation with the priest in the final chapter that Meursault comes to realize that these are not the qualities of an ordinary man. 'Why should the death of other people or a mother's love matter so much?', he yells at the priest (TO: 127). He takes the lack of objective meaning to imply that these things do not matter, because there can be no objective reason why they should. But through his outburst, he finally comes to see that these things matter simply because people care about them.

Part of what he comes to understand is that he is not alone in his guilt. He realizes that everyone in the story is guilty of making the error of thinking that ethical value must be grounded in some intelligible meaning of life, such as religion or the structure of society. For everyone else, this takes the form of mistaking the value that is actually grounded in their own hearts for an objective order of the universe. Because he lacks the relevant kind of emotions, Meursault has made the error in the opposite direction: he has been right about the lack of objective meaning, but wrong to insist on nihilism. Where he previously thought of everyone else as guilty of false belief in objective morality, he now has a deeper understanding of their mistake, one that implicates his own form of this guilt. Rather than affirm his drive for order by insisting on nihilism, he now affirms it by accepting that ethical value is grounded in a kind of emotion that he lacks but that people generally do have. And he affirms the general human longing for order in his diagnosis of the mistaken moral objectivism of his society, all the while affirming the lack of an objective meaning to life. He remains a hero of absurdity, but has come to see the absurd in a new light.

2.4 The Origin of Meursault's Estrangement

Meursault's emotional strangeness is therefore integral to his role as a hero of absurdity. His role is not simply to embrace absurdity, but to disclose the source of ethical value in an absurd universe. It is a mistake, therefore, to think that *The Outsider* is intended merely to dramatize the absurd attitude described in *The Myth of Sisyphus*, or to draw out its implications without attempting to move beyond it (Foley 2008: 13). The novel builds on the essay in presenting a view of the falsehood of nihilism against the backdrop of absurdity. The naturalistic picture of ethical value that it presents is rather unfocused and suggestive. It falls very short of the precision that we would expect from a philosophical treatise in metaethics and no clear rational argument for it can be formulated on the basis of the novel. But this is exactly what we should expect. Our demands for rational intelligibility are frustrated, Camus argues in *The Myth of Sisyphus*, because life is always richer and more nuanced than any abstract thought designed to capture it. Literary fiction can present 'in images rather than in reasoned arguments' what is 'simultaneously relative and inexhaustible knowledge' (MS: 92–3).

The novel does convey, however, with admirable concision, a sophisticated position on the origin of ethical value. For the logic of its narrative carries implications about the origin of the emotional engagement with other people that it presents as grounding that value. To see this, we need to consider Beauvoir's comments on this novel. For she recognizes that Meursault's strangeness consists in his lack of emotional concern for other people, arguing that this lack results from his lack of projects. 'Only I can create the tie that unites me to the other', she wrote in her analysis of *The Outsider*, and 'I create it from the fact that I am not a thing, but a project' (P&C: 93). Her comments here are ambiguous. They can be read either as an analysis of Meursault as Camus has presented him or as showing how some aspects of his behaviour could illustrate her own view of the origins of emotional concern for other people. How plausible are these comments as a reading of the novel itself?

If we read *The Outsider* this way, then Meursault's strangeness echoes Roquentin's strange experiences in Sartre's first novel *Nausea*, published four years earlier. Towards the end of this novel, Roquentin experiences the world and his own body as mere matter lacking any structure or meaning beyond those he chooses to give them. The tram seat he is sitting on 'could just as well be a dead donkey, for example, swollen by the water and drifting along, belly up on a great grey river', the bark of the chestnut tree could be 'boiled leather' partly covered in rust (N: 180, 183). 'Things have broken free from their names', he tells us, and 'the diversity of things, their individuality' has 'melted, leaving soft, monstrous masses, in disorder' (N: 180, 183). These experiences come about after the only projects that have given Roquentin's life any shape and purpose, his relationship with Anny and his work on a biography of the obscure M. Rollebon, have come to an end. This is the first draft of an idea that will become in *Being and Nothingness* the core of Sartre's existentialism. At this stage, the idea is that the meanings we experience in the world are manifestations of the projects that we choose to engage in. Sartre develops this into the theory that while the meanings of objects are generally socially determined, the value we experience them as having depends on our projects (see 3.2–3.3 below).

Should we accept Beauvoir's presentation of Meursault as exemplifying the idea that our emotional concern for other people is likewise grounded in our own projects? Camus was inspired by *Nausea* in writing *The Outsider*. In his review of *Nausea* four years before *The Outsider* was published, Camus praised its philosophical ambition in presenting the absurdity of life through literary images, but argued that it fell short of the ideal of philosophical literature in its reliance on Roquentin explaining and analysing his experiences rather than allowing their philosophical import to shine through the experiences themselves (SN: 199–202). These comments are echoed in the comments in *The Myth of Sisyphus* that philosophical reasoning abstracts away from the rich nuance of existence that can be preserved in literary treatments of the same themes. However, this does not show that Camus is merely attempting to provide a superior literary presentation of the ideas dramatized in *Nausea*.

Moreover, there is little direct textual evidence to support Beauvoir's comments as a reading of *The Outsider*. It is true that Meursault drifts along in life without any sense of direction. He does not seem to mind whether he marries Marie. When offered the opportunity to move to

Paris, he says that he does not care one way or the other. 'When I was a student, I was very ambitious about having a career', he tells us, but 'when I had to give up my studies, I realised quite soon that none of that sort of thing mattered very much' (TO: 45). But he does not lack commitments. He loves the pleasures of the sea and the sun and prefers not to give them up for a career move to Paris. His indifference about marrying Marie is part of his general lack of emotional engagement with other people. Perhaps most importantly, the whole story rests on his commitment to absurdity, along with his consequent commitments to nihilism and to honesty about his own feelings. These are the projects that structure his life through the novel.

Rather than assimilating Meursault's emotional strangeness to the experiences recorded by Roquentin towards the end of *Nausea*, we can make more sense of *The Outsider* by understanding this strangeness as essential to Meursault's personality. The prosecutor is right to declare that Meursault 'had no soul, and that nothing that makes a man human, not a single moral principle, could be found within' him (TO: 106). Meursault's lawyer disagrees, but the positive characteristics he lists do nothing to counter the prosecutor's point that Meursault lacks the foundations of ethical value. Earlier, the magistrate had recognized that Meursault's nihilism was a manifestation of a deep deficiency at the core of his being, which more than Meursault's atheism is why the magistrate calls him 'our Antichrist' (TO: 75). This too is why Meursault ends the novel feeling that the indifferent universe is 'so like me, so like a brother, in fact' (TO: 129). He has realized that his lack of emotional engagement with other people's feelings sets him apart by making him as coldly indifferent as the universe whose lack of meaning he had always recognized. Meursault is an outsider not only to his society, but to everyone, including his readers.[2]

---

[2] This reading agrees with Philip Thody's claim that Meursault has been explicitly and reflectively aware of the absurdity of life throughout the novel, but does not agree with his conclusion that at the end of the novel Meursault simply comes to publicly proclaim what he had always privately held (1961: 37–41). Brian Masters is right to criticize this conclusion as failing to account for Meursault's progress from apathetic, insensitive bewilderment to passionate, assertive lucidity (1974: 32). Thody and Masters, however, both fail to see that Meursault's progress here concerns his understanding of the place of ethical value in an absurd life.

2.5 A Literary Moral Cogito

Meursault's emotional strangeness is thus essential to his being the hero of absurdity that he is, but is not essential to embracing absurdity itself. There is no contradiction between affirming the human longing for rational intelligibility, accepting that this longing is inevitably frustrated, and being emotionally concerned with the feelings of others. Indeed, the rhetorical purpose of the novel is precisely to recommend this combination of attitudes. Camus has presented this tale told by a narrator who cannot empathize with the reader to bring us to recognize that we possess what Meursault lacks. The novel is a literary attempt at the moral cogito that Camus dedicates *The Rebel* to elucidating (TR: xi–xii, 10). Just as Descartes employed his famous cogito argument to secure the foundations of knowledge against the backdrop of universal doubt, Camus intends this novel to isolate the ground of ethical value through a meditation on absurdity, thereby demonstrating both the falsity of nihilism and the error that leads to it.

Meursault comes to this conclusion gradually across the second part of the novel, with its culmination in his rant at the priest. He later feels as though 'this great release of anger' has 'purged me of evil, emptied me of hope' (TO: 129). This feeling is right. It has purged him of his nihilism, since he now recognizes the ground of ethical value. He has realized that everyone shares in the guilt of mistaking the value grounded in their emotions for an objective meaning. But we should not conclude that he has recognized an existential guilt common to us all (Sherman 2009: 78). On the contrary, he has recognized an existential guilt that is uniquely his: that he is constitutionally incapable of the kind of emotion that others possess and that grounds ethical value. His recognition that he is incapable of it, rather than simply currently lacking it, explains why he has been emptied of hope: there is no prospect of rehabilitation. It is this recognition of his status as an existential outsider that would be confirmed by crowds at the guillotine shouting their hatred of him.

Although this literary moral cogito operates through Meursault's progress and final understanding itself, the purpose of presenting it is to bring about a parallel recognition in the reader. Although his honest indifference may bring us to admit to ourselves that we do not always care about the lives of others as we think we should, Camus wants to convey a more significant point. He tells us this story to bring us to realize the deep significance of our natural emotional engagement with the feelings of other people. Camus indicates this purpose in his famous description of Meursault as 'the only Christ we deserve' (PS: 337). This is hardly perspicuous, given the wide variety of interpretations of that title provided by two thousand years of Christian theology. But it does seem that he thinks that reflecting on the story of Meursault can save us from the fundamental evil of nihilism, just as Christians might think that the life of Jesus saves us from sin, or at least that our reflection on it can do.

None of this is meant to deny that Camus intended to convey some more immediate social critiques through this novel. At least two aspects of the injustice of the trial and sentencing embody important moral concerns. One is the stark presentation of the lack of value accorded to the lives of the colonized people by the French colonial system. The novel has been criticized for denying the reality of colonialism by presenting the court as treating the colonized equally with the colonizers (O'Brien 1970: 26). But this criticism overlooks that the court is far more concerned with whether Meursault cried at his mother's funeral than with his murder of one of the colonized people, and that the murder victim remains nameless throughout the trial. The court treats the murder merely as an occasion to try, convict, and sentence Meursault for being an outsider. This embodies the novel's second social critique. It is not exactly right to say that Meursault is condemned for his lack of social conformity (Foley 2008: 14, 17–22). It is rather because he lacks the capacity for emotional engagement with the feelings of others. He is rejected and condemned to death on grounds of an inherent part of his personality. These two specific moral aspects of the novel contribute to the larger ethical message that Camus intends it to bring. It is through our emotional engagement with these fictional characters that we come to see the moral problems here, if we do see them. It is through their commitment to their imagined objective meanings of life that Meursault's society fails to see these problems.

2.6 Why Camus is not an Existentialist

We can now see more clearly why Camus did not want to be classified as an existentialist. He rejected the label at the time of what Beauvoir calls 'the existentialist offensive', during which Beauvoir and Sartre published articles and books and gave lectures and interviews using the term 'existentialism' to expound their shared philosophy. Their core claim that 'existence precedes essence' is the idea that each person's set values are ultimately the result of their own choices. Although, as we will see in more detail in Chapters 4 and 5, Beauvoir and Sartre disagreed at this point over the precise meaning of this, what they agreed upon is enough to exclude Camus from the existentialist category. For according to this existentialism, there are no inbuilt desires, values, or personality traits that explain any part of an individual's behaviour. It follows that there are no inbuilt desires, values, or personality traits that all or nearly all people have in common, which could constitute a basic human nature.

Camus, by contrast, believes in an emotional fraternity inherent in human nature. The idea that he wants to convey in *The Outsider* is that we are naturally emotionally engaged in one another's lives. It is perhaps not surprising that the literary presentation of this idea contains some ambiguities. It is unclear whether Meursault is intended as an impossible character, lacking a trait that Camus considers strictly essential to human existence and presented merely to illustrate that essentiality, or whether Camus would allow that people can lack this trait, just as people can lack other normal features of human existence. But either way, his position contradicts the basic tenet of existentialism. For the difference between Meursault and the rest of his society is a difference in their inbuilt traits. He lacks a normal feature of human nature.

How deep is this difference between Camus and the existentialists? We have seen that Meursault's emotional strangeness is sufficiently central to the narrative and narration of *The Outsider* that without it there simply could not be this novel. But does the idea that existence precedes essence require the rejection of this idea that emotional concern for others is part of human nature? Could there be a form of existentialism that held all human motivations to be grounded ultimately in each individual's choices and actions within the constraint of a natural emotional concern for other people? It might be argued that this move could be made for the other personality trait that Camus postulates in *The Outsider* and *The Myth of Sisyphus*, the inescapable drive to make rational sense of things. For it seems perfectly coherent to think that this is simply the structure of the human mind, which by its nature categorizes and seeks explanation, and is therefore a purely formal trait that sets no limits on the other goals and values that the individual may have.[3]

---

[3] Indeed, a similar view is often ascribed to Sartre. On this reading, the motivation he calls 'the desire to be God', which is the desire to have the impossible ontological structure

However, a natural emotional concern for other people would not be purely formal, since it places substantive value on the happiness and well-being of those other people, at least in the subjective sense of their feelings of happiness and well-being. An argument would be required to explain why human nature can include this substantive trait but no others. Moreover, a substantive trait constrains the range of other goals and values an individual could have. To the degree that it does so, the scope of the claim that existence precedes essence would be eroded, perhaps to the point at which it is merely the uncontroversial and unexciting claim that many of our motivations result from our choices.

A more significant reason why the message of *The Outsider* cannot be accommodated within existentialism concerns not the claim that Camus makes about human nature itself, but the ethical significance that he ascribes to it. For classical existentialism is not simply a theory of what it is to be human. It is an ethical theory. It is a form of humanism that holds the structure of human existence, that existence precedes essence, to itself be the ground of ethical value (Sartre EH: 51–3). Camus makes precisely the opposite claim that ethical value is grounded in motivations that are natural to human beings.

2.7 Human Nature and Political Violence

Camus had first expressed his ethical outlook in *The Outsider*, published a year before Beauvoir and Sartre first presented their idea that existence precedes essence in *She Came To Stay* and *Being and Nothingness*, two years before the first detailed statement of the ethical outlook of existentialism in Beauvoir's *Pyrrhus and Cineas*, and three years before Beauvoir and Sartre widely publicized their philosophy under the name

---

of a fixed nature and a conscious mind, is itself an essential structure of human existence. The claim that existence precedes essence, on this reading, can be rewritten as the claim that our choices determine exactly what kind of fixed nature we aim to identify ourselves with. I have argued that this reading is mistaken and that the 'desire to be God' is Sartre's label for the fundamental form of bad faith that he thinks we can and should overcome (Webber 2009: ch. 8). It may be that the more common reading is partly motivated by the parallel with the idea of absurdity described in *The Myth of Sisyphus* on the assumption that Camus and Sartre are rightly understood as contemporaneous existentialists. This kind of misreading is likely to occur if a diverse group of thinkers are categorized together without any clear definition governing the category. It is also found, for example, in the idea that Meursault is an exemplar of Sartrean bad faith, even though *The Outsider* was published before Sartre had published his thoughts on bad faith and before Camus had met Beauvoir and Sartre (Sherman 2009: 70–6; Solomon 2006: 33).

of existentialism. From the outset, Camus was fundamentally opposed to their existentialist theory of human existence and its grounding of ethical value. He outlined his view of natural human solidarity as the ground of ethical value in an anonymous article published in *Combat* just before the liberation of Paris in 1944, where he contrasted the Nazi attempt to impose meaning on a meaningless world with the morally right expression of natural human concern for one another manifested in the Resistance (LGF: 26–32). It is hardly surprising, then, that Camus should reject the label 'existentialist' in 1945, just as Beauvoir and Sartre were busy defining it as the claim that existence precedes essence with the entailment that there is no human nature (IJD: 345).

Camus crystallized his thought about the grounds of ethical value into a sophisticated theory of moral right and wrong in *The Rebel*, published in 1951. He presents this theory in the context of political violence, but it can equally well be applied to less extreme situations. He argues that our natural human solidarity makes rebellion against systematic political violence morally necessary. The protection of one another against oppression is required by that natural ground of ethical value. But at the same time, the use of violence in this rebellion is immoral precisely because it offends against that same solidarity. When violent rebellion is the only way to resist systematic political violence, we must either violate solidarity by acquiescing in oppression or violate solidarity by rebelling violently. Such a situation thus condemns us to immoral action, though it may still require one immoral action rather than the other (see especially TR: 1–10, 119–20, 221–35). This dilemma is not in principle restricted to violence: any situation of oppression, subjugation, or injustice might require resistance in the name of solidarity that takes the form of contravening our solidarity with the perpetrator or their witting or unwitting accomplices.[4]

Camus develops this theory of solidarity in explicit contrast with existentialism, which he claims sees history as the sole determinant of

---

[4] Paul George Neiman has recently argued that this dilemma of rebellion arises because the rebel perceives a conflict between two values, solidarity and justice (2017: § 2). Stated in this way, however, it is unclear why the dilemma should not be resolved by ranking those two values in order of importance. The answer is that the commitment to justice is itself an expression of the value of solidarity, so the dilemma is generated by one value rather than two. Since this value is grounded in human nature, according to Camus, it is inescapable. The dilemma does not arise simply from the individual's recognition of it, moreover, but from that objective value itself. The rebel's recognition of the dilemma is required only for violent rebellion to be clear-eyed and authentic (e.g. TR: 226–7).

human action, first in his notebooks soon after the existentialist offensive and then in *The Rebel* (CN: 136; TR: 4, 240-1). This might seem to misrepresent existentialism. Beauvoir and Sartre emphasize the role of freedom in motivating action through chosen projects that structure one's experience of situations. But history does play a determining role in their view, since it provides the context in which projects are undertaken and pursued, even though it does not fully determine those projects. Camus is right, moreover, that in their view history is the only determinant, whereas he takes human nature to be a second determinant. The aspect of human nature that Camus considers to shape human action is precisely the one isolated in *The Outsider* and the one that he considers to ground ethical value: our innate emotional engagement with the feelings of other people.

Just as Camus was finalizing *The Rebel*, Sartre had reached his own conclusion that revolutionary political violence is required to bring about a world in which the value of human freedom can be fully realized (Aronson 2004: 112-13). It is not surprising, then, that Sartre did not approve of *The Rebel*, which holds violence to be justified only in rebellion against systematic political violence. But it might seem surprising that Sartre viewed *The Rebel* as a kind of betrayal of its own author's earlier work. 'Where is Meursault, Camus? Where is Sisyphus? Where are those Trotskyites of the heart who preached permanent revolution?', asked Sartre in his defence of the negative review of *The Rebel* written for *Les Temps Modernes* by his colleague Francis Jeanson. 'Murdered, no doubt, or in exile', he concludes (P: 125). On the contrary, Meursault is alive and well in the pages of *The Rebel* and never was intended to preach permanent revolution of the heart. He was the first attempt Camus made to present the grounding of morality in an unchanging human nature, the same idea elaborated in *The Rebel* in greater detail.

In his review of *The Outsider* almost ten years earlier, Sartre had understood Meursault simply as experiencing life as a meaningless sequence of events and then coming to recognize this absurdity explicitly at the end of the novel. Sartre was unsure whether to chastise Camus for misrepresenting the phenomenology of experience, or whether to read the misrepresentation as an ironic satire (OE: 173-80). Sartre's error there had been to attribute to Camus his own obsession with the phenomenology of experience. This led him to overlook that for Camus the absurd is not the lack of meaning itself, which might be found in

Meursault's experience, but the clash between the lack of meaning and the inescapable human desire for meaning.

Had he kept sight of this richer conception of absurdity, Sartre would have had to look into Meursault's particular character and motivations in order to unravel his role as a hero of absurdity, which should have led him to Meursault's emotional strangeness. By failing to see this dimension of the novel, Sartre has overlooked from the outset the deep difference between the existentialist philosophy he shares with Beauvoir and the sharply contrasting ethical outlook that Camus presents in *The Outsider*. He has instead misread Camus as agreeing with the existentialist idea that value is dependent on human projects, then a decade later been shocked to find this view contradicted in *The Rebel*. It is hardly surprising, therefore, that Camus was so puzzled by Sartre's reaction, which was after all only a sophisticated development and detailed articulation of ideas that Camus had been working on since the beginning of his published career, indeed since before he and Sartre had even met.

3

Freedom and the Origins of Reasons

Merleau-Ponty had been a friend of Beauvoir and Sartre since they were all students together in the 1920s. They discussed philosophy regularly throughout the years in which their philosophical outlooks were forged. They founded *Les Temps Modernes* together in 1945 and all three were still editors when the dispute between Camus and Sartre was played out on its pages in 1952. Although he had previously been a communist, by this time Merleau-Ponty was very sympathetic to the moderate and democratic politics that Camus was articulating. At the end of that year, Sartre published the first part of his book *The Communists and Peace* in *Les Temps Modernes* without first showing it to Merleau-Ponty, probably because his co-editor was likely to ask for its pro-communist message to be toned down. This was the start of a series of infractions and breaches of collegial etiquette that increased the tension between them until Merleau-Ponty resigned from the journal a year later.

This private dispute became public when Merleau-Ponty published *Adventures of the Dialectic* in 1955. The fifth chapter, comprising half the book, is a sustained attack on Sartre's politics that traces the problems Merleau-Ponty finds with it back to the central claim of Sartre's existentialism. Beauvoir responded with an essay in *Les Temps Modernes* arguing that what Merleau-Ponty has criticized is merely a crude caricature of Sartre's philosophy. Beauvoir's response might seem rather surprising. Could it really be that Merleau-Ponty has misunderstood the central philosophical ideas of someone who had been a close friend and colleague for so long? Or is he rather aiming to portray a view of the philosophy that Sartre is committed to by his underlying ontological categories, whether Sartre agrees with this resulting position or not?

There is some misunderstanding on Merleau-Ponty's part, as we will see, particularly in his failure to distinguish between the meanings present in a situation and the reasons that situation presents. But we will also see that he is right that one of Sartre's fundamental ontological claims is inconsistent with the idea of projects at the heart of his theory of freedom. Merleau-Ponty's conclusion that we should reject Sartre's theory of freedom is not fully justified by this argument, however, since an alternative would be to deny that ontological claim and retain the rest of the theory of freedom. Indeed, a careful reading of Beauvoir's response to Merleau-Ponty suggests that this was already Sartre's position by the time *Adventures of the Dialectic* was published.

3.1 Freedom, Reasons, and Projects

Freedom is the central concept in Sartre's initial form of existentialism. To say that existence precedes essence, according to the Sartre of *Being and Nothingness*, is to say that an individual is always free to change the goals and values that shape their outlook and behaviour. Sartre is often ascribed a view of freedom much simpler and less credible than the one he actually held at this stage of his career. This is partly because he develops his theory across the whole of *Being and Nothingness* without ever providing a concise statement of it. Although one sizeable tract of the book is specifically devoted to this topic (part 4, ch. 1, §§ 1–3), much of its groundwork earlier in the book is incautiously worded. As a result, Sartre is often read as a kind of staccato voluntarist who holds that we decide at every moment how to respond to the world. In its starkest form, this overlooks Sartre's account of action as responding to invitations, demands, and proscriptions that we find in the world (Smith 1970). More precisely, it ignores the distinction Sartre draws between unreflective engagement in a world that presents us with reasons inviting particular responses and the recognition available through reflection on my experience that these reasons are not features of the world independent of my experience of it (B&N: part 1, ch. 1, § 1; part 4, ch. 2, § 2). A more sophisticated form of this misreading ascribes to him the view that we are free simply to decide how the world appears to us in unreflective experience (Føllesdal 1981).

Although it is true that Sartre understands us to have freedom over how the world seems to us and the reasons it presents us with, he does not locate this freedom in voluntary decision. He does not hold that we have to make an explicit decision at every moment about how to behave.

Neither does he hold that we can change the set of reasons we find in the world simply by deciding to do so. For decisions, he argues, are themselves responses to the reasons that we find in the world, even though these reasons depend on our experience of the world. 'What we usually understand by "will" is a conscious decision that most of us take only after we have made ourselves what we are', he tells us in *Existentialism Is a Humanism*, because such decision 'is only a manifestation of an earlier and more spontaneous choice' (EH: 23). This remark summarizes a passage in *Being and Nothingness* which argues that the deliberation leading to a voluntary action can only be a procedure of weighing up the reasons for competing actions, where the weight of each reason is silently conferred upon it by the projects that I am pursuing (B&N: 472-3; Webber 2009: 33-4).

Deliberation, decision, and voluntary action, therefore, express a prior and more fundamental choice that shapes the reasons they embody. This deeper kind of choice, according to Sartre, consists in adopting or abandoning a 'project' (*projet*). It is unfortunate that he does not provide any single, comprehensive, and precise analysis of these actions of undertaking or abandoning a project, for they are fundamental to his theory of freedom. Given that he does not, it is quite natural to assume that he means them in their ordinary sense and to think of writing a book or raising a child as paradigm cases. Such projects are generally undertaken and pursued in clear knowledge of doing so. These projects require continual effortful commitment, which can be ended by an explicit decision to do so. If projects are like this, then it is difficult to see how they can be prior to reasoned decision in the way that Sartre describes. However, he has a broader conception of project in mind. He argues, for example, that I might accept a job for the reason that I will starve if I do not get some money soon, but this presents a strong reason for getting money only because I am already committed to a project of staying alive. I might never have deliberated about whether to stay alive. It might never have crossed my mind to even consider this. But staying alive is a project rather than simply a habit because it embodies an evaluative stance, that being alive is worthwhile (B&N: 459).

Undertaking or maintaining a project, for Sartre, thus means orienting oneself towards a specific 'end' (*fin*) which is valued (B&N: 459; see also B&N: 471). He does not deny that this could be a voluntary action. Reasons grounded in some of one's existing projects might indeed motivate a decision to adopt a new project or abandon an existing one. But in Sartre's view, such reasoned deliberation is neither necessary nor sufficient for altering one's projects. That it is not necessary is shown by the example of the project of staying alive, which one might never have deliberated over. That it is not sufficient is well illustrated by Sartre's example of the gambler who has resolved never to gamble again but who finds his resolution powerless in the face of the temptations of the casino (B&N: 56-7). This character's decision not to gamble again is the result of deliberation on the basis of reasons rooted in some of his projects. Yet he has not succeeded in fully orienting himself towards this new value. In his novel *The Age of Reason*, Sartre gives another example: Daniel wants to prove that he is not the sentimental person that people take him to be, so he gathers up his cats in a bag and goes to the river to drown them, but when he gets there he finds to his dismay that he cannot go through with it (AR: 81-91).

The patterns in a person's deliberations, decisions, and actions, for Sartre, thus result from the reasons they find in their situations, which are determined by the projects they are pursuing, the goals and values they are oriented towards, whether or not they are explicitly aware of this. When we describe people in terms of character traits, we are referring, whether we know it or not, to the projects they are pursuing, whether they know it or not (Webber 2009: ch. 2). It is a mistake to think that Sartre's theory of freedom entails that character trait terminology refers only to the patterns in a person's past actions, rather than to anything that explains those patterns and disposes towards their continuation (Morris 1976: ch. 4; Gilbert 2006: 48-9; Harman 2009: 239, 242). We should rather understand Sartre in *Being and Nothingness* as holding that freedom consists in the ability to change one's own character, thereby changing the invitations and demands that one experiences the world as presenting and to which one responds.

3.2 The Field of Meaning

What, precisely, is Merleau-Ponty's criticism of this theory of freedom? Its presentation in *Adventures of the Dialectic* is woven into a critique of Sartre's political philosophy and analyses of the post-war global political developments. As a result, it can be difficult to disentangle the arguments targeted specifically at Sartre's theory of freedom from the larger critique. But the comments on freedom in this later critique of Sartre simply restate the points Merleau-Ponty had made ten years earlier in *Phenomenology of Perception*. This earlier statement is entirely focused on the theory of freedom, so is clearer than the later statement. However, this version presents other challenges. It explicitly mentions Sartre only once across a lengthy discussion, but is structured as a dialectical argument that begins from a theory like Sartre's that is described in Sartre's terminology and develops towards Merleau-Ponty's own position through critical consideration of examples drawn from Sartre's discussion of freedom in *Being and Nothingness*. This implicit sparring with Sartre makes it difficult to distinguish the points Merleau-Ponty raises in his own voice from those he intends to ascribe to Sartre, which makes it difficult to see how the various points raised are intended to fit together as a single argument. Indeed, it can read like a mere scattergun attack on a range of distinct claims that Sartre makes about freedom, but read in this way it seems that each of the shots Merleau-Ponty fires misses its target (Stewart 1995; Wilkerson 2010: § 2).[1]

We can make better sense of this chapter of *Phenomenology of Perception* if we read each of the central objections that Merleau-Ponty raises against Sartre as ultimately a facet of his rejection of the claim central to Sartre's existentialism. According to Sartre's original version of the idea that existence precedes essence, the situations that an individual faces are articulated by that individual's freely chosen projects. On this view, freedom is ontologically prior to situations. Merleau-Ponty, by contrast, holds that an individual's situations are articulated by their bodily abilities and their social context. On his view, freedom is ontologically consequent upon situations: one is free only to the extent that the material and social situation allows. Whether a rock appears to me as a climbing challenge, a beautiful object, or an obstacle in my path, Sartre argues in *Being and Nothingness*, depends entirely on my projects (B&N: 504). Merleau-Ponty replies in *Phenomenology of Perception* that

---

[1] This strategy of critiquing aspects of Sartre's theory without ever presenting a clear formulation of the target position is perhaps explained by an article Merleau-Ponty published in *Les Temps Modernes* soon after *Phenomenology of Perception* appeared, 'The Battle over Existentialism', which is a defence of Sartre's *Being and Nothingness* against Catholic and Marxist critics. Here, he describes Sartre's thoughts on freedom as incomplete and in need of further clarification (BE: 72–3, 77). By the time he wrote *Adventures of the Dialectic*, it seems he had concluded that the required clarification could not be provided.

'given the same project, this rock face over here will appear as an obstacle while this other more passable one will appear as an aid' (PP: 464). Similarly, the world around me is already filled with objects, languages, customs, opportunities, and limitations inscribed there by generations of people and an economic situation dependent on the activities of the people I live alongside (PP: 467–76). Together, these physical and social meanings constitute a 'field of freedom' that determines my range of possibilities and the degree of resistance to the pursuit of each possibility (PP: 481).

Sartre does not deny that an individual's situations are replete with meanings that reflect their bodily abilities and social context. Merleau-Ponty ascribes to Sartre the view that even these meanings are dependent on the individual's projects, that 'it is consciousness which gives meaning' (AD: 159; see PP: 461; AD: 196–201). But as Beauvoir points out, Sartre devotes a considerable amount of *Being and Nothingness* to articulating precisely the point that these meanings of the situation are not dependent on the individual's projects (Beauvoir MPPS: § 1). How did Merleau-Ponty get this wrong? He had known Beauvoir and Sartre throughout the years in which their existentialism was formed and discussed philosophy with them regularly. How could he have been mistaken on this central aspect of their view of freedom?

Part of the answer lies in the development of Sartre's thought on this point. Beauvoir is mistaken to claim that Sartre's position on this matter had remained the same from *Nausea* onwards (MPPS: 210). The strange experiences that Roquentin records after his only projects have come to an end include the disappearance of the instrumental and social meanings of the environment. 'Words had disappeared', he tells us, 'and with them the meaning of things, the methods of using them, the feeble landmarks which men had traced on their surface' (N: 182). Merleau-Ponty has not noticed that Sartre has moved on from the view presented in *Nausea* that even the instrumental and social meanings of objects are experienced only as a result of the individual's projects. This is why Merleau-Ponty ascribes to Sartre a theory of 'centrifugal *Sinnbewegung*', the idea that all sense or meaning is bestowed outwards onto the situation from the individual subject at the centre (PP: 461; 'centrifugal' also appears at AD: 198). Indeed, it is why he effectively classifies Sartre as a kind of 'intellectualist' who sees the mind as distinct from an objective reality that possesses no meanings of its own (AD: 124, 137–44; Whitford 1979).

3.3 The Field of Reasons

In fact, what Sartre holds in *Being and Nothingness* is that although the meanings of objects are given by our bodily abilities and social contexts, these meanings provide *reasons* for us only in relation to our projects. Alarm clocks, tax forms, police officers, and signs that tell us to keep off the grass are all socially constituted meanings, but it is only as a result of my projects that I experience them as having any directive significance for me (B&N: 62-3).[2]

This development from the position illustrated in *Nausea* is slightly obscured by Sartre's imprecision of expression in *Being and Nothingness*. He writes, for example, that it is my set of projects 'which causes the existence of values, appeals, expectations and in general a world' for me (B&N: 63). Although values, appeals, and expectations are all reasons, the addition of the phrase 'in general a world' does suggest the whole meaningful structure of the experienced world. But all the kinds of structure that he identifies as dependent on projects have directive significance, not merely meaning.

Sartre sometimes indicates this directive significance by use of the term 'value' (*valeur*), as when he claims that 'in this world where I engage myself my acts cause values to spring up like partridges' (B&N: 62). Sometimes, he uses the term 'exigency' (*exegence*), as when he writes that 'it is I who confer on the alarm clock its exigency—I and I alone' (B&N: 62). This term nicely captures those reasons that are experienced as making such normative demands as requiring or forbidding a particular response. But some directive significance is experienced as merely favouring some outcome, which can be outweighed by other considerations. Sartre

---

[2] This might appear to be the reverse of the idea presented in *Nausea*, where the ending of Roquentin's projects leads him to experience the raw being of objects as 'monstrous' and 'frightening', revealing the 'horrible' contingency and superfluity of everything (N: 183, 188). Although these emotions are repellent, however, they have no directive significance. There is nothing that they are inviting Roquentin to do. So this is not a case where reasons persist in the absence of a field of meanings. Rather, these feelings are a symptom of the failure to constitute a meaningful world at all. They belong to the species of emotion that Sartre identifies towards the end of *Sketch for a Theory of Emotions*, where the sudden appearance of an inscrutable face at the window, for example, can leave one frozen in terror, fixated on that face until it indicates something of its possessor's intentions, because until then one's immediate environment cannot be constituted into a field of meanings at all (Webber 2018: § 4). This terror is not a reason inviting one to scrutinize the face. It is just the fixation itself. Roquentin's nausea, likewise, is just the dizzying absence of meaning.

sometimes uses the term '*motif*' to mean the overall motivating reason for an action, 'the ensemble of rational considerations which justify it' (B&N: 468). This encompasses aspects of the situation that require or forbid an action and those that merely favour it.

Sartre does not seem to have a term, however, for each of those aspects of the situation that could contribute to the overall *motif* of an action, each rational consideration. For our purposes, the term 'reason' is a good fit, even though the same word can be used to name the whole set of rational considerations that in fact motivate the action. Unlike a motive, a reason in this narrower sense need not actually motivate a response. For a situation can contain conflicting reasons in this sense, and crucially, for Sartre at this stage of his career, such a reason can be resisted even in the absence of some conflicting reason. The use of the term 'reason', moreover, should not be taken to indicate any philosophical account of how reasons are structured. To say that the pain in my foot is experienced as a reason to stop walking, in this sense, is just to say that the pain figures in my experience as favouring or demanding that I stop walking.

Merleau-Ponty does not use any term that is equivalent to 'reasons' as I am using it here either. In a short discussion of the directive significance of pain or tiredness, he describes this significance as a 'valuation' (*valorisation*), but in the preceding paragraphs uses this same term of features of experience that present no directive significance (PP: 465–6). Despite this, Merleau-Ponty does briefly argue for a claim about the origin of experienced reasons. If the soldier resists torture, he writes, 'this is because the historical situation, his comrades, and the world around him seemed to him to expect this particular behaviour from him' (PP: 480–1). He accepts that these experienced reasons are dependent on the individual's projects, but argues that those projects are the product of the individual's nature and history. 'I am a psychological and historical structure', he writes, and all 'my actions and thoughts are related to this structure' (PP: 482). The reasons that I find in the world, on Merleau-Ponty's view, are the necessary products of my innate nature as this has developed in response to my experience of life. There is no place in this theory for the freedom that Sartre envisages as the origin of experienced reasons. Instead, I am free to the extent that my bodily and social situation tolerates my attempts to express the motivations produced by my nature and history (PP: 481).

Should we accept Merleau-Ponty's account of the origin of reasons rather than Sartre's? Some further aspects of Merleau-Ponty's critique of Sartre can be read as attempting to answer that question. But before we turn to those, it is worth considering Sartre's phenomenological analyses of the experience of reasons in more detail. For those analyses contain powerful motivations for Sartre's theory of freedom that Merleau-Ponty has entirely ignored. Indeed, those analyses form an argument against Merleau-Ponty's account of freedom, even though they are to be found in *Being and Nothingness*, first published two years before Merleau-Ponty published his theory of freedom in *Phenomenology of Perception*. Only once we have fully understood why Sartre thinks that experienced reasons must manifest a freedom that is ontologically prior to the constitution of situations will we be able to assess Merleau-Ponty's arguments against this conception of freedom.

3.4 The Phenomenology of Reasons

Sartre argues that reasons feature in our experience in two different ways. The way we experience them in our unreflective engagement with the world is not the same as the way they seem to us if we reflect on our experience of the world. More precisely, Sartre argues that there are two different ways of reflecting on experience. One way is to focus attention on the relation between the world and oneself, keeping both of these things in view. This is what Sartre calls 'impure reflection'. This can show us that the reasons the world presents are matched by our existing desires. To borrow one of Sartre's examples, if I reflect in this way on my experience of running after the tram to catch up with it, it is clear that the tram appeared to me as something to be caught up with and that I had the desire to get onto that tram. Sartre thinks that this is the kind of reflection that Husserl employs in developing the method of phenomenology (Webber forthcoming, § 4).

But this kind of reflection distorts the original experience, according to Sartre. This becomes clear, he thinks, if we engage in a different kind of reflection on our experience, which he calls 'pure reflection'. In this kind of reflection, we do not focus on the relation between the world and ourselves. Rather, we focus attention on the appearance of the world, on how things seem. My unreflective and engaged experience of chasing after the tram is focused on the tram, which appears as receding and as something to catch up with. In pure reflection on that experience, I focus attention not on the tram, but on its appearance as receding and to be caught up with. This kind of reflection is the one Sartre employs in his phenomenology, because he considers it to provide undistorted access to how the world appears in unreflective experience. One thing that it makes clear, he argues, is that unreflective experience directed towards the world does not include explicit reference to oneself. As I run after the tram, my experience is just of the tram as something to be caught up with. The experience does not present me or my desire to catch up with the tram, although these might be inferred from what the experience does present (TE: 11–13; Webber forthcoming: § 4).

Pure reflection also reveals, according to Sartre, something else about the experience of reasons that is not revealed in impure reflection: that a reason for action is not experienced simply as a motivation pulling one towards a particular action or outcome, but as presenting a directive claim that is to be questioned, considered, compared with other reasons, and then affirmed, reassessed, rejected, overridden, or even ignored in action. In short, a reason is recognized in experience as to be respected or negated (B&N: 55–7, 470–1; Eshleman 2011: 37–40; Poellner 2015: 236). This is why Sartre considers it a form of bad faith to ascribe one's actions simply to one's character traits. Impure reflection indicates the correlation between the reasons one finds in the world and one's desires. The patterns in these desires indicate one's character traits. But impure reflection does not show that action is mechanically produced by one's character traits via the experience of reasons. It does not disclose anything about the force that reasons actually exert over behaviour. Pure reflection on the way reasons seem to us reveals that action is not mechanically produced by their influence over us. It reveals that in our unreflective engagement with the world, reasons are experienced as making directive claims on us to which we respond by following those claims or by resisting them. To treat action as though it is simply produced by character is thus not merely to make a mistake, according to Sartre; it is to falsify our experience of reasons.

Sartre has therefore already dismissed Merleau-Ponty's theory of freedom in *Being and Nothingness* as a form of bad faith that exploits the indications of impure reflection while ignoring our actual experience of reasons in unreflective engagement with the world, an experience revealed in pure reflection. The same analysis of the experience of reasons is intended to support Sartre's view of freedom as ontologically prior to one's character traits, to the projects that one pursues. For if freedom were only as Merleau-Ponty describes it, the degree to which one can achieve the goals set by one's motivations within the constraints of the material and social environment, then one would not be free to reassess or reject the reasons that one experiences in the world as a result of one's character. One would not, on Sartre's view, experience reasons in the way that we do experience reasons, as making claims to which we can respond in a variety of ways.

Freedom is not simply a matter of the ability to pursue one's projects, therefore, but includes the freedom not to pursue those projects. This is what Sartre means by his regular use of the term 'radical freedom': freedom over the projects at the very root of our actions, a freedom indicated by our experience of reasons. Our projects have no strength or inertia of their own, but are sustained only by our continuing to endorse the value or 'end' at their core. Merleau-Ponty does not engage with this argument in either statement of his critique of Sartre. He seems to have entirely overlooked Sartre's sophisticated phenomenological analysis of the difference between the way pure reflection reveals reasons to figure in unreflective experience and the way they seem in impure reflection.

We might reply on Merleau-Ponty's behalf that even if we agree that Sartre has shown that one must be able to reject or revise the reasons presented in experience, even if we accept that freedom must include the freedom to change the projects that underlie our character traits, then we still do not need to accept that freedom is prior to all reasons. For we could maintain instead that to revise or reject a reason is always to do so for some other reason. We need not be able to reject all of our reasons together, or to overthrow our entire character or set of projects, in order that Sartre's account of the phenomenology of reasons be correct. But to accept this, Merleau-Ponty would need to abandon his view that freedom is only the degree to which our situations permit the pursuit of our aims. For he would need to accept that freedom is the ability to respond negatively to the reasons we find in our situations as a result of our projects, and thus the freedom to revise those projects. Does his critique of Sartre contain any convincing arguments against accepting this?

3.5 Freedom Without Reasons

Merleau-Ponty focuses his critique on the idea that one can refine or reject a reason without any reason to do so. It is not simply that a reasoned decision is not necessary for a change in projects, on his reading of Sartre, but more strongly that one can orient oneself towards a new set of values, set oneself to pursue new goals, without having any reason to do so provided by one's existing set of values and goals. This is a consequence of Sartre's ontology of being and nothingness: because consciousness is not part of the ordinary causal realm, on this reading of Sartre, my values and goals can persist only so long as I continue to accept them and nothing can prevent me from rejecting them and adopting a new set. Merleau-Ponty usually frames his response to this as a rejection of the temporal claim that my past can influence my future only through my continued acceptance of past commitments (Wilkerson 2010: § 3). He objects that this would mean that 'my habitual being in the world is equally fragile at each moment', since no matter how long I have been committed to my goals and values 'freedom's gesture can effortlessly shatter them at any moment' (PP: 466–7; see AD: 106).

There are at least two ways in which we can understand this objection, both of which echo David Hume's influential critique of what he called 'the liberty of indifference' (1739: book 2 part 3 § 2). One is that an action that is entirely unmotivated by reasons is not an expression of freedom, but is either an action out of the agent's control or no action at all. Merleau-Ponty makes this point when he argues that 'choice assumes a previous commitment' that provides the reasons for it; 'freedom must have *a field*; that is, it must have some privileged possibilities or realities' to serve as reasons (PP: 462). A second way to understand the Humean point is that if abrupt changes in projects need not be motivated by reasons, then the broad consistency and continuity that we regularly find in the behaviour of individuals would be entirely unexplained. We should instead expect people to be abandoning projects and beginning fresh ones all the time. Yet 'after having built my life upon an inferiority complex, continuously reinforced for twenty years, it is not *likely* that I would change' (PP: 467).[3]

---

[3] The phrase 'it is not likely' here somewhat underplays Merleau-Ponty's point. A more idiomatic rendering of his '*il est peu probable*' would be 'it is hardly likely'.

Peter Poellner has recently argued for an interpretation of Sartre's theory of freedom in *Being and Nothingness* that does not include the claim that Merleau-Ponty targets. On this reading, Sartre holds only that overriding reasons cannot be imposed on the individual by objects in the world. This is consistent, according to Poellner, with the idea that features of the world do provide reasons for an individual independently of that individual's projects, an idea which he finds in *Being and Nothingness*. It is also consistent, he argues, with Sartre's basic ethical claim that the freedom of oneself and others is objectively valuable. There are two parts to Poellner's interpretation. First, the holism of reasons means that any reason that the world provides for me independently of my projects is one that exerts its influence on me only in the context of all of my reasons, including those that are dependent on my projects (2015: 231–3). Second, although the objective value of the freedom of oneself and others does provide an overriding reason for me, this freedom is never an object in the world (2015: 238). Sartre's repeated claims that nothing outside of the individual can determine their choice of projects should be read, according to Poellner, only as making these claims, not as making the further claim that projects can be chosen for no reason, the claim that is subject to the Humean objections (2015: 226).

Poellner is certainly right to draw attention to both the holism of reasons and the objective value of freedom in Sartre's philosophy, two features of his existentialism that are usually overlooked in analyses of his theory of motivation. Sartre's claims about the origins of experienced reasons and values, however, cannot be fully explained in this way. Poellner gives the example of a soldier fleeing an enemy attack: the danger to the soldier's life presents an objective reason to flee, which the soldier's fear correctly registers (2015: 229). This fear can motivate action only in the context of the soldier's set of reasons, but so long as that set does not include any directly countervailing reasons, on Poellner's reading, the soldier has reason to flee and does so. Taking another of Sartre's examples, Poellner argues that the tiredness felt by the hiker is an objective reason to stop walking, but whether the hiker will act on that reason depends on the hiker's other reasons, some of which depend on the hiker's projects (2015: 231–2). But this is not how Sartre describes these examples. He describes the fear of dying not as a recognition of an objective reason to act to preserve my life, but as a manifestation of a project that sets my life as valuable (B&N: 459). He describes the hiker's tiredness as having its value and practical significance for the hiker conferred on it by the hiker's projects (B&N: 476–7).

Sartre does indeed hold that the freedom of myself and others is objectively valuable. We will consider this claim in detail in Chapter 9. Sartre's point, however, is not that this value is experienced as a reason, overriding or otherwise, irrespective of the individual's projects. His point is normative: the value of freedom ought to be recognized by every individual as an overriding reason. We should not accept, therefore, Poellner's revisionary interpretation. Sartre's claim that nothing in the world can impose values or reasons on the individual cannot be understood as claiming only that reasons function holistically and that the only objectively overriding reason does not feature in experience as an aspect of an object in the world. Rather, we should take at face value his claim that 'my freedom is the unique foundation of values' and that a value cannot be founded in the world independently of my projects (B&N: 62). Sartre does hold the view that Merleau-Ponty attributes to him here.

3.6 Projects as Commitments

What has Sartre to say in defence of his idea that projects can be modified or abandoned for no reason? He does anticipate the objection that he has described as 'a pure capricious, unlawful, gratuitous, and incomprehensible contingency', as he puts it, and that his theory entails 'that my act can be anything *whatsoever* or even that it is *unforeseeable*' (B&N: 475). His response is that the interdependence of an individual's projects provides them with stability. Projects peripheral to the set could be altered without much noticeable change in the individual. But to alter a project that is more central to the set would require substantial changes across the set of projects, with implications for the individual's self-image and relations with other people. It should not surprise us, Sartre argues, that people tend to preserve their projects, at least the ones that we most identify with them, given these implications of changing an important project. We tend to act on reasons presented in our situations because the cost of doing otherwise is generally high. 'There is no doubt that I could have done otherwise' in any given situation, he writes, but 'at what price?' (B&N: 476). His eventual conclusion is that the price is often 'a fundamental modification of my original choice of myself', 'another choice of myself and my ends' (B&N: 486).

We might question whether projects are indeed as holistic as Sartre suggests here. Or we might question why we should expect people to be so committed to the overall coherence of their projects. We might wonder why that coherence could not be preserved by temporarily suspending a project in order to resist a reason it grounds, rather than permanently altering or abandoning that project. But we need not consider these questions here. For even if we accept what Sartre says about the cost of changing projects, this point does not fully address the Humean objection that Merleau-Ponty raises. That objection presents a problem for the very idea of pursuing a project at all. Freedom 'could not commit itself' to any goal, Merleau-Ponty writes, if 'it knows quite well that the following instant will find it, in every way, just as free and just as little established'. If a commitment is to be made then 'what it does must not immediately be undone by a new freedom'; rather, 'I must benefit from my momentum, and I must be inclined to continue' (PP: 462). If one can simply change course at any moment for no reason at all, then one cannot be committed to anything and it makes no sense to talk of undertaking or maintaining a project (McInerney 1979).

We can approach this same problem from another angle. One of Sartre's most famous examples concerns a student who asked him during the war whether he should stay at home to look after his mother or instead leave home to fight against the Nazis (EH: 30). What makes this a difficult decision, argues Charles Taylor, is that each of the two mutually exclusive options embodies a value that the student cannot simply choose to abandon. For otherwise, 'the grievous nature of the predicament would dissolve' (1976: 291). If the student could simply abandon the set of projects that grounds the reasons in favour of one course of action, then he would have no difficulty in deciding and would not really be facing a dilemma at all. The difficulty stems from his being deeply committed to values that seem to make incompatible demands in this situation, unable simply to refuse one of those demands in favour of the other. Sartre even recognizes this kind of commitment that resists a simple decision to abandon it, as we have seen in his cases of the gambler who has resolved not to gamble again and Daniel's attempt to drown his cats. In the face of such commitments, decisions made against them can be, in Sartre's apt phrase, merely 'cheques without funds to meet them' (AR: 86).

The very idea of commitment to a project, therefore, already requires that one cannot simply abandon the project on a whim. One could not respond to the Humean objection to Sartre's theory of freedom by appealing to the holism of projects, therefore, since this move would presuppose that there could be such things as projects, which is what is in question. It would be to define commitment to a project in terms of that project's relation to other projects to which one is already committed, which is clearly circular. This is perhaps why Merleau-Ponty often presents his objection to Sartre's theory of freedom in temporal terms: at its core, the objection concerns the fundamentally temporal idea of a project or a commitment. Beauvoir accuses Merleau-Ponty of employing a 'ruse of paradox' in claiming that Sartre does not hold various claims that he in fact does hold (MPPS: 210). We can be more sympathetic and read Merleau-Ponty's claim that Sartre's theory does not accommodate projects or commitments as the claim that, given his underlying ontology, Sartre cannot accommodate them.

However, we should accept Beauvoir's further point that Merleau-Ponty develops this critique of Sartre in an arbitrary way (MPPS: 234). Rather than reject Sartre's entire theory of freedom because of one ontological claim, why not just reject that claim? We should agree with Poellner, therefore, that Sartre's texts suggest a theory that does not include the idea that projects can be abandoned for no reason. But rather than explain away the passages in which Sartre endorses that idea, we should accept that he does hold it in *Being and Nothingness* even though it is inconsistent with the rest of his theory. Despite its ambition of systematicity, then, we should accept that this monumental work contains a deep inconsistency between the idea of pursuing a project and the idea of radical freedom.

3.7 Sartre's Progress

Merleau-Ponty aimed to establish that freedom is nothing more than the extent to which one's material and social situation permit the pursuit of aims determined by one's nature and development. His strategy was to argue for this through a critique of Sartre's contrasting view that the projects we freely choose and maintain ground the reasons that we find in our situations. Merleau-Ponty has not properly addressed Sartre's theory, however, because he has not appreciated the distinction between the meanings and the reasons that a situation presents. His argument that meanings are not dependent on the individual's projects misfires, because the Sartre of *Being and Nothingness* holds only that reasons are dependent on projects. Sartre here is in agreement with part of what Camus has Meursault discover towards the end of *The Outsider*, that values are not grounded in the meanings of situations themselves but in something that the subject brings to those situations. Camus and Sartre differ over just what it is about the subject that grounds the values they experience in the world and, consequently, as we will see in Chapter 9, over what truly is valuable.

Sartre's distinction between meanings and reasons is partly phenomenological. In our unreflective engagement with the world, reasons are presented as to be considered, compared, accepted, or rejected. This is revealed in pure reflection, but is not manifest in the impure reflection that simply reveals the correlation between our motivations and the reasons we find in situations. It is this phenomenology of reasons that grounds Sartre's view that the reasons we find in the world reflect our prior commitments, the values at the heart of our projects. Merleau-Ponty has overlooked this phenomenology of reasons and so has failed to engage with Sartre's motivation for postulating a metaphysical freedom that is ontologically prior to our experience of the world. We should agree with Merleau-Ponty, however, that Sartre is wrong to think that this metaphysical freedom allows us to revise or abandon a project for no reason, because this is inconsistent with the very idea of a project. But we should take this inconsistency as a reason to reject Sartre's claim that projects can be abandoned for no reason, rather than agreeing with Merleau-Ponty that it is a reason to reject Sartre's entire theory of freedom.

There are indications in Beauvoir's response to Merleau-Ponty that she considered Sartre to have refined his theory of freedom in this way by the time *Adventures of the Dialectic* was written. Sartre does not hold that projects can be abandoned at any moment for no reason, she argues, for this would be incompatible with the 'temporal thickness' required by his conception of projects (MPPS: 242–3). The claim that Sartre already agrees with Merleau-Ponty on this point contrasts sharply with her review of *Phenomenology of Perception* ten years earlier, where she describes Sartre's view of 'the nihilating power of the mind in the face of being, and the absolute freedom of the mind' as setting him clearly apart from Merleau-Ponty (RPP: 163). Towards the end of her later article, moreover, she writes that 'throughout the development of his work Sartre has insisted more and more on the *engaged* character of freedom' (MPPS: 252). She does not tell us precisely what she means by this, but she clearly intends to indicate that Sartre has been moving away from some details of the theory of freedom articulated in *Being and Nothingness*. Merleau-Ponty, by contrast, repeated in *Adventures of the Dialectic* the critique published a decade earlier in *Phenomenology of Perception* precisely because he thought that Sartre's core philosophical theory of freedom had not changed in the interim, but had simply been restated in a new social and political context (AD: 188–93).

As we will see in the next chapter, Beauvoir's own theory of freedom, her form of the basic existentialist claim that 'existence precedes essence', differed from the one Sartre articulated in *Being and Nothingness* even at the time that book was published and, ironically, the central difference concerns a point on which Beauvoir agrees with Merleau-Ponty. We will see in Chapter 7 that Sartre had accepted Beauvoir's form of existentialism by the time he wrote *Saint Genet*, published in 1952. By the time Beauvoir wrote her response to Merleau-Ponty's critique of Sartre in *Adventures of the Dialectic*, then, Sartre's theory of freedom had developed in a way that brought it closer to the view that Merleau-Ponty had articulated in *Phenomenology of Perception* ten years earlier. However, as we will also see in Chapter 7, the reason that Sartre is required to accept Beauvoir's form of existentialism is distinct from Merleau-Ponty's critique of his initial theory of freedom.

This progress of Sartre's thought can help to explain something that otherwise seems rather odd about the dispute with Merleau-Ponty: why was it Beauvoir, rather than Sartre, who responded in defence of Sartre and why does her response display the comprehensiveness and vehemence that one might expect only from someone's defence of their own work? Beauvoir had discussed philosophy with Sartre and had given him detailed critical feedback on his writing for all of their adult lives, of course, so in a sense everything he published is partly a product of her work. This would also go some way to explaining why she considered herself better placed than Merleau-Ponty to understand Sartre's philosophy, despite his long friendship with them both. But these points do not fully explain the firmness of her endorsement of Sartre's theory of freedom. This is not at all puzzling, however, if the theory of freedom underlying Sartre's *The Communists and Peace*, ostensibly the target of Merleau-Ponty's attack in *Adventures of the Dialectic*, and articulated in *Saint Genet*, to which Beauvoir refers in her response to Merleau-Ponty, is essentially the theory that she had held for over a decade and to which Sartre had only recently been converted.

4
Why Xavière is a Threat to Françoise

Beauvoir's first publication, *She Came To Stay*, set the agenda for much of the rest of her philosophical career, both in its form and in its content. The use of literary fiction remained central to her articulation of her own brand of existentialism. The use of autobiographical material to provide much of the narrative is echoed not only in her subsequent works of fiction, but also in her use of autobiography itself as a medium of existential thought. The themes of gender and age in relation to human freedom and fulfilment are central to the novel, just as they are central to her work as a whole and are the subjects of her two major theoretical treatises. Published in 1943, the same year as Sartre's *Being and Nothingness*, this novel constitutes the first major statement of Beauvoir's form of existentialism.

Merleau-Ponty recognized the novel's significance early on, describing it as heralding a new kind of literature in his 1945 article 'Metaphysics and the Novel'. Existential philosophy, he argues, shifts the focus of metaphysics from the abstract categories of thought onto our experience of the world, which precedes and underpins that thought. It thus aligns the central task of philosophy with that of literary fiction, to explicate our experience and explore its implications, and Beauvoir's novel is a paradigm of this new 'metaphysical literature' (MN: 27–8). Beauvoir confirmed this in 'Literature and Metaphysics', a lecture delivered during the 'existentialist offensive' later in 1945 and published in *Les Temps Modernes* the following year. Metaphysics, she argues, is the attempt to elucidate one's own existence. Philosophy does this in abstract concepts, but literature allows us 'to describe the metaphysical experience in its singular and temporal form' (LM: 274). Existentialist thought uses both forms because it aims 'to reconcile the objective and the subjective, the absolute and the relative, the timeless and the historical' (LM: 274).

We should not accept, therefore, any reading of the novel that aims to capture it fully in a few abstract themes or ideas. Beauvoir points out that a metaphysical novel would fail if it merely attempted to provide 'a fictional, more or less shimmering garment' for 'a preconstructed ideological framework' (LM: 272). Rather, such a novel is an 'adventure of the mind' in which the novelist tries to present a rich metaphysical vision of the human condition through language and the reader aims to participate in this vision (LM: 275–6). To try to decode the novel for its abstract philosophical meaning is to take up the wrong attitude as a reader. But having read the novel properly, the reader can express aspects of that vision in the abstract terms of philosophy, however inherently limited those terms may be. This simply requires the reader to respect the richness and sophistication of the vision in which it is embedded. One aspect of the novel that can be isolated in this way is an image of freedom over time that is central to Beauvoir's distinctive form of existentialism.

4.1 A Metaphysical Novel

The novel centres on the threat that Xavière poses to the relationship between Françoise and Pierre. This is indicated by the novel's original title, *L'Invitée*, an indication preserved by the title of the English translation, *She Came To Stay*. Françoise and Pierre have a relationship that allows them to have affairs with other people. But the threat Xavière poses is not simply that Françoise finds the reality of this openness more difficult than she had imagined. Xavière is not the first person Pierre has had an affair with during their relationship, but his previous affairs have not caused Françoise any anguish. What is more, he repeatedly offers to break off this affair. One aspect of the problem is certainly that Françoise is herself attracted to Xavière. But we should not agree that the problem Françoise faces is simply that Xavière brings out in her something taboo in her society (Heath 1998: 177–80). We should agree with Merleau-Ponty that the psychological aspects of the novel are merely superficial and look deeper for a metaphysical problem (MN: 32). Otherwise we would not have succeeded in participating in the metaphysical vision that Beauvoir attempts to capture in the novel that centres on this problem.

What is the aspect of the human condition exemplified, then, in the problem that Xavière poses for Françoise? 'What the characters in this book discover', argues Merleau-Ponty, 'is inherent individuality' (MN: 32).

The relationship between Françoise and Pierre was premised on a common project, a common set of values, which they pursued together, even where this meant them each having affairs with other people. Xavière is brought into the relationship as part of this project, but then undermines it. She does this not only through her rejection of their common values, but more importantly through Pierre's increasing sympathy with that rejection. She thus ruptures the mythical status that Françoise and Pierre have assigned themselves as a couple in harmony (Heath 1998: 176–7). But this is not merely a psychological point: through Pierre's complicity in bringing about this rupture, Françoise is forced to confront the metaphysical fact of her individuality, her irrevocable existential isolation. As her illusion of being part of a metaphysical 'we' is shattered, Merleau-Ponty points out, the artificial world she has built on this foundation collapses (MN: 32–3).

Xavière's challenge to the projects at the heart of the relationship between Françoise and Pierre is not simply that she presents an alternative set of values. It is rather that she directly attacks those values, objecting to their endless conversations about how best to live as a kind of narcissistic pedantry and portraying their creative endeavours as no different from the tediously regimented lives that they think they have escaped. This aspect of the rupture that she effects in their relationship reveals to Françoise that her own image of her life is no more significant than the ways in which it might be seen by other people. It is not merely a psychological fact, according to Merleau-Ponty, that 'it is our inevitable fate to be seen differently from the way we see ourselves' (MN: 38). It is a metaphysical fact. 'As long as Xavière exists, Françoise cannot help being what Xavière thinks she is' (MN: 37). Indeed, much of the novel explores the various ways it is possible to respond to the images of oneself presented by another person, and the ways in which these strategies can be infused with sexual desire (Barnes 1998).

The confrontation with Xavière, therefore, destroys Françoise's confident image of herself as part of a deeply connected couple engaged in a noble project of experimental living. Although this does capture an essential aspect of the problem that Xavière poses for Françoise, it does not seem to capture the whole of it. For it leaves some important aspects of the novel unexplained. We can ask why Xavière's behaviour has this effect on Françoise but not on Pierre. This suggests that their collective project played a more significant role in her life than in his.

Pierre's more sympathetic reactions to Xavière's challenges to their values, moreover, seem essential to the problem that Françoise faces. This suggests that the problem is as much to do with Pierre's commitment to their shared values as it is with Xavière's criticisms of them. And if we see the metaphysical story only as Françoise's realization of her individuality and her dependence on the ways other people see her, then her finding Xavière sexually attractive plays no metaphysical role.

Merleau-Ponty's interpretation has therefore left some aspects of the drama unexplained and others metaphysically redundant. An account of the problem Xavière poses for Françoise that does not have these shortcomings would better fit Beauvoir's idea of a metaphysical novel. Furthermore, in her essay on the metaphysical novel Beauvoir is clear that the temporal dimension of literary narrative is a feature of this way of articulating a metaphysical vision that sets it apart from mere description in the abstract language of philosophy (LM: 274). Merleau-Ponty's interpretation casts time merely as the arena in which the metaphysical vision is articulated, playing no essential role in that vision itself. Beauvoir's emphasis on the role of time in metaphysical literature, however, suggests that the metaphysical vision that Beauvoir is presenting through this novel is itself inherently temporal.

4.2 The Sedimentation of Projects

At the heart of Beauvoir's existentialism is the idea of a project. Human existence just is 'engagement in the world', a 'surpassing of the present toward a future' (EPW: 212; see also SS: 17). Projects are, as their name suggests, inherently temporal: not only are they oriented towards goals, but these goals are pursued only on the basis of what one has already become in the past (PC: 94). These projects are not determined by innate natures as they develop through our circumstances, but rather are freely chosen. 'I am free, and my projects are not defined by pre-existing interests; they posit their own ends' (EPW: 212). Since these freely undertaken projects are the whole basic structure of my existence, I have no innate nature. 'I am not a thing, but a project' (PC: 93). Beauvoir therefore agrees with Sartre and disagrees with Merleau-Ponty on the origins of projects.

But there is one crucial respect in which the metaphysical vision that Beauvoir presents through the threat Xavière poses to Françoise agrees with Merleau-Ponty's theory of freedom and disagrees with Sartre's initial form of existentialism. Merleau-Ponty argues that 'we must recognize a sort of sedimentation in our life', such that 'when an attitude toward the world has been confirmed often enough, it becomes privileged for us' (PP: 466). If I have been committed to a particular project, then 'this past, if not a destiny, has a specific weight' that makes it not merely a past decision and set of actions but 'the atmosphere of my present' (PP: 467). This is why one cannot easily abandon a project that one has been pursuing for a significant amount of time, he claims. But what exactly does he mean by an attitude becoming 'privileged' or carrying 'weight' or being 'the atmosphere of my present' due to 'a sort of sedimentation'?

Merleau-Ponty's concept of 'sedimentation' is central to the account of human existence articulated in *Phenomenology of Perception*, with the result that it has accrued a complicated meaning before it is employed in the chapter on freedom. He first uses the term to refer to the persistence of the conclusion of some reasoning as an acquired concept or judgment that can be drawn on without the need to work through that reasoning again (PP: 131). In part, this account of concept formation and its influence over thought is intended as a critique of rationalist epistemology. Explicit reasoning to a conclusion or the immediate judgment that something seems evidently true both deploy such sedimented ideas, so that the structure and meaning of such rational thought could not be fully spelled out without articulating all of the prior experience that formed the content and degree of influence of these sedimented ideas (PP: 416).

But the role of sedimentation is not limited to forming a stock of ideas that can be recalled and deployed in explicit reasoning. Rather, the knowledge that I gain about my environment becomes sedimented in my ability to navigate the world intelligently and even adeptly without the need for explicit thought about what I am doing (PP: 132). Perception 'is a reconstitution' of a meaningful environment, argues Merleau-Ponty, and therefore 'presupposes in me the sedimentations of a previous constitution' (PP: 222-3). The world that I live in, my milieu, is not simply a realm of physical objects, but is replete with my sedimented knowledge of their spatial arrangement and the meanings that they have for me. Indeed, it is also replete with meanings that have become 'sedimented on the outside': meanings encoded in language (PP: 195-6, 202) and those conferred on objects by people who have designed or used them for a specific purpose (PP: 363).

When he talks of a 'sort of sedimentation' of motives (PP: 466), Merleau-Ponty is therefore drawing a parallel with the role of one's own sedimented knowledge in constituting the world that one experiences. The sedimentation of motives would thus have two aspects. The first is that it would structure the world of one's experience. This structuring of the experienced environment by one's motives is central to both Beauvoir's and Sartre's forms of existentialism. Merleau-Ponty does not provide any distinction between this aspect of sedimented motives and the parallel aspect of sedimented knowledge. This contrasts sharply with Sartre, who analyses the phenomenology of the motivational structure of one's experience as a field of directive reasons to be questioned, considered, compared, affirmed, reassessed, rejected, overridden, or ignored, but does not ascribe such a directive structure to the manifestation of knowledge in experience as a field of meanings (see 3.2–3.4 above).[1]

The second aspect of this sedimentation, however, is that it is a gradual strengthening: each time a motive is acted upon, it increases in 'weight', becomes a little more 'privileged', becomes more firmly embedded in the agent's outlook, with the effects that its influence over behaviour is increased and that it is more difficult to reject. Merleau-Ponty argues for the sedimentation of motives through his critique of Sartre's idea that a project can be revised or abandoned at any point without any reason to do so. However, this argument fails to establish its conclusion. This idea of sedimentation is indeed inconsistent with the claim that one can revise or abandon a project for no reason. But the rejection of that claim does not entail the idea of sedimentation. For there is no inconsistency between the claim that reasons can only be opposed by other reasons and the claim that reasons are grounded in projects that are sustained only by the subject continuing to endorse the value at its core. Beauvoir does present an argument against this idea that projects have no inertia of their own, however, albeit in dramatic form.

---

[1] This contrast between Merleau-Ponty and Sartre seems to be grounded in their different underlying philosophical interests: Margaret Whitford argues that although both were 'concerned to elucidate the relation between consciousness and the world', Merleau-Ponty's purpose in this was 'to define the nature and limits of our *understanding* of the world', whereas Sartre's was 'to provide the basis for a philosophy of *action*' (1979: 306).

4.3 Why Xavière is a Threat to Françoise

Beauvoir explicitly endorses Merleau-Ponty's idea of sedimentation in her review of his *Phenomenology of Perception*, where she contrasts it with Sartre's theory of 'the absolute freedom of the mind' (RPP: 163). Although she does not specifically mention motives or projects in that review, we can derive from her novel published a couple of years earlier a reason to believe in this sort of sedimentation. For the sedimentation of projects is an aspect of the metaphysical vision of human existence that Beauvoir articulates in *She Came To Stay*. Françoise has pursued her shared project with Pierre for many years, has built her life around the values enshrined in that project, with the result that those values have gradually become deeply sedimented for her. They now exert a strong influence over her outlook in general and it would be very difficult for her to give them up. Indeed, this project and these values are now at the core of her identity. Because this is a joint project with Pierre, moreover, his commitment to these same values is essential to her understanding of what is worthwhile, her sense of purpose in life, and indeed to who she herself is. Because of the sedimentation of the project over a substantial tract of time, a threat to this project is a threat to Françoise herself and her whole world.

The threat Xavière poses is not simply that she might replace Françoise in Pierre's affections. If that were the problem, then Françoise would encourage Pierre to break off the affair with Xavière when he offers to do so. She does not want this because she is committed to the joint project that allows them each to have affairs with other people. Neither is the threat Xavière poses simply that she criticizes the values around which Françoise has built her life. Living an unconventional life means facing such criticisms regularly from many people, so Françoise must be used to this. Xavière does not criticize from an alternative set of values, moreover, but simply as a flippant rejection of organizing one's life around any values at all. It is difficult to see how this could be taken as serious criticism by someone living according to values that have been and continue to be carefully thought through.

Rather, it is Xavière's own lack of commitment to any values that is at the heart of the threat she poses to Françoise. More precisely, the problem is Pierre's admiration for Xavière's rejection of such commitment. For in taking seriously her claims that the values he shares with Françoise are worthless, or at least are no more important than any other set of values that they could have adopted instead, Pierre betrays his own lack of commitment to the shared project. Xavière is much younger than Françoise and Pierre. She is only just starting out in adult life. Her playful and sceptical view of their values is perfectly appropriate for someone beginning to find her own way in the world. 'Her life had not yet begun; for her everything was possible', as Françoise herself puts it (SCS: 23). But having pursued his joint project with Françoise for many years, Pierre by contrast ought to have developed a deep attachment to the values enshrined in that project that would preclude his admiration for Xavière's rejection of that project.

Or this, at least, is the problem Françoise faces. Pierre's admiration for Xavière indicates that he has not been committed to their shared values in the same way that she has been, the way that she had thought he had been. For if he had, then those values would now be as sedimented in his outlook as in hers. 'These thirty years were not only a past that she dragged along behind her; they had settled all about her, within her', Beauvoir tells us. 'That was her present, her future, that was the substance of which she was made' (SCS: 143). Had he really been committed to their shared project, he would not be able to mistake Xavière's frippery for profundity. This is what brings Françoise to realize her individuality. She discovers that even what she was most sure of in another person, Pierre's commitment to their project, has turned out not to be true. The problem is not that she has discovered the inevitable mismatch between her image of herself and the ways in which other people see her. It is that Pierre's sympathy for the way Xavière sees the two of them brings Françoise to realize that her entire adult life has not been what she thought it was. Her identity as someone engaged in this joint commitment is undermined.

In this light, her attraction to Xavière takes on a metaphysical aspect. So long as she could subordinate this to the aim of incorporating Xavière into her life with Pierre, it posed no problem for her. But once she realized the implications of Pierre's admiration for Xavière's outlook, her continuing attraction to Xavière threatened to erode her own commitment to the values of the shared project and her sense that she ever took them seriously. The final scene of the novel is not motivated simply by Françoise's jealousy or by her inability to live with her taboo attraction (Heath 1998: 177–80). Read in such psychological terms, this scene seems excessive and melodramatic, as Toril Moi has pointed out (2008: 117).

Given that Beauvoir intended the novel as a work of metaphysical literature, however, we should not be satisfied with Moi's psychoanalytic reading of it (2008: 139–43). Rather, we should agree with Mary Sirridge that the shortcoming of the psychological narrative in the final scene is essential to the novel's design: it forces the reader into the metaphysical perspective (2003: 147). In one act, Françoise departs from the shared project with Pierre while removing the threat to her commitment to the values that she had believed herself to share with Pierre, thereby establishing her individual life project on the ruins of their shared one.

4.4 Beauvoir's Critique of Sartre

We should therefore understand this metaphysical drama to be the fundamental structure of the novel. It is not that 'the metaphysical narrative is constantly destabilized by the presence of a second, commonplace level of narrative' (Sirridge 2003: 146). Rather, this more commonplace psychological intrigue of attractions and jealousies is the vehicle for the metaphysical narrative. Although the novel might contain valuable psychological insights, it is the metaphysical vision that drives the entire story. In this respect, *She Came To Stay* is the most accomplished of Beauvoir's works of metaphysical literature, perhaps the most accomplished existentialist novel of all. For it is the unfolding of the drama itself that embodies the metaphysical vision, rather than the lessons learned by the characters, the ideas they discuss, or their analyses of their experiences. By accomplishing this through a plot which is psychologically plausible until the end, Beauvoir has allowed the metaphysical content to structure the novel without disrupting the literary artifice that allows the reader to enter fully into the world it portrays. Her novel therefore meets the stringent literary standard that Camus outlines for philosophical novels in his review of Sartre's *Nausea*, a novel he praises highly despite thinking that it fails to meet that standard (SN: 199–202).

The novel's metaphysical purpose also drives its deployment of autobiographical material. It is clear from their shared project in life that Françoise and Pierre are modelled, however loosely, on Beauvoir and Sartre. The unstable ambivalence towards their shared project that Françoise sees in Pierre's admiration for Xavière dramatizes the philosophical instability that Beauvoir sees in Sartre's theory of projects. Just as Pierre claims to be committed to their shared project while also open to the idea that it is no more valuable than any other possible project, so Sartre's theory of freedom in *Being and Nothingness*, published in the same year as *She Came To Stay*, holds that human existence is fundamentally both a commitment to projects and an ability to revise or reject any project at any time. Just as Françoise sees Pierre's admiration for Xavière's frippery as incompatible with his professed commitment to their shared project, so Beauvoir sees Sartre's idea of the freedom to revise or reject a project without difficulty as incompatible with the sedimentation involved in the genuine pursuit of a project.

Beauvoir's critique of Sartre's theory of freedom embedded in this novel goes further than the critique offered by Merleau-Ponty two years later. For, as we saw in Chapter 3, all that is required to protect Sartre's theory from Merleau-Ponty's argument is to excise the claim that a project can be revised or rejected for no reason. One could reject that claim without thereby accepting that projects, or the values they enshrine, are gradually strengthened over time as the individual's commitment to them is repeatedly affirmed in thought and action. The existential threat that Xavière poses to Françoise dramatizes Beauvoir's view that such sedimentation is an essential aspect of commitment to a project or value. It is because the values of their shared project are not deeply sedimented in Pierre's outlook that Françoise comes to realize that he has never really been committed to them.

Sartre, by contrast, does not offer a clear positive account of what he means by commitment to a project. He does hold that it requires one to orient oneself toward the value enshrined in the project and that an explicit decision to do so is neither necessary nor sufficient for doing so, just as it is neither necessary nor sufficient for physically turning to face in a new direction (see 3.1 above). But since orienting oneself towards a value is not a bodily action, it is not clear what this imagery really indicates. Why does the gambler find the casino tempting despite his recent resolution not to gamble? How can he establish that resolution in place of his old project of gambling? Why does Daniel find it so difficult to drown his cats? The conception of radical freedom in Sartre's initial form of existentialism precludes any non-circular explanation of what it is to undertake or be committed to a project (see 3.6 above).[2]

---

[2] Christina Howells has argued that Merleau-Ponty's talk of the sedimentation of a project and Sartre's conception of the holism of projects (see 3.5 and 3.6 above) are 'using a

Beauvoir's vision of the metaphysics of commitment in *She Came To Stay*, by contrast, provides clear answers to these questions: the gambler has become deeply committed to gambling by regularly affirming in action the value it has for him; Daniel has become deeply attached to his cats by looking after them.

The metaphysical drama of *She Came To Stay*, therefore, is driven by an inherently temporal view of what it is to commit to a project. Françoise's view that Pierre has not really been committed to their shared values because they have not become sedimented dramatizes Beauvoir's view that Sartre cannot provide an account of commitment unless he accepts the sedimentation of projects. To accept sedimentation would require him, as Beauvoir points out in her review of Merleau-Ponty's *Phenomenology of Perception*, to revise his belief in 'the absolute freedom of the mind' (RPP: 163). For the influence of a sedimented project over one's thought and behaviour can be overcome only through an extended pattern of thought and action, a process that Françoise is concerned might result from her own attraction to Xavière. This is the 'temporal thickness' of projects that Beauvoir mentions in her response to Merleau-Ponty more than a decade later (MPPS: 242). But by that time, Beauvoir ascribed this idea of sedimentation to Sartre.

4.5 The Weight of Situation

In some of the most influential work in anglophone Beauvoir scholarship, Sonia Kruks has argued that Beauvoir and Sartre disagreed about the metaphysics of freedom as early as 1940, that Beauvoir developed her own account of freedom across her theoretical publications of the 1940s, and that she eventually persuaded Sartre to adopt her position (Kruks 1995; Kruks 1998). This disagreement and development, according to Kruks, concerns the impact of the individual's situation on their freedom. Sartre holds in *Being and Nothingness* that the social and physical structure of a situation limits the range of possibilities open to the

---

different vocabulary' but 'making the same point', which is that 'personal transformation is not easy' (2011: 45). However, there are two reasons that they are not making the same point. One is that sedimentation provides a non-circular explanation of what it is to be committed to a project, whereas the holism of projects cannot. The other, as we will see in Chapter 7, is that the idea of sedimentation affords a theory of the development of cultural values, whereas Sartre's initial form of existentialism does not.

individual, so limiting their freedom of action, but the significance of these limits is provided by the projects sustained by the individual's metaphysical freedom, since it is these projects that transform a pre-existing situation into a field of reasons. Beauvoir, according to Kruks, develops the contrary idea that situations weigh down metaphysical freedom itself, such that social oppression severely atrophies that freedom, and eventually persuades Sartre to agree.

This analysis has been claimed to misrepresent Sartre's theory of freedom. 'Sartre abandons his initially exaggerated view of absolute freedom', argues Matthew Eshleman, when he 'recognises social limitations to freedom' in the latter half of *Being and Nothingness* (2009: 69; see also Eshleman 2011: 43). Sartre begins with an abstract characterization of metaphysical freedom, on this reading, but then revises this to form his considered view, which includes the claim that 'the Other's existence brings a factual limit to my freedom' (B&N: 544).

Eshleman overlooks, however, the distinction between metaphysical freedom and freedom of the person. Sartre argues in the first part of *Being and Nothingness* for absolute freedom over the projects that structure the world of experience as a field of reasons. Later in the book, he argues that our freedom over our public image, or being-for-others, is limited by the freedom of other people: they have freedom over the projects that shape the way things in their world, including myself, appear to them. But this does not limit my freedom over the projects that shape my experience, because my being-for-others is a distinct aspect of my existence (B&N: 545–6; Webber 2011: 188–9). Beauvoir is right, therefore, to ascribe to *Being and Nothingness* a theory of 'the absolute freedom of the mind' (RPP: 163), where this indicates the metaphysical or ontological freedom to alter the projects that shape one's perceptions, thoughts, and feelings.

Eshleman further argues that Kruks is mistaken because Beauvoir's *Pyrrhus and Cineas*, published the year after *Being and Nothingness*, agrees with Sartre's initial abstract characterization of freedom rather than endorsing the fully considered view that emerges by the end of *Being and Nothingness*. Beauvoir here distinguishes metaphysical 'freedom' from the 'power' to influence the world. While 'power is finite and one can increase it or restrict it from the outside', she argues, 'freedom remains infinite in all cases' (PC: 124). Kruks does cite this passage, but concludes only that Beauvoir's idea that metaphysical freedom can be modified by restrictions on the agent's power remains 'still undeveloped' in this work (1998: 50–1). We should not agree with Eshleman, however, that this shows that it is Sartre rather than Beauvoir who has the more situated conception of freedom at this stage. Rather, we should recognize that Beauvoir has here provided a terminological distinction to capture the philosophical distinction also present in Sartre's thought, coining 'power' for the freedom of the person, reserving 'freedom' for metaphysical freedom.

Finally, as Eshleman points out, Kruks provides only one quotation from all of Beauvoir's theoretical works of the 1940s that directly describes metaphysical freedom as reduced by oppressive situations, a sentence from the Introduction to *The Second Sex*: when 'transcendence lapses into immanence, there is degradation of existence into "in-itself", of freedom into facticity' (SS: 17). The significance of this sentence is questionable. The use of quotation marks around 'in-itself' suggests that it is not to be taken literally as a metaphysical change, as Eshleman points out (2009: 85 n15). Taking it to indicate a metaphysical change does not fit well with the preceding sentence, which identifies transcendence as essential to 'every subject' (SS: 17). And perhaps more importantly, Eshleman points out that *The Second Sex* was first published in 1949, by which time Sartre seems to have been changing his mind about metaphysical freedom anyway (2009: 67).[3]

Should we conclude that Kruks is mistaken to claim that Beauvoir and Sartre disagreed about freedom at the time *Being and Nothingness* was published? As we have seen, the metaphysical vision that Beauvoir articulates in her novel published at that time does disagree with Sartre's theory of freedom, even drawing attention to this in the characters that she uses to dramatize her metaphysics of commitment. Kruks and Eshleman have both restricted themselves to Beauvoir's theoretical writings, even though Beauvoir argued that literary fiction is more appropriate than abstract philosophical thought for articulating metaphysics (LM: 274–5). What we find in *She Came To Stay*, however, is not the view that Kruks ascribes to Beauvoir, that situations can directly reduce

---

[3] We will return to this passage of *The Second Sex* in Chapter 11 (section 11.1), where we will see that the degradation of transcendence that Beauvoir describes here is not a reduction of metaphysical freedom, but the sedimentation of projects aimed at maintaining rather than transforming the current situation.

metaphysical freedom. It is rather the view that the longer one has been genuinely pursuing a project, committing oneself to the value it enshrines, the more sedimented that project and value become. Given that projects are undertaken and pursued in socially constructed contexts, projects that become sedimented incorporate aspects of the individual's social situation. It is through the sedimentation of one's projects, therefore, that the influence of social situation on oneself and one's outlook can become steadily stronger and more difficult to overcome.

This is consistent with the contrast that Beauvoir draws between freedom and power in *Pyrrhus and Cineas*. Power can be restricted from the outside, by imprisonment for example, but freedom cannot. The increasing influence of social situation on the mind occurs only through the sedimentation of projects that are themselves freely formulated and undertaken by the individual. Although actions can be effectively forced from the outside, the attitude with which they are done cannot. The sedimentation of projects, moreover, does not set external limits on freedom, because sedimentation is inherent in the freedom to commit oneself to projects and the values they enshrine. Sedimentation is therefore intrinsic to metaphysical freedom, as Beauvoir sees it, not something external to it. In this sense, metaphysical freedom remains 'infinite' (PC: 124) even though overcoming a sedimented project would be a difficult temporally extended task: freedom is infinite because it has no external boundaries, no limitations set by anything other than the operation of freedom itself. This conception of the sedimentation of social meanings through freely endorsed projects is the cornerstone of Beauvoir's theory of gender in *The Second Sex*, as we will see in Chapter 5.

4.6 Why Beauvoir is an Existentialist

We should agree with Kruks, therefore, that even when *Being and Nothingness* was being written, Beauvoir was developing an alternative theory of freedom which recognized that metaphysical freedom can become weighed down by the social structures that constrain the individual's life. But this effect of situations is mediated, on Beauvoir's view, through the sedimentation of freely chosen projects. Although she has this idea of sedimentation in common with Merleau-Ponty, we should not conclude that her theory of freedom is closer to his than it is to Sartre's. For as we saw in Chapter 3, Merleau-Ponty holds freedom to be the degree to which the material and social structure of the individual's situations permits the pursuit of their preferred projects. The projects themselves, on Merleau-Ponty's view, are the result of an innate nature as it has developed through the individual's experience. Beauvoir, by contrast, agrees with Sartre that there is a prior metaphysical or ontological freedom over the pursuit of projects: we freely choose the projects we pursue and the values they enshrine, according to Beauvoir, even though abandoning a project becomes more difficult the longer it is pursued.

This contrast with Merleau-Ponty can be found in Beauvoir's view of the relation between the sedimentation of motives and the sedimentation of knowledge. In her review of *Phenomenology of Perception*, Beauvoir praises Merleau-Ponty's detailed theories of the sedimentation of knowledge in thought and action (RPP: 160–3). She does not mention his point towards the end of the book that we should also recognize 'a sort of sedimentation' of motives (PP: 466). Merleau-Ponty describes this sedimentation as something merely additional to the sedimentation of knowledge, operating in an analogous way. Beauvoir, however, sees the sedimentation of knowledge as an aspect of the sedimentation of projects. She agrees with Sartre, that is to say, that the classifications and techniques that make up the social world cannot impinge on metaphysical freedom directly, but become incorporated into the individual's outlook and behaviour only through forming the detail of the projects that the individual pursues. Sartre calls this subsumption of social meanings into projects 'interiorization' (B&N: 544). Beauvoir differs from Sartre only in her further view that these meanings become sedimented in one's thought and behaviour through the sedimentation of the projects within which they are subsumed.

Beauvoir's position is a form of existentialism precisely because it accords this priority to the individual's projects. But her form of existentialism differs from Sartre's on a fundamental matter. For her, the slogan 'existence precedes essence' captures a temporal relation as well as a logical one: as time goes on, for Beauvoir, the values and meanings that comprise the individual's projects become sedimented, thereby developing an individual Aristotelian essence that explains why that person thinks and behaves in the particular ways that they do. This is not a fixed essence, since the idea of sedimentation entails that this character continues to develop and that, in principle, any sedimented project could be weakened and removed over time. But it contrasts with the kind of individual essence that we have according to Sartre's initial theory of freedom. In his meaning of the slogan, the term 'essence' refers only to the set of projects that the individual is pursuing and can revise or reject at any moment. These projects carry no weight, for Sartre, beyond the individual continuing to affirm them. Beauvoir's meaning of the slogan recognizes that the values and social meanings enshrined in these projects can become very firmly embedded in the individual's outlook and behaviour, so that the individual can find it difficult to overcome them and is even unlikely to want to do so.

This form of existentialism has a political aspect that Sartre's cannot have. Beauvoir's theory allows that social structures can make the exercise of metaphysical freedom over one's own projects increasingly difficult as a result of the sedimentation of social meanings and of values formulated against the backdrop of these meanings. Sedimented meanings can influence the individual's thought and outlook to such a degree that alternatives to their current situation become very hard to imagine and sedimented values built on those social meanings can make such alternatives seem very unattractive, even if the individual is strongly dissatisfied with their current situation and projects. Such internalized oppression cannot be explained without a theory of sedimentation, so cannot be explained by Sartre's initial form of existentialism. It can be characterized as a repression of freedom only if we accept that the ability to imagine and adopt new projects is central to human freedom, which is not accepted by Merleau-Ponty's theory of freedom as the degree to which one's situation tolerates the pursuit of one's projects. This way of understanding the internalization of oppression is central to Beauvoir's analysis of gender in *The Second Sex*, as we will see in Chapter 5. It rests on a theory of freedom and projects that is neither Sartre's nor Merleau-Ponty's, though it has aspects in common with each of these.

What, then, should we make of Beauvoir repeatedly claiming that she had simply adopted Sartre's philosophical system? These claims have been taken to justify reading her work as simply providing literary illustrations and ethical applications of Sartre's philosophy. But they have also been dismissed as disingenuous, since the evidence shows that her philosophical thought departs substantially from his (Kruks 1995: 80–2; Kruks 1998: 46). One way to reconcile Beauvoir's distinctive form of existentialism with her claim that she followed Sartre in philosophical matters, however, is to apply the distinction she herself drew between metaphysics and philosophy. 'Metaphysics is, first of all, not a system', she writes; 'one does not "do" metaphysics as one "does" mathematics or physics' (LM: 273). One rather adopts an attitude towards existence that enables 'an original grasping of metaphysical reality' (LM: 273). Philosophy makes this vision explicit by forging a conceptual apparatus to capture abstract structures of it. Literature, by contrast, can present it in full. In her theoretical works, Beauvoir presents her original metaphysical vision through her appropriation of the conceptual apparatus of *Being and Nothingness*.

4.7 The Ambiguity of Influence

This is not to deny that Beauvoir influenced that conceptual apparatus. Sartre's sophisticated and detailed philosophical terminology undoubtedly developed through his continual discussions of philosophy with Beauvoir throughout his adult life, just as it undoubtedly developed through discussion with other philosophers, including Merleau-Ponty, and through his readings and perhaps misreadings of many works across the years of its formation. Neither is it to deny that these discussions substantially shaped the metaphysical views that Beauvoir, Sartre, and Merleau-Ponty each went on to articulate. But it is to accept Beauvoir's distancing herself from the precise meanings of these terms that can be found in *Being and Nothingness* and elsewhere in Sartre's work, even though she deploys those same terms. For on this reading of the development of existentialism, Sartre's primary concern was with the articulation of his metaphysical view in an abstract philosophical framework, whereas Beauvoir was sceptical of the power of such conceptual work to capture the rich nuance of her metaphysical vision. That she nevertheless tried to capture her vision in the terminology of a closely similar metaphysics has some strategic advantages over developing an entirely new terminology, but comes with inevitable limitations.

When some detail of her philosophical fiction or her theoretical works is incompatible with those of Sartre's concepts she deploys, we should read this as a manifestation of these limitations, rather than as mere inconsistency in Beauvoir's thought itself. We should prefer, so far as is plausible, to revise our understanding of her use of the relevant concept rather than to dismiss the apparently troublesome detail. Given the role of the sedimentation of projects in structuring the narrative of *She Came To Stay*, we should read her use of Sartre's language of metaphysical freedom in *Pyrrhus and Cineas*, for example, not as an endorsement of his concept of freedom in its entirety, but only as much as is consistent with this sedimentation. Given the development of existentialism through their continual discussion and given her views of the relation between metaphysical thought and philosophical vocabulary, we are not justified in drawing the stronger conclusion, which some Beauvoir scholars have put forward, that she employs his terminology only out of personal loyalty at the cost of significantly distorting her own thought (Langer 2003: 88–9; Le Doeuff 1995: 62–5; Kruks 1998: 58; Tidd 1999: 48). We should rather accept the view that Beauvoir transforms the terms she appropriates from Sartre, just as she does with the terms borrowed from other thinkers (Deutscher 2008: 14–18).

These transformations are often subtle. Her alterations to Sartre's concepts are obscured if we read her work through the lens of his philosophy. There have been two forms of reading *She Came To Stay* in this way. One has been to read it as an illustration of the philosophical analyses found in *Being and Nothingness* (Barnes 1998). The other has been to analyse the biographical record with the aim of establishing which of the ideas in common between these two books were originally Beauvoir's and which were originally Sartre's (Fullbrook and Fullbrook 1995; Fullbrook 2004). Both of these ways of reading Beauvoir risk occluding philosophical contributions unique to her works of the relevant period. Drawing attention to the parallels between her thought and Merleau-Ponty's, on the other hand, risks simply recasting Beauvoir as his intellectual disciple rather than Sartre's, or at best characterizing her work as a synthesis of theirs (Bergoffen 2009: 17).

These kinds of analysis of Beauvoir's work are tempting if we start with her theoretical works of the 1940s, since they were all published after *Being and Nothingness* and all but *Pyrrhus and Cineas* were published after *Phenomenology of Perception*. We might then read our conclusions about her theoretical works back into her earlier novel. But if we start by trying to make sense of the novel in its own terms, then we are led to a metaphysical vision that can in part be explicated in terms of the philosophies of Sartre and Merleau-Ponty, but since it was published at the same time as *Being and Nothingness* and two years before *Phenomenology of Perception*, it is less tempting to take her work to be derivative of theirs. We could then attempt to disentangle the lines of influence through analysing the biographical record, but since this is patchy and mostly limited to correspondence between two of the three it is not at all clear why we should expect such an endeavour to be successful.

One of Merleau-Ponty's observations on *She Came To Stay* is instructive here. 'It is impossible to calculate each one's role in the drama, impossible to evaluate the responsibilities, to give a true version of the story', he writes, because it is part of the novel's metaphysical vision that each person 'is inextricably and confusedly bound up with the world and with others' (MN: 36). Beauvoir, Merleau-Ponty, and Sartre had been discussing their ideas with one another for fifteen years by the time *She Came To Stay* was published (Bakewell 2016: 111–14, 144, 238–40). We can identify Beauvoir's philosophy, just as we can identify Françoise's view that Pierre had never really been committed to their project. What we cannot hope to do is to break the thought of any one of these philosophers down into distinct units and determine its provenance, just as we cannot break Beauvoir's novel down into discrete events and assign responsibility for each to a particular character. But this ambiguity of influence does not matter. For what is interesting about Beauvoir is not whether this or that particular idea crossed her mind before it crossed either Sartre's or Merleau-Ponty's. What is interesting is the metaphysical and ethical outlook, the form of existentialism, that she developed in part through her extended conversations with them both.

# 5

Psychoanalysis and the Existentialist Mind

Existentialism is often portrayed as fundamentally antagonistic to the Freudian psychoanalytic view of the mind that pervaded the intellectual and cultural atmosphere in which Beauvoir and Sartre developed their philosophical theories. The basic tenet of existentialism, that existence precedes essence, rules out explaining an individual's preferences or behaviour in terms of inbuilt aspects of their mind, whereas Freud ascribes problematic thought and behaviour to the repression of innate drives. The same basic tenet grounds the existentialist affirmation of the metaphysical freedom of the individual, whereas Freud's theory of the origins and effects of repression is deterministic. Despite these oppositions, however, existentialism should be classed as standing in the Freudian tradition, rather than an alternative to that tradition.

For both Beauvoir and Sartre seek to preserve in their existentialism what they find valuable in Freud's work. What they reject, primarily, is what has become known as Freud's 'metapsychology', his schematic division of the mind between those aspects the individual can easily become aware of, those they cannot easily become aware of but which are expressed in their thought and behaviour anyway, and those that police the boundary between the two. Beauvoir and Sartre both retain some of Freud's central insights, in particular that emotional outbursts are often covertly directed at achieving the individual's goals and that problematic thought and behaviour can stem from a deeply embedded sense of inferiority. They are both quite clear that their existentialist theory of the mind is intended to explain these features of human existence better than Freud's own theory of mind.

Sartre criticizes Freud's theory of mind early on in *Being and Nothingness* as unable to explain the findings of Freud's own psychoanalysis, then devotes a large section towards the end of the book to elaborating an 'existentialist psychoanalysis', partly by arguing that it can explain many of Freud's insights. Beauvoir devotes an early section of *The Second Sex* to separating out those aspects of Freud's theory of gender that she thinks ought to be accepted from those she considers philosophically untenable. She elaborates her own theory of gender partly through critical dialogue with Freudian psychoanalysis across the whole book. Beauvoir and Sartre both develop their forms of existentialism as contributions to the Freudian tradition of psychoanalysis, therefore. But the two end up with markedly different varieties of psychoanalysis, reflecting the difference between Beauvoir's idea of sedimentation and Sartre's idea of radical freedom. Beauvoir's version has greater explanatory power, as we shall see, but she does not advertise this or even make the contrast with Sartre explicit.

5.1 The Puzzles of Repression and Resistance

One reason why this relationship between existentialism and Freudian psychoanalysis has been overlooked is that it is no easier to find a clear and definitive statement of a theory of the basic structures of the mind in the works of Freud than it is to find one in the works of Beauvoir or Sartre. Freud's theory was in continuous development throughout his long career and very little of his voluminous published work is focused directly on this issue. The meanings of particular Freudian concepts alter subtly from work to work and occasionally a whole new set of terms is introduced. This makes it difficult to compare Freud's theory of the mind with any other way of thinking about it, not just with existentialism (Gardner 2000).

Despite these challenges, however, we can discern the basic structure of the Freudian mind with some degree of precision from two works, 'The Unconscious', published in 1915, and *The Ego and the Id*, published in 1923. Freud holds in these works that there are two senses in which a 'drive' or motivation can be unconscious. For it to be 'descriptively unconscious' is simply for the agent to be unaware of it. Some drives are not merely descriptively unconscious, but are also 'dynamically unconscious', meaning that the individual actively tries to keep them out of conscious awareness (TU: § II; EI: ch. 1). Sexual desires that are taboo in one's society, for example, are drives that become repressed as one does not want to admit to oneself that one even has such desires.

This activity of repression is psychologically puzzling: how is it possible to actively try to keep something out of conscious awareness, without thereby being aware of it as the thing one is trying to repress? The activity of repression, moreover, continues even as the psychoanalyst is trying to help the patient to identify the cause of their problematic behaviour. When the analyst comes close to correctly identifying the repressed drive, according to Freud, the patient tends to resist by refusing to cooperate or by denying the diagnosis (TU: 166; EI: 17). This is also puzzling: the patient has sought out precisely this help in uncovering the source of their problems, so why do they resist it just as it reaches fruition? Sartre argues that these puzzles cannot be solved within the framework of Freud's theory of mind and develops his own account of the deep motivations for thought and action partly to explain how the repression and resistance observed by Freud is possible. Beauvoir augments this theory with her idea of the sedimentation of projects and the social meanings they subsume.

What these two existentialist accounts of mind have in common, as we have seen in Chapters 3 and 4, is the claim that the individual's projects are at the core of their existence. Projects are directed towards goals that the individual is trying to achieve and enshrine values that the individual endorses. One way to think of this view of the mind is as the Freudian view pulled inside out: where Freud saw the individual's goal-directed behaviour as manifesting deep desires, or drives, that precede and shape their choices, the existentialists see desires as manifestations of deep projects that have themselves been chosen. This language of choice does not indicate explicit reasoned decision making. 'It can happen', according to Beauvoir, that 'one suddenly becomes aware of engagements that have been lived without being thought' (PC: 94). Sartre gives the example of staying alive as a project that might be pursued without being considered (B&N: 459). To undertake a project is rather to set oneself toward achieving its purpose, to orient oneself towards the value that it enshrines.

Sartre's initial form of existentialism cannot explain what undertaking or being committed to a project consists in, but on Beauvoir's theory it consists in the sedimentation of a project through repeated thought and behaviour that endorses it (see 3.6 and 4.4 above). This difference in their theories of projects grounds a divergence between their overall existential outlooks that neither philosopher explicitly acknowledges. Beauvoir's elaboration of her form of existentialism in *The Second Sex* departs from Sartre's initial form of existentialism not only in its inclusion of sedimentation, but consequently in its theories of freedom and responsibility, and its framework for psychoanalysis. It is because Beauvoir allows for the sedimentation of socially determined meanings internalized into projects that she can ascribe to the individual's social context a more substantial role in shaping their behaviour than is available on either Freud's theory or Sartre's initial form of existentialism. Indeed, as we will see, the progression from Freud to Beauvoir can be seen as overcoming the influence of fundamentally Cartesian ideas about the mind, first through Sartre's critique of Freud, then through Beauvoir's rejection of the vestige of Cartesianism remaining in Sartre's own position.

5.2 In the Shadow of Descartes

Sartre's critique of Freud is often characterized as an insistence on aspects of the Cartesian view of the mind that Freud considered himself to have clinical reasons to reject. Cartesian dualism is usually defined as the view that mind and body are distinct substances. But this substance dualism is motivated by a prior conceptual dualism between rational and spatial processes: I can clearly and distinctly conceive of my thinking without conceiving of it as spatially extended, according to Descartes, and I can clearly and distinctly conceive of spatially extended body without conceiving of it as thinking (1984: 54). The argument for substance dualism in the Sixth Meditation rests on this distinction between thought and extension. Descartes concludes that these inhere in distinct substances from a general claim that conceptually distinct items can really exist apart from one another (1984: 54). Moreover, he is clear in the Second Replies that what he means by 'thought' is 'everything that is within us in such a way that we are immediately aware of it', which he claims covers 'all the operations of the will, the intellect, the imagination and the senses' (1984: 113). The conceptual dualism that underlies his metaphysical dualism of substances is therefore between conscious, rational, mental activity and nonconscious, nonrational, spatial processes.

Freud's theory of dynamically unconscious drives clearly departs from this conceptual dualism: these drives are purposive mental activity, aiming to be expressed in behaviour, but they are mechanistic and operate without the agent's conscious awareness of them. Sartre is sometimes read as objecting to this departure from the Cartesian picture. On this reading, Sartre wants to retain both the Cartesian identification of all mentality with consciousness and the Cartesian denial that anything mechanistic or material could be part of the mind. This reading is usually accompanied by the argument that Freud had good reason to abandon these Cartesian shibboleths, so Sartre's descriptions of bad faith, though illuminating in some respects, cannot capture the full range of self-deceptive strategies that the human mind is capable of (Soll 1981; Neu 1988). This reading of Sartre emphasizes his claim that consciousness is ontologically distinct from the material realm, a claim exemplifying his own Cartesian heritage and suggestive of a dualism between the rational mind and the causal material world. But this reading overlooks an important strand of the theory of human existence developed in *Being and Nothingness* that stands in tension with this ontological claim, a strand that entails the rejection of aspects of the Cartesian conceptual dualism between rationality and spatiality that Freud's theory of mind retains.

Once these features of the disagreement between Sartre and Freud are in view, it is Freud who seems the more Cartesian of the two. To see this, we need first to consider Freud's characterization of the essential difference between conscious thought and dynamically unconscious drives (TU: § V; EI: chs. 1–2). For this employs a conceptual dualism between two kinds of mental item. One kind are sensitive to evidence about the way the world is, are structured in such a way as to make them evidentially and inferentially related to one another, and are thereby available for beliefs to be formed about them, beliefs that can then be linguistically articulated. These kinds of mental item may be conscious or descriptively unconscious. They form the part of my mind of which I can easily become aware and with which I identify. The other kind are mere drives and impulses that are structured in such a way that they do not stand in any rational relations with one another or with anything else. They compete and combine according to the causal laws unique to their 'cathectic energy'. They can motivate actions aimed at satisfying them, so that the sex drive, for example, can motivate sexual activity. But when the person does not accept the drive, or cannot reasonably engage in activity to satisfy it, that person represses it: they refuse its expression through denying that they even possess it. This is what makes a drive 'dynamically unconscious'.

This is a departure from Cartesian conceptual dualism, but it is also a descendant of it. For the conceptual dualism that Descartes formulated combines three distinguishable dualisms. First, it contains a dualism of the consciously accessible and the rest: for Descartes, as we have seen, the term 'thought' that covers everything in the mind is defined by availability to self-awareness. Second, it contains a dualism of the representational and the nonrepresentational: every mental item is an 'idea' which represents something, some 'object', but this 'objective reality' is a feature only of ideas (1984: 28–9, 113). Third, it contains a dualism of the rational and the spatial: on the Cartesian picture, everything in the mind is a form of thought and operates on rational principles; everything else is spatially extended and operates accordingly.

Freud's theory of the mind employs all three of these conceptual dualisms. His departure from Descartes is simply in recognizing that the three need not be understood as forming a single conceptual duality. Instead, on Freud's view, it is the dualism between the representational and the nonrepresentational, rather than that between the consciously accessible and the consciously inaccessible, that forms the boundary around the mind: what 'psychical' items have in common, on Freud's theory, is that they represent the way the world is, if they are beliefs, or the goal that would satisfy them, if they are desires or drives. This does not coincide with the dualism between consciously accessible and consciously inaccessible: only some items within the realm of the representational are accessible to consciousness, others can be uncovered only by psychoanalysis.

Most importantly, on Freud's theory, the dualism of rational and nonrational does not coincide with either of the other two. Rationally structured mental items are governed by 'the reality principle': they are sensitive to the way things really are, a sensitivity that operates by the rules of inference. But mental items lacking this structure, the drives, are governed by 'the pleasure principle': they aim to be satisfied through processes described in spatial metaphors; drives with the most 'cathectic energy' dominate over those with less, but cathectic energy can be 'displaced' from one drive to another, or by 'condensation' one drive can take on the cathectic energies of several drives (TU: § V). All rationally structured mental items are consciously accessible. Some drives are consciously accessible, but the dynamically unconscious ones are not.

5.3 Sartre's Critique of Freud

Early on in *Being and Nothingness*, Sartre rejects Freud's theory of the mind by arguing that it cannot explain the activities of repression and resistance that motivated it in the first place (B&N: 74–7). His argument targets Freud's retention of the conceptual dualism of the rational and the nonrational. On which side of this divide do the activities of repression and resistance belong? The process of repression requires that each drive is recognized as either permitted or to be repressed and that impulses toward specific actions are tested for whether they express one of the drives to be repressed. The process of resistance requires comparing the psychoanalyst's suggestion of a possible repressed drive with the set of drives being repressed, in order that a denial or other evasive strategy can be formulated if the analyst's suggestion accurately describes a member of that set, or is close to doing so. These are all rational activities. They involve sensitivity to evidence and inferential reasoning. They cannot be understood as operating in the nonrational part of the mind. But neither can they be understood as operating in the rational part of the mind, for if they were then the processes themselves and therefore the drives they attempt to repress would be consciously accessible to the subject by rational inference.

Freud is not unaware of this problem. He raises it himself at the end of the first chapter of *The Ego and the Id*. The activity of repression, he writes, 'produces powerful effects without itself being conscious' and 'requires special work before it can be made conscious' (EI: 17). Repression is itself a dynamically unconscious process, so we cannot accept the initial definition of the dynamic unconscious as the set of drives that have been repressed (EI: 18). Freud then struggles to settle on a satisfying description of repression in the terms of his own theory. In the second chapter, he introduces two new terms, 'ego' and 'id', defining the ego as 'that part of the id which has been modified by the direct influence of the external world' and now 'seeks to bring the influence of the external world to bear upon the id' (EI: 25). He also tells us that the 'ego represents what may be called reason and common sense, in contrast to the id, which contains the passions' (EI: 25). The rational activity of repressing drives that are socially unacceptable therefore belongs in the ego. Yet this just compounds the puzzle: we are left asking not only how the ego's rational activity of repression is dynamically unconscious, but also how the ego can engage in resistance to the analysis when the person who identifies with the ego actively sought out and is now engaging with this analysis (EI: 26–7).

Freud's next move, in chapter 3, is to introduce the idea of the 'superego' or 'ego ideal'. This is an internalized model of the individual's parents, particularly the father figure, that replicates the parental work of repressing particular drives. Freud describes this construction as 'a precipitate in the ego' and as a 'modification of the ego' (EI: 34). Since the ego is the region of the id that is structured rationally and the superego carries out the rational function of selective repression, it is clear that the superego must be an aspect of the ego. But he also contrasts the ego as 'essentially the representative of the external world, of reality' with the superego as 'the representative of the internal world, of the id' (EI: 36). There are two features of the superego that justify this description. One is that it is the expression of the id's drive to identify with, or at least emulate, the parents, particularly the father figure (EI: 34–5). The other is that it responds to the drives of the id generally, otherwise it could not carry out its work of repression, whereas the rest of the ego is sensitive only to its own contents and reality beyond the mind.

This might help to explain how resistance occurs: it is the superego that resists the analyst's questions, in conflict with the ego's goal of identifying the cause of the problematic symptoms. This would be an example of the conflicts between ego and superego that, Freud tells us, 'ultimately reflect the contrast between what is real and what is psychical, between the external world and the internal world' (EI: 36). But none of this resolves the initial puzzle: how can the superego's rational activity of repression occur beyond the reach of conscious accessibility, given the conceptual dualism of the rational and the nonrational that Freud has deployed to develop this whole theory? At this point, Freud gives up on the attempt to solve this puzzle about repression. 'It would be vain', he argues, 'to work it into any of the analogies with the help of which we have tried to picture the relation between the ego and the id' (EI: 36–7). Freud has paved the way for this retreat by first complaining of 'a general refusal to recognize that psychoanalytic research could not, like a philosophical system, produce a complete and readymade theoretical structure', but should instead be understood as an empirical science whose conceptual structures evolve with the accumulation of evidence (EI: 35–6).

Sartre does not frame his argument against Freud particularly clearly. Indeed, he has been read as firing a variety of disparate and undeveloped criticisms at Freud's theory (Brown and Hausman 1981). However, his various comments centre on this problem that Freud fails to solve in *The Ego and the Id*. Sartre's central claim is that the problem simply cannot be solved within the conceptual dualism of the rational and the non-rational on which Freud's theory is ultimately founded. Sartre is right that we must 'abandon all the metaphors representing repression as the impact of blind forces', because repression and resistance are inherently rational activities (B&N: 75). But they therefore cannot be beyond the reach of the rational mind. For their rational structure is sufficient for the inferential formation of beliefs about them and spoken reports of them. Sartre recognizes the pragmatic status of psychoanalysis, such that the criteria of success for a theory or hypothesis are 'the number of conscious psychic facts which it explains' and 'the success of the psychiatric cure which it allows' (B&N: 74). His critique of Freud's theory is not simply motivated by a philosopher's preference for theoretical precision and completeness. Rather, he is arguing that psychoanalysis, despite its successes, is hamstrung by the incoherence of its fundamental conceptual structure. If this is right, then pragmatically what psychoanalysis needs is a whole new conceptual framework.

5.4 Bad Faith in a Unified Mind

Sartre's proposal is not to return to the Cartesian alignment of the three conceptual dualisms of consciously accessible and consciously inaccessible, representational and nonrepresentational, and rationally structured and spatially ordered. Neither is his solution to rearrange these dualisms differently from the way Freud has rearranged them. Rather, his more radical solution is to abandon these Cartesian conceptual dualisms altogether and instead build a theory of the mind on the basis of his conception of a project. Sartre's idea of a project, as we have seen in Chapter 3, is not merely the idea of a goal that one is pursuing, although it does include that, but is an orientation of oneself towards a value that then informs the structure of one's experience. More specifically, one experiences the world as a field of reasons to act in particular ways as a result of the projects one is pursuing. It is because I aim to keep my job that I experience the sound of the alarm clock as a reason to get out of bed, or because of my project of defiance towards social authority that the sign ordering me to keep off the grass strikes me as a reason to stride across the lawn.

It is this role of projects in structuring experience that is central to Sartre's transformation of psychoanalysis. The contrast with Freud is well illustrated by their differing conceptions of the inferiority complex. Freud argues that feelings of inferiority to other people, which he considers common to certain psychiatric conditions, have their origin in an overactive superego. The function of the superego, after all, is to condemn aspects of the individual's desires in order to prevent their expression. If this critical role is overplayed, the individual will suffer the feeling of inferiority (EI: 51). Sartre, by contrast, sees this problem of perceived inferiority as a project. He holds that some people aim to present themselves to themselves and to the world at large as intrinsically inferior, either to carve out a distinctive identity or to evade taking responsibility for their lives. This project requires that one sets oneself goals that one cannot hope to achieve, or goes about pursuing perfectly achievable goals in hopeless ways, so that one will then fail to achieve these goals and be able to cite these failings as evidence of one's inferiority. One must consider oneself to be genuinely trying to achieve these goals, however, since otherwise one would not be able to see one's failure to achieve them as evidence of inferiority (B&N: 493–5).[1]

How can one manage to trick oneself in this way? The inferiority project, according to Sartre, structures one's experience of the world so that particular goals seem achievable when they are not, or achievable by means that are not in fact good ways of trying to achieve them. One's field of reasons is distorted, inviting and reinforcing behaviour that is unlikely in fact to produce the promised results. One's voluntary decisions are therefore responses to considerations that have been selected and weighted by this underlying project. But this is not sufficient for the project to be a success. It is crucial that one's awareness of oneself is also shaped by the inferiority project. Sartre holds that there are two forms of

---

[1] The idea of the inferiority complex was most thoroughly developed by Alfred Adler in the first three decades of the twentieth century. It was the centrepiece of his theory of individual psychology, which emphasized conscious thought and social dynamics in opposition to Freud's focus on unconscious mechanisms. Adler's influence on existentialism has not been explored in detail, perhaps in part because he is not usually identified as an existentialist or existential thinker himself.

reflection on one's own experience: pure reflection presents only the way the world seems, so does not ascribe any specific motivations to oneself; impure reflection, on the other hand, views one's experience as a relation between the way the world seems and one's own motivations (see 3.4 above). Impure reflection structured by the inferiority project, therefore, would collude in presenting one's motivations in pursuing one's doomed projects as genuine aims rather than mere ruses to prove one's inferiority (B&N: 495).

This way in which the inferiority project buries itself, according to Sartre, is just one form of a more general structure of bad faith. For this is also a project, 'a type of being in the world' which 'tends to perpetuate itself' (B&N: 92). At its core, it is the project of seeing oneself as having some specific fixed nature that explains one's thoughts, feelings, and actions. It structures one's experience of the world in such a way that other people's behaviour appears as expressing their fixed natures. Like the inferiority project, it also shapes one's reflections on oneself. One's own thoughts, feelings, and actions will seem, through this lens, as expressions of one's fixed nature. This will remain true even for the project of bad faith itself: any reflection on seeing people as having fixed natures will present this as itself an aspect of one's own fixed nature (Webber 2009: 99–101). In this way, someone can pursue the project of bad faith, like the inferiority project, while also hiding it from themselves. An underlying project can thus repress itself, without needing any of the apparatus that Freud's theory describes.

This structure can also explain the phenomenon of resistance to psychoanalytic treatment, according to Sartre. Although bad faith is socially pervasive, Sartre thinks, and so considered a normal outlook, the inferiority project is a particular problem that can lead the person to seek the help of a psychoanalyst. Seeking this help can itself be an attempt to establish one's inferiority. After all, not everyone needs to see a psychoanalyst! This goal then governs the person's engagement in the psychoanalytic procedure: all of the patient's 'efforts will have as their goal causing the attempt to fail', in order to establish that they have an incurable psychological problem, which makes them inferior to other people (B&N: 496). If the analyst begins to make progress towards the correct diagnosis, then the patient will respond with emotional outbursts aimed at preventing that diagnosis. Thus, according to Sartre, the idea of projects can accommodate the puzzling psychological phenomena that motivated Freud's theory of the mind without using Freud's theoretical framework or deploying any of the three conceptual dualisms that Freud inherited from Descartes.

5.5 A Psychoanalysis of Radical Freedom

Existentialist psychoanalysis differs from its Freudian forebear in ways that follow directly, according to Sartre, from this alternative conceptual structure of the minds that it investigates. Freudian psychoanalysis, Sartre argues, was content to trace an individual's choices back to some set of basic desires or drives by considering how these have interacted with one another and the social environment in this particular person's history. Sartre objects that there is no justification for treating these desires or drives as basic, or 'irreducible', rather than seeking to explain them in terms of something deeper (B&N: 578–85). His own view of the mind pulls the Freudian structure inside out: the desires that can be identified are to be explained in terms of the deeper projects that the individual has chosen to pursue, until we reach a project that is evidently genuinely irreducible in itself. The fear of death, for example, cannot be understood as a basic drive: it makes sense only within the deeper project of living (B&N: 585). 'There is not a taste, a mannerism, or a human act which is not *revealing*', writes Sartre (B&N: 589). He differs from Freud over what it reveals, a project rather than a complex (B&N: 590).

Because the structure of projects can explain both repression and resistance, Sartre points out, existentialist psychoanalysis agrees with Freud that the subject is not in a privileged position to uncover the underlying attitude. Psychoanalysis requires specialist knowledge of both the method and the conceptual framework, which in principle can be applied to oneself if one is suitably trained, but which is likely to be applied better by someone who does not share the motivations produced by the attitude that is to be uncovered (B&N: 591). Sartre then argues that existentialism can explain a further phenomenon encountered in psychoanalysis that Freud's theory cannot explain. This is the collapse of resistance when the patient finally recognizes the diagnosis as correct. There seems no clear reason why the Freudian superego should ever give up resisting the analyst's diagnosis. On the existentialist view, the analyst's diagnosis does not force out into the open something that was hidden from the patient, but rather teaches the patient how to conceptualize the project that they have always been nonconceptually aware of pursuing (B&N: 592).

These two forms of psychoanalysis further agree, according to Sartre, that the individual's behaviour is not due to an innate human nature or any hereditary personality traits. Rather, they both trace the individual's outlook back to the ways in which that individual has interacted with their social environment (B&N: 590). But whereas Freud sees this as a mechanical interaction between basic drives and the environment to produce the complexes that define the individual, Sartre argues that the individual's projects are prior to this influence because the 'environment can act on the subject only to the exact extent that he understands it, transforms it into a situation' (B&N: 593). The social meanings in the environment can be interiorized into my projects only to the extent that I understand and respond to them as reasons, which on the existentialist view is itself a manifestation of my projects. The attitude to be uncovered, therefore, is a project freely undertaken, a value freely endorsed, rather than the mechanical product of the social context.

Finally, the two forms of psychoanalysis agree that conscious desires and actions symbolize the deep attitude to be uncovered (B&N: 590). The differences in the two theoretical frameworks, however, entail that this symbolization is to be understood differently. Repressed drives are symbolized in dreams, slips of the tongue, and other phenomena, according to Freud, because they evade the censorship of the superego when in symbolic form. But these are not ways of satisfying the drive: a taboo sexual desire is not satisfied by being symbolized in a dream. Anything that would satisfy the taboo desire would not evade censorship. Sartre's theory holds that the expressions of the underlying project, by contrast, are ways of achieving that project's goal. Sartre puts this by saying that the deeper project is internal to the desire or action that expresses it (B&N: 586; see STE: 29–33). It is internal because it is part of the motivational structure of that desire or action. The conscious desire to be a concert pianist, for example, and the actions that express that desire might symbolize an underlying inferiority project, which itself provides their motivational structures in order to ensure their failure.

Because a desire or action symbolizes the project that it expresses in this way, argues Sartre, this form of psychoanalysis cannot accept the Freudian idea of a 'universal symbolism': the symbolic meaning of a desire or an action is given by the project that motivates it; what seems superficially to be the same desire or action, even in the same person, may differ in this symbolic meaning (B&N: 593-4). Not everyone who wants to be a concert pianist and acts on that desire is suffering the inferiority project: some of them are genuinely, all the way down, trying to become concert pianists. The action of regularly playing the piano that once expressed the inferiority project might now express the same person's genuine project of becoming a competent musician. Because every desire and action expresses some project, according to Sartre, this view of symbolism means that there are no privileged aspects of mental life. Whereas the Freudian psychoanalyst has a particular reason to be interested in dreams, the Sartrean psychoanalyst should be just as interested in 'the thoughts of waking life, successfully adjusted acts, style' and indeed everything else (B&N: 595-6).

5.6 Sedimentation and the Origins of Gender

Sartre ends his outline of his approach to psychoanalysis by observing that it 'has not yet found its Freud' and then promising to produce case studies of Dostoevsky and Flaubert (B&N: 596). The projected work on Dostoevsky never appeared. The work on Flaubert appeared nearly three decades later in the form of the gargantuan and unfinished *The Family Idiot*, but by this time Sartre's thought had evolved significantly. Sartre did produce two shorter works of existentialist psychoanalysis soon after *Being and Nothingness*: his book on anti-Semitism and its effects on Jewish identity and his biography of Baudelaire. But the first major application of existentialist psychoanalysis is Beauvoir's *The Second Sex*, a work that sets out to provide an analysis of the origins of what she takes to be the characteristic outlook and behaviour of women in her culture. 'The perspective we have adopted is one of existentialist morality', Beauvoir writes in the Introduction, which requires finding the origin of woman's femininity in 'the feminine condition' that has been designed in order to 'freeze her as an object' (SS: 17).

The psychological and behavioural differences between men and women are not due to any innate traits, that is to say, but result from the different conditions in which they develop their projects. 'One is not born, but rather becomes, woman', as she puts it in what is undoubtedly her most famous sentence (SS: 293). In this, she is in agreement not only with Sartre, but also with Freud. Boys and girls are not psychologically different from birth, according to Freud, but take different paths early in life when girls generally identify with their mothers and boys with their fathers as a result of the early development of their sexual drives (EI: 31-3). Beauvoir praises Freud's insight that because 'the existent is a body', the person is formed through the experience of being a body among other bodies (SS: 69). But the error in Freud's theory, she claims, is to construe the individual as a collection of disparate basic drives, rather than a chosen project that underlies their desires (SS: 55-6, 59-60). 'Sexuality must not be taken as an irreducible given', as Freud takes it, because 'the existent possesses a more primary "quest for being"; sexuality is only one of its aspects', she writes, adding that 'Sartre demonstrates this in *Being and Nothingness*' (SS: 56).

Beauvoir's famous sentence, however, opens a chapter on the role of childhood in shaping gender, one of the four chapters that comprise a division of *The Second Sex* entitled simply 'Formation'. The process of 'becoming a woman' that Beauvoir details here is not simply a Sartrean one of undertaking projects that carry no weight beyond the individual's continual endorsement of them. Rather, her description of childhood articulates the different sets of social meanings that structure the situations of girls and boys, within which they choose their projects and which then become sedimented along with those projects. Girls are praised for their looks and gracious deportment. They are forbidden from engaging in the more physical and exploratory pursuits that are positively encouraged among boys, such as climbing trees. The boy 'undertakes, he invents, he dares' and so it is 'by doing that he makes himself be' (SS: 305). The girl, by contrast, learns to be passive rather than active, pleasing to other people rather than exploratory and conquering (SS: 305). This difference is implicitly and explicitly enforced by family and wider society, through role modelling by adults and fictional characters, and through toys and play (SS: 305-7, 311, 316).

This situation 'defines what is called the woman's "character"' through 'conditioning' (SS: 653). Childhood 'imperiously modifies her consciousness of herself' (SS: 312). This is partly through the skills that she develops and those she does not develop. But it is also a matter of the social meanings that become incorporated into her projects and the values she is rewarded for having. Her childhood teaches not just that she is different from boys and men, but that she is inferior to them (SS: 311-14). Boys learn to dominate their situations, girls learn to navigate theirs.

These values and social meanings become sufficiently habituated that they shape the way she sees herself and her surroundings. She comes to value masculine authority, for example, seeing law and order as inherently masculine (SS: 655–6); 'she sees the man from head to toe as the valet sees his master' (SS: 669).

In this respect, Beauvoir resembles Freud rather than Sartre. Freud describes the process of childhood as 'forming a precipitate in the ego', a sedimented internalization of parental dictates that he calls the 'ego ideal or super-ego' (EI: 34). Beauvoir does not object to this internalization itself, only to Freud's explanation of it in terms of basic drives that he leaves unexplained (SS: 52, 56). Beauvoir's view is that childhood shapes the individual's outlook through the projects they choose to undertake in response to the enforced social meanings of the situation (SS: 59–61). She therefore rejects the claim made by both Freud and Merleau-Ponty that character and projects result simply from innate traits developed through the individual's environment (SS: 57). The sedimentation of social meanings through the sedimentation of projects, however, means that a woman who has become economically independent and so can afford to ignore the enforcement of these meanings still 'has a different perspective on the universe' from that of a man, because 'she does not have the same past as a boy'; to renounce her sedimented femininity would be a 'mutilation' of who she is (SS: 739).

5.7 A Psychoanalysis of Sedimented Projects

Beauvoir's analysis of femininity embodies a development of Sartre's existentialist psychoanalysis. Beauvoir agrees with Sartre in rejecting Freud's metaphysics of mind in favour of the existentialist view of the individual as fundamentally the pursuit of projects, or values, that they have chosen in the context of their social environment (SS: 52, 62). But she departs from Sartre in her theory of sedimentation. For once sedimented, projects and the social meanings they incorporate shape the individual's outlook in ways that cannot be overcome simply by adopting new projects. Femininity is a set of values and meanings sedimented through upbringing; 'later, it would be impossible to keep woman from being what she *was made*, and she will always trail this past behind her' (SS: 777). At least, it is impossible for a woman to escape what she was made simply by deciding on new projects, the kind of decision that Sartre describes as a 'radical conversion' (B&N: 486). But if we understand sedimentation correctly, then 'it is obvious that her destiny is not fixed in eternity' (SS: 777). A sedimented outlook can be overcome by gradual erosion, or 'an inner metamorphosis' (SS: 780).

Beauvoir thereby eliminates the last vestige of Cartesian dualism retained in Sartre's initial form of existentialism. Despite his repudiation at the start of *Being and Nothingness* of all forms of dualism and his extensive theory of the embodiment of consciousness, Sartre's concept of radical freedom is a form of the Cartesian idea that the mind is immediately responsive to rational decision. Judith Butler is right, therefore, to say that in *Being and Nothingness* Sartre both affirmed and denied that the mind is distinct from the body and in *The Second Sex* Beauvoir 'sought to exorcise Sartre's doctrine of its Cartesian ghost' (1998: 32–3, 41). However, there is more to this attempted exorcism than Butler recognizes, which explains why she thinks that Beauvoir is not entirely successful (1998: 32). Butler focuses exclusively on Beauvoir's theory that gender norms shape the body's abilities, looks, and behavioural styles, but constitute a gender identity only as they are subsumed into the individual's projects. Therefore, on Butler's reading, the individual is always able to transform their gender simply by adopting new projects (1998: 34, 40–1). What this reading overlooks is Beauvoir's theory that values and social meanings become sedimented aspects of the individual, thereby constraining the adoption of new projects.

Despite rejecting the Cartesian idea that the mind is immediately sensitive to rational decision, Beauvoir retains the existentialist conception of the mind as structured by the individual's projects. 'Every subject posits itself concretely as a transcendence through projects' (SS: 17). Femininity is designed to deny women their freedom, but it cannot succeed because this freedom is essential to human existence. 'Woman's drama lies in this conflict' (SS: 17). Even though men and women occupy different social conditions, 'freedom is entire in each' (SS: 680). It is because the oppressed person remains free but their freedom is frustrated that they feel their oppression in dissatisfaction (SS: 322–3, 661). The only solution, Beauvoir argues, is to revolt against the oppressive condition (SS: 661, 680). Beauvoir holds that when women accept their condition for its compensations rather than embrace the harsh reality of revolt, they do so from a perspective in which femininity is already instilled; 'her outlook is limited; her wings are cut' (SS: 660; see also SS: 322, 669).

This is why women's complicity is not the moral fault of bad faith, but is itself a form of oppression (SS: 17).

Beauvoir, therefore, is not philosophically committed to blaming women for their own oppression, as is sometimes alleged (Le Doeuff 1987). But neither does she exonerate women from this charge by arguing that their oppression has removed their freedom (Kruks 1995: 87–8; 1998: 60). Rather, she rejects the idea Sartre articulates in *Being and Nothingness* that human freedom entails the individual's responsibility for their situation, which gains its evaluative structure from their projects (B&N: 574–5). Where an individual's behaviour expresses a sedimented outlook socially instilled in them from childhood precisely in order to produce this behaviour, on Beauvoir's view, responsibility for the choice lies with the society rather than with the individual who is shaped by it. It is society's oppression of freedom operating internally within the woman herself.[2] This ethical departure is matched by one in the theory of existentialist psychoanalysis. Sartre sees the inferiority complex as an individual's chosen project, as we saw in section 5.4, but Beauvoir understands it as a sedimented social meaning. Sartre cannot fully explain why an individual freely chose inferiority. But for Beauvoir inferiority is sedimented into the outlooks of girls raised in a society that distinguishes them from boys in this way.

Finally, her theory of sedimentation allows Beauvoir to formulate an original theory of the symbolic meanings of dreams, desires, and actions. Beauvoir contrasts her view with those of Freud and Sartre in a single sentence: 'symbolism did not fall out of heaven, or rise out of subterranean depths: it was elaborated like language' (SS: 58). That is, Beauvoir agrees with Sartre in rejecting Freud's theory of a universal symbolic code, but rejects Sartre's idea that the symbolic meaning of a dream, desire, or action is the deeper project it expresses. On her form of

---

[2] Susan James traces this conception of blameless complicity in one's own oppression to the influence of late seventeenth-century French philosophy on Beauvoir's thought. She argues that there is an important discrepancy between the conception of embodiment that this influence requires and Beauvoir's adherence to Sartre's distinction between transcendence and facticity (2003: 152). This reading overlooks Beauvoir's account of the sedimentation of social values, which departs to some extent from both of these influences, since it entails not only the rejection of Sartre's conception of radical freedom but also of the seventeenth-century understanding of the passions as simply manifesting 'a natural and functional sensitivity to the harms and advantages that people, objects, and states of affairs may bring to us' (James 2003: 153–4).

existentialism, symbolism is the expression of sedimented social meaning. The implicit political desire that law and order be controlled and enforced primarily by men, for example, symbolically expresses the superiority of men over women (SS: 656). Sartrean psychoanalysis cannot uncover the individual's projects through their symbolic representations in dreams, desires, or actions, because on the Sartrean view these symbols can be read only after the projects are identified. Beauvoir, by contrast, allows these symbols to be read with reference to social meanings, so that the underlying cause of an individual's problem can be found in a conflict between the values that they explicitly endorse and the sedimented meanings that implicitly structure their desires (SS: 779).

6
Why Inez is not in Hell

Beauvoir and Sartre offered markedly different forms of existentialism in the 1940s. Beauvoir held that the individual's chosen projects become progressively more embedded, limiting their outlook, constraining the range of possible projects they might choose, and requiring that any replacement of projects could only be gradual. Sartre, by contrast, held that individuals can simply replace their projects at any time, though generally prefer not to. We have seen that Beauvoir's theory explains what it is to pursue a project where Sartre's ultimately does not and that her theory grounds a form of psychoanalysis in *The Second Sex* that departs in important ways from the one outlined in *Being and Nothingness*. We will see in Chapter 7 that Beauvoir's version of existentialism is preferable to Sartre's initial version, as Sartre realized by 1952, and that the reason for this lies in their different theories of the role of other people in the development of the individual.

Sartre's initial existentialist theory of relations between people is dramatized in his play *Huis Clos*, which he wrote in the space of two weeks after Camus and two other friends asked him for something they could perform. This was in 1943, the year *Being and Nothingness* and *She Came To Stay* were both published. As it turned out, these three never did perform the play. Sartre staged it the following year, shortly before the liberation of Paris, under the title *Les Autres* (*The Others*). This title and the play's claustrophobic atmosphere of continual surveillance and judgment were taken as an allegory of the occupation. Sartre does seem to have intended this dimension of the play, making it all the more remarkable that it was cleared for production by the Nazi censors. Despite its initial mixed reviews, which were perhaps partly because of the occupation, *Huis Clos* has proved to have an enduring and widespread appeal.

It has been produced on stage, on radio, and on film countless times. 'Hell is . . . other people!' (*L'enfer, c'est les autres*), a line at the end of the play (HC: 223), has become the most widely quoted, paraphrased, and parodied sentence of existentialism, perhaps even of the whole history of philosophy. Although this does seem to have been a call to resist the Nazis, colloquially known as *les autres*, the cultural reach of this sentiment far beyond wartime Paris reflects the play's deeper existential theme. This is the scope for dissonance between someone's own self-image and the image other people have of that person. Sartre's point about this dissonance, both in this play and in the section of *Being and Nothingness* that it dramatizes, however, are often misconstrued. Before contrasting his theory with Beauvoir's, therefore, we need first to clarify what he meant by that famous line about other people.

6.1 A Metaphysical Play

The play's three central characters focus their dialogue on the images they each have of one another. This is played out through a triangle of sexual desire. Garcin is attracted only to Inez, who is attracted only to Estelle, who is attracted only to Garcin. These desires structure the play's dynamic, as the narrative unfolds through each character's attempts to seduce one of the others while resisting the advances of the third. Moreover, it is this sexual tension that gradually forces the characters to reveal more information about themselves. But we should not accept the triangle of desire as the basic structure of the play. For according to Sartre's existentialism, as we have seen, desires are expressions of the individual's projects. So we should ask why each character has the sexual desires that they have. In particular, we should ask why their anxiety about their self-image is manifested in this sexual desire in this particular situation.

It is clear throughout the play that Estelle's image of herself as a paragon of femininity is fundamental to her entire outlook. Being attractive to men is the essential structure of femininity, as Beauvoir was soon to argue in *The Second Sex*, in line with a long tradition of philosophical analyses of gender (e.g. Wollstonecraft 1792: ch. 2; Mill 1869: ch. 1). Estelle's basic project is therefore threatened if she cannot confirm her femininity in seducing men. Once she comes to see herself as trapped forever in the company of Garcin and Inez, it is Garcin's desire she needs. The fact that Inez desires her cannot confirm her self-image. She rather takes it as a threat to her femininity. But it is this very need to be desired by men that prevents Garcin from desiring her. For his project is to see himself as a tough and courageous character who is not the coward that he fears other people think he is. Estelle's affirmation of his self-image is too easily won, given her need to please him, so he needs his affirmation from Inez, who seems as tough as he wants to be (HC: 217–18, 222).

By desiring Estelle and refusing Garcin's advances, Inez therefore threatens both their images of themselves. This much fits the standard reading of the play as a morality tale about the dangers of caring too much about one's image in the eyes of other people. On this reading, each of these three is condemned to an eternity of frustration simply by being made to share a room. None of them can be secure in their image of themselves, because they are each permanently seeking confirmation of that image from people who threaten to undermine it. Because they are dead, according to this reading, they can no longer change. None of them can stop seeking the affirmation of their self-image and none of them can affirm the self-image of either of the other two. The moral of the story, on this reading, is that we should not be too concerned with the image other people have of us, but should instead continue to develop our projects (Azzi 1981: 452–3; Bernasconi 2006: 30–4; Cox 2009: 132, 136–8; Detmer 2008: 149–56; O'Donohoe 2005: 85–6; Solomon 2006: 177–85).

Inez, however, poses a problem for this standard reading of the play. What grounds her sexual desires? She sees herself as fundamentally cruel: 'I can't get on without making people suffer', she says, describing herself as a 'live coal in others' hearts'. 'When I'm alone I flicker out', she adds (HC: 203–4). She is quite clear about the suffering she caused other people through the sexual relationship that led to her death (HC: 203). Her place within the triangle of desire therefore manifests this underlying self-image, just as Garcin's and Estelle's desires manifest theirs. But she does not face the predicament that Garcin and Estelle face. Their inability to establish their preferred image in the eyes of the other two threatens their view of themselves as being tough or feminine. Inez, by contrast, is in no doubt about her cruelty and neither is anybody else.

How should we understand this difference? We could view Inez as correctly understanding her cruelty as a project. On this reading, she would be a kind of hero of authenticity despite her cruelty. But this sits uneasily with her descriptions of herself as cruel by nature rather than as a chosen project. Alternatively, we could see her as wrongly taking this image of herself as cruel to be a correct description of her fixed nature

(Azzi 1981: 438). But then the play would not have the moral that the standard reading ascribes to it, because Inez would be a counterexample to the idea that reliance on other people's image of oneself inevitably leads to frustration. The third option is to see Inez as metaphysically different from the other two characters, as genuinely having the fixed nature that she claims to have. These interpretations agree that the psychological drama of the play is driven by an underlying metaphysical framework, but disagree on what that framework is. To decide between them, we need to consider which view of Inez is best supported by the details of the play.

6.2 An Ambiguous Situation

The play is routinely described as set in Hell, where these three unfortunate protagonists have been selected to spend eternity in a room together effectively torturing one another by their mutual inability to give one another what they each most want. But why should we accept that this is their situation? Two of them say that it is, Garcin rather speculatively and Inez much more firmly. But if the standard reading is right that these three characters are ordinary mortals who have found themselves here after their deaths, then why should they have any insight into the nature of their new predicament? It is obvious that they are not in Heaven, because they are not enjoying their new situation. But within the Christian eschatological mythology that frames the play, there are two other options. They might be in Purgatory, being punished until they are purged of their sins so that they can progress to Heaven. Or they might be at the Last Judgment, where their eternal destinies are to be decided. The only character who knows for sure is the valet who brings each of them into the room. Under the guise of tact, he studiously avoids saying where they are.

This ambiguity is reflected in the play's title, which has always caused trouble for English language editions and productions. It is often given the title *No Exit* or *No Way Out*, which reflects the standard reading that these characters are now locked into this situation forever. The title *No Exit* is also a nice theatrical pun, since none of the three main characters ever leaves the stage, even when the door to their room is wide open and there seems to be nothing to prevent them from walking out. But these titles are neither literal nor even figurative translations of the original.

For the phrase 'huis clos' is taken from French legal terminology and designates a proceeding taking place behind closed doors, in a room with no public or media gallery, as opposed to a proceeding in an open court. For this reason, *No Admittance* might be a better English title than *No Exit*, though it might hinder ticket sales. The literal translation of 'huis clos' into English is 'in camera', which has the same technical meaning, but is unattractive precisely because it is legal jargon.

On the standard reading of the play, this title must be taken to indicate simply that the characters are now locked away from their own world, their own families, friends, and other acquaintances, who cannot see the torture they are facing for the rest of eternity. But the title suggests more than that they are locked away from their own world. For legal proceedings in camera have a specific objective. The participants do exit the room once the objective has been achieved. Such proceedings are not forms of punishment, eternal or otherwise, but are rather parts of the process of establishing guilt. What the title suggests, therefore, is that the characters are neither in Hell nor in Purgatory, but are facing the Last Judgment of what they have made of their lives. If this is indeed their predicament, then we the audience must be a part of this process itself. We cannot be merely spectators external to the logic of the play. For if we were, we would be analogous to people in the public gallery of an open courtroom, witnessing the proceedings but playing no role in them. This would be a performative contradiction of the play's title.

Since the action is taking place behind closed doors, therefore, we the audience must be in that room as part of the story. Productions of the play are often staged in a way that is consistent with this. Rather than employing the traditional theatrical layout of a raised and lit platform in front of rows of audience seated in darkness, the action often takes place on a floor surrounded by an audience who can see one another's reactions. One advantage of this layout is that it heightens the atmosphere of paranoia. Another is that it subtly reminds us that our self-image depends partly on other people's judgments of our behaviour, which is a central theme of the play. But a third advantage is that it allows each audience member to see the audience itself as sitting in judgment over the characters in the play. Each character's confessions, appeals, and strategies are all met with the facial expressions and bodily postures, as well as occasional laughter and other audible reactions, of an array of people gradually coming to understand what motivates these characters.

If the audience are internal to the logic of the play in this way, internal to the closed room in which the drama unfolds, then not only are the characters facing the Last Judgment, but we the audience are their judges. The characters themselves do not seem to see it this way. For they neither address the audience directly nor are affected by the audience's reactions. They seem oblivious to being watched, as in traditional theatre. But this is exactly as we should expect. The true situation should be withheld from the people being judged for the same reason that psychologists withhold the purpose of an experiment from its participants until it is finished. If the characters knew that their lives were being judged, their words and actions would be calibrated to present themselves in the best light. Each of us wants other people to affirm our positive self-image, as the play itself dramatizes. The ambiguity, from their perspective, of the situation that they are thrown into allows them to think that judgment has already happened and that they are now in Hell, destined to question one another for all eternity. Under those conditions, there would be no point in hiding anything. So they gradually bare their souls, which allows us to judge them.

6.3 Why Inez is an Insider

If we read the play in this way, then we can resolve the puzzle about the role Inez plays in the narrative. For, as we have seen, Inez seems to be different from the other two characters. She seems remarkably unperturbed by the whole situation. She is not struggling to establish her preferred self-image in the eyes of the others in order to convince herself of it. On the contrary, she seems very sure that she is cruel and her behaviour clearly demonstrates her cruelty. She differs too in her relation to the room they are in. Garcin and Estelle are annoyed by features of it that seem to have no purpose other than to annoy these particular people. The heat, the style and colour of the furniture, the ugly statue that cannot be moved, the paper knife that serves no function, and the lack of any mirrors or other reflective surfaces irritate Garcin and Estelle, but Inez remains entirely unruffled by them.

It is Inez, moreover, who assures the other two that they are all in Hell torturing one another. Garcin assumes at the outset that he has arrived in Hell, immediately asking the valet where the torture equipment is

(HC: 182). The valet's answers, however, neither confirm nor deny the assumption. Inez arrives next and the first thing she does is to reinforce the assumption by accusing Garcin of being the torturer (HC: 186). Estelle arrives without any apparent presumption of where she is, but Inez alludes to being in Hell in conversation with her before asserting it firmly without any hint of doubt or regret. 'We're in hell, my pets, they never make mistakes, and people aren't damned for nothing', she declares (HC: 194). She even taunts Estelle with the idea. 'A damned soul', she tells her gleefully, 'that's you, my little plaster saint' (HC: 194). It is Inez who then claims that the reason there is no torturer is that they have been selected to torture one another, 'as in the cafeteria, where customers serve themselves' (HC: 195). Earlier on, it was Inez who described the annoying features of the room as evidence that they are in Hell, even though she is not annoyed by them. 'Nothing was left to chance', she declared. 'The room was all set for us' (HC: 192).

All of this is rather puzzling if Inez is what she claims to be. But if her role is to bring the other two to admit the reality of their lives, then the room does not need to be designed to annoy her and she has nothing to fear from her situation. She can play her role best by leading the other two to believe that they are already in Hell so they think they have nothing to gain from hiding anything about themselves. If this is her role, moreover, then it would make sense for her not to have the metaphysical structure of human existence, but rather to have precisely the fixed nature that she believes herself to have. Given the aim and strategy, her role in this Last Judgment would be filled better by a demon than by a mortal or by an angel. Inez is indeed, as she says, dependent on making people suffer; her essence precedes her existence (HC: 203–4). But she can play this role only if the others do not realize that she is different from them. Her story of her past life is thus essential.

Her declaration that they will all torture one another is also essential, despite its tension with her saying she is uncommonly nasty, which itself implies that she will in fact do most of the torturing. Her mask slips a little again when Estelle asks why anyone would set up the room exactly as it is. 'I only know they're waiting', Inez replies, perhaps truthfully. 'You don't even know what they expect', she adds (HC: 192). Garcin becomes suspicious about her calmness and apparent knowledge of the situation. 'You've given us quite enough hints', he tells her; 'you might as well come out with it' (HC: 193). Inez replies that she is 'as much in the dark as you are', but soon asks directly what the others have done that has led to them being 'here' (HC: 193). At one point, she calls the other two 'my pets' and at another she praises Estelle's facial expression as 'quite diabolical' (HC: 194, 198).

Sartre has used these slips, I suggest, to indicate her role to us, an audience who can read or watch the play more than once, while allowing her to cover her tracks quickly within the temporality of the play itself, in order to prevent Garcin or Estelle from reaching the conclusion that she is different from them. Sartre gives us a clear hint in a brief exchange when Inez starts to describe her cruelty. Garcin responds by claiming to be rather cruel himself, to which Inez responds 'No, you're not cruel. It's something else.' Garcin asks what she means and she replies simply 'I'll tell you later', before returning quickly to describing herself (HC: 203). Sartre's clearest hint to us about her centrality to the play, however, is her name. He called her 'Inès', which English translators have rendered 'Inez' to avoid mispronunciation. The theatre director Ralf Tognieri has pointed out that her original name thus comprises the final two letters of 'Garcin' and the first two of 'Estelle', indicating her position 'at the heart of the play' (2013: 1).

If her position were too obvious to us, however, the play would be less captivating. Two structural features of the play prevent this. One is that the three main characters share the audience's attention equally. They have an equal number of lines. Their triangle of sexual desire allows the narrative to incorporate conversations between each pair, attempting to exclude the third. Each character delivers soliloquies. It is this equality that leads to interpretations of the play as presenting three characters facing the same situation together, differentiated only by their social backgrounds. The second feature is that if any of the three is focused on as the lead character, it is more likely to be Garcin than either of the other two. He enters the stage first and his conversation with the valet initially sets the scene. He delivers the eminently quotable line 'Hell is...other people!' and soon afterwards delivers the final line of the play, 'Well, well, let's get on with it...' (HC: 223). Inez, by contrast, enters the stage neither first nor last, but between Garcin and Estelle. This nicely echoes the structure of her name that Tognieri points out, but nevertheless serves to obscure her centrality.

6.4 Garcin's Progress

These features that make Garcin more prominent than the other two, however, are not merely a device for ensuring that Inez remains a subtle and intriguing character rather than too obviously a demon forcing Garcin and Estelle to face the reality of their lives. For although Inez is central to the dramatic structure of the play, the metaphysical picture presented by the play is best illustrated by the progress that Garcin makes. According to the standard reading, there is no quest or discovery in this narrative because none of the characters can make any progress. 'They are all *done with*', writes Robert Solomon, for example, 'with nowhere to go, nothing to learn, and nothing to do' (2006: 179). The moral of the tale, on this reading, is found in contrasting their inability to change with the inherently dynamic structure of our existence. While they cannot escape their predicament, we can choose to concentrate on developing ourselves through our own projects without being too concerned with other people's views of us. But this reading is mistaken. For the characters do change: they come to a settled view on where they are, learn about one another's pasts, and realize that they will continue to irritate each other.

Garcin's progress structures the narrative of the play: he begins by exuding a false bravado about the torments he thinks he is about to face, then relates his exploits in life through a similarly macho persona, but under questioning from Inez he soon admits that he is genuinely unsure whether he is courageous or cowardly. Was his attempt to escape across the Mexican border really the courageous act of a pacifist taking an immense risk in order to stand up for his principles, as he would like it to have been, or was it simply a cowardly desertion driven by fear of gunfire? This action is genuinely ambiguous. Had he succeeded in setting up a pacifist newspaper, his escape might come to be seen as heroic. But that would not entail that it had been heroic at the time. The newspaper might rather have later redeemed an act that was cowardly at the time. This problem is compounded for Garcin by the fact that he died before reaching the border.

In coming to understand this ambiguity, Garcin makes progress away from his initial position of viewing himself as tough and courageous by nature. The ambiguity is repeated in the play itself when the door to the room opens, apparently allowing any or even all of the three to leave. None of them do. How should Garcin understand his decision to remain? Is he courageously staying to continue his project of convincing Inez of his toughness despite the problems that she and Estelle pose for him in this room? 'It is because of her I'm staying here', he declares (HC: 219). But is he really just scared that leaving might result in worse torture in another room? Garcin comes to realize that he is tortured by the divergence between the way he sees these ambiguous events and the ways in which other people might see them. His view of himself as fundamentally tough and courageous is perennially challenged by the fact that these actions can be read in the opposite way. Hell is other people for Garcin because the source of his torture is ultimately that there are perspectives on his behaviour that conflict with his own.

Garcin ends the play with an unambiguously courageous attitude. 'Well, well, let's get on with it', he says, finally having abandoned his attempts to avoid other people's judgments of his behaviour (HC: 223). In making this progress, Garcin contrasts not only with Inez, who has been certain and clearly right about her own character from the very beginning, but also with Estelle, who faces a similar predicament to Garcin's but seems to be making no progress at all. From the start of the play right to the end, Estelle is concerned only with confirming her femininity. Garcin's concern with his self-image is accompanied by a drive to find his salvation. He encourages the three of them to 'bring our spectres into the open' in the hope that this might 'save us from disaster' (HC: 201). This aim leads him to make progress towards correctly understanding himself. Estelle, by contrast, seems to think that her salvation lies in seducing Garcin and thereby affirming her self-image. She is, in a sense, a one-dimensional character. But her lack of depth is not a flaw in Sartre's portrayal of her. It is a feature of the character herself, one that he has portrayed very well.

If the characters are in Hell, then neither Garcin's progress nor Estelle's inertia amounts to anything at all. For if nobody is going anywhere, any change is insignificant. But if we read the play as set at the Last Judgment, with Inez as a demon whose job is to bring the deceased to admit the reality of their lives, as I have argued that we should, then Garcin's progress and Estelle's inertia make sense. Garcin is mistaken to think he is in Hell being tortured. He is simply finding painful the process of coming to recognize, confess, and regret his sins. We the judges are coming to understand his basic sin, just as we understand Estelle's. But unlike Estelle, Garcin is also starting to understand it himself. He is making progress towards the point at which he might be absolved by genuine remorse. By the end of the play, he might indeed be approaching his salvation. Estelle, by contrast, ends the play in the same position she was in at the start. She has not even begun the process of discovery that her situation is designed to elicit.[1]

6.5 Why Garcin is in Hell

One of the disadvantages of Garcin being more prominent than the other characters has been a tendency among readers and viewers of the play to take him as a role model throughout the play whose lines express Sartre's existentialism. 'Hell is other people' is thus often taken to be the central message of the play, a moment of insight that encapsulates Sartre's pessimism about human life. Personal and social relations can only ever be based on conflict, on this reading; 'no human relationship can ever be either stable or satisfying' (Thody 1981: 423). Twenty years after the play was first published, Sartre pointed out that this was a misunderstanding. 'It has been thought that what I meant by that was that our relations with other people are always poisoned', he said, but 'I mean that if relations with someone else are twisted, vitiated, then that other person can only be hell' (NE: 199). Far from being a role model articulating a deep insight into the human condition, then, Garcin has misread his twisted, vitiated relationships with his roommates as revealing the basic structure of all relations between people.

In what way are these relationships twisted? It is not simply that Garcin takes seriously the views that other people have of him. In describing the

---

[1] If this interpretation is correct, the play is a neat inversion of Franz Kafka's novel *The Trial*. The protagonist of that novel, Josef K, knows that he is undergoing legal proceedings in relation to an accusation made against him, does not know what the accusation is, but is sure that he is innocent. Estelle and Garcin, by contrast, are aware that they have done something wrong, are in fact being brought to confess this wrong, but do not know that they are in such proceedings. This is perhaps no coincidence. Sartre tells us in *Being and Nothingness* that *The Trial* expresses two essential aspects of the meaning of an action: that this does not depend solely on the agent's own intentions or interpretations, but on how the action is seen from a variety of perspectives; and that it depends on the place of the action in the overall sequence of the agent's life (B&N: 289, 523). On this interpretation of *Huis Clos*, both these points are essential to its plot.

play, Sartre affirms that 'other people are basically the most important means we have in ourselves for our knowledge of ourselves' (NE: 199). From the unreflective perspective of the individual, the world appears as a set of social meanings and directive reasons. This dimension of 'being for-itself' is structured by the projects that the individual has undertaken, the values that they pursue, as we saw in Chapter 3. But this reliance of the reasons encountered in experience on one's own projects is not evident from that unreflective perspective. Impure reflection on our experience does reveal, according to Sartre, that the reasons we find in our experience match our desires at the time, as we have seen (3.4). But impure reflection does not reveal the origin of those desires. Moreover, like the rest of an individual's experience, impure reflection is itself structured by the individual's own projects.

Garcin's impure reflection on his own experience and motivations, for example, is structured by his project of seeing himself as a courageous hero. Through that lens, his desire to escape to the border does not look like a cowardly desire to escape from the war, but looks instead like a heroic desire to make a stand against the war. The public dimension of our existence, according to Sartre, provides a useful corrective to the inevitable distortions of impure reflection. As our words and actions can be witnessed by people who do not share our projects and might not have projects in common with one another, the views that other people form of us can be useful sources of information about ourselves. Other people mostly lack the extent of our own experience of our behaviour, of course, and are viewing us through the lenses of their own projects. But it remains that I would know myself better if I took a variety of partial perspectives into account than if I relied only on my own. I would come to know myself through what Sartre calls my 'being-for-others' (B&N: 245–6).

The play should not be read as recommending that we should prefer our own image of ourselves to the views that other people have of us, therefore. The idea that we should get on with pursuing our projects without regard for other people's judgments of our behaviour is profoundly opposed to Sartre's existentialism. For on his view, we cannot be sure what our underlying motivations, our deepest projects, are without considering other people's judgments. Indeed, as we saw in Chapter 5, Sartre's existentialism stands in the Freudian tradition of viewing our behaviour and more immediate motivations as manifestations of deeper motivations that might be hidden from us. We might need the help of an existentialist psychoanalyst to uncover the projects that are causing thoughts and actions that distress us, according to Sartre, where one effect of those projects themselves is precisely to distort our own reflective thought about ourselves in such a way as to conceal those projects.

If the problem Garcin faces is not generated by his taking seriously the judgments that Inez and Estelle make about his behaviour, then what does generate it? In his discussion of the play, Sartre went on to say that 'I am indeed in hell' if 'I am situating myself in total dependence on someone else' (NE: 199). Garcin has made himself too dependent on other people's views of him by trying to understand his own behaviour as the manifestation of an inner nature. He sees himself as having a set of essential properties that explain his behaviour. He wants to be essentially a hero, but worries that he is essentially a coward. He is thus reliant on other people to affirm that he is essentially courageous. For if they collectively see any of his actions as cowardly, this undermines his self-image because courageous heroes simply do not do cowardly things. According to Sartre's existentialism, Garcin should see himself as no more than a set of projects that he pursues and can change. The views of other people could then help him to identify his projects, so help him to change them if he is unhappy with his behaviour. He would not be locked into the Hell of having his most fundamental conception of himself perennially challenged by those around him.

6.6 The Sins of Garcin and Estelle

It is not Garcin, therefore, but Inez who delivers the line that encapsulates Sartre's central message in the play: 'You are', she tells Garcin, 'your life, and nothing else' (HC: 221). This is what Garcin, under the leadership of Inez, is making progress towards understanding. He first comes to understand that his own actions are ambiguous, so cannot be seen as unequivocally manifesting some particular fixed nature, whether it is the one he insists on or the one he denies. By the end of the play, he is beginning to undertake a genuinely courageous project towards the situation he takes himself to be in. These are necessary steps towards understanding and overcoming his underlying state of existential sin, which, according to Sartre's existentialism, is the state of bad faith, the project of viewing oneself and others as having fixed natures. This is what

Sartre meant when he said that the play describes the 'living death' of people who have become 'encrusted in a set of habits and customs' that they are unhappy with but they 'do not even try to change'; this project of bad faith makes people 'victims of judgments passed on them by other people' (NE: 200).

Estelle is in the same position. Her relations with other people, like Garcin's, are poisoned by her project of seeing people as having fixed natures. Estelle sees herself as being essentially defined by femininity as traditionally understood, which symmetrically matches Garcin's view of himself as essentially tough and courageous, since these are features of the traditional view of masculinity. Her underlying sin is bad faith, just as Garcin's is. Both of these characters have behaved terribly towards the people around them while they were alive. But they recount these stories as though these actions are not what is most important. They each focus their attention instead on the question of the kind of people they really are. In a sense, they are right to do so. For it is this obsession with their natures, with seeing themselves as essentially feminine or masculine, that is the basic state of sin underlying the more immediate sins for which they think they are now being punished in Hell, although they do not yet understand this.

It is because Estelle simultaneously saw herself as essentially feminine and tried to prove this femininity through her behaviour that she made the decisions that led to her crime. It is because Garcin wanted to prove his essential machismo through his behaviour that he treated his wife abominably. In both cases, their bad faith, their project of seeing people's behaviour as manifesting fixed natures, allowed them to see their own behaviour as the inevitable result of their own fixed natures, even though they were choosing to behave that way in order to prove that they have a particular fixed nature. For on their view, people are courageous or feminine in the same way that people are tall or thin, or objects are hard or soft. Rather than accept responsibility for their behaviour, therefore, Garcin and Estelle viewed these as simply products of the interactions between their essential characteristics and those of the people around them. This is part of what Sartre means when he describes bad faith as akin to the Christian notion of original sin (B&N: 431–2, 434n; see Webber 2009: 143–4). It is an ongoing state that explains why the individual commits the particular sins they commit.

We should not conclude from this, however, that the play presents a consequentialist argument that bad faith is wrong because it leads to morally bad behaviour. Such an argument would need to rely on a further moral theory to substantiate the intuitive view that the ways that Garcin and Estelle behaved towards the people around them were indeed morally wrong. Sartre does want to condemn their behaviour as morally wrong. But he holds that this kind of behaviour is wrong because it is a manifestation of bad faith. More precisely, he wants to argue that we are morally required to treat people as beings whose existence precedes their essence, rather than as having any fixed nature. Bad faith is wrong, in Sartre's view, because it is the failure to meet this moral requirement, not because it causes behaviour that fails to meet some other moral requirement. We will consider Sartre's argument for this moral requirement in Chapter 9, then in Chapter 10 will see that Beauvoir presents a more promising argument for the same conclusion.

Estelle and Garcin, meanwhile, are struggling with the same underlying existential sin, which has taken the form of identifying with the socially dominant view of femininity for her and with the socially dominant view of masculinity for him. Inez, by contrast, identifies with a fixed nature that defies the social norms for women. But she is also different in not facing any dissonance between her preferred self-image and the way other people see her. Everyone can readily agree that she is cruel. She demonstrates what people would be like if they did have fixed natures. Our actions would not be ambiguous, there would be no ineliminable disagreement over our character traits. The standard reading of the play is mistaken, therefore, to view the three characters as fellow mortals facing the same predicament. It is equally mistaken to see the characters as condemned to an eternity without change: Garcin's progress towards his salvation structures the play; Estelle's lack of progress serves as his counterpoint. And the standard view is mistaken to see the play as dramatizing a pessimistic view of our relations with one another, as though it were a basic existential truth that other people are Hell.

6.7 Bad Faith and Other People

The message of the play is rather that bad faith inevitably vitiates our relations with one another. The standard reading is partly due to Sartre's treatise *Being and Nothingness*, published the year before the play, having standardly been read as arguing that relations between people are fundamentally based on conflict (e.g. Howells 1988: 21). But this misunderstands the structure of *Being and Nothingness*. It is not a series of discrete analyses of aspects of the basic structure of human existence, but the progressive elaboration of a single vision of both the basic structure of human existence and the particular form that Sartre considered it to have in his cultural context. The theory of bad faith near the start of the book aims not only to uncover the structures of human existence necessary for self-deception to be possible, but also to diagnose a particular attitude towards human existence that Sartre considered to be socially pervasive. His analysis of relations between people is developed within the context of that diagnosis. It aims to show that relations between people are always conflictual when they are poisoned by bad faith (Webber 2011; see also Beauvoir EA: 46; Fanon BSWM: 24, 117 n24).

Because it is framed by his theory of bad faith, it is a mistake to think that Sartre's theory of relations between people could be assessed by comparing it with the findings of early developmental psychology or animal psychology. For example, Kathleen Wider has argued against Sartre's theory on the basis of evidence that babies and toddlers can imitate the facial expressions of other people and recognize when other people are imitating them, an ability that seems to demonstrate an innate sense of fraternity with fellow human subjects that is not present in the child's dealings with other objects. Moreover, the way infants pursue shared goals through this imitation may well be fundamental in developing their ability to set and pursue goals and projects of their own. For these reasons, argues Wider, Sartre is mistaken to think that 'the self's fundamental relation with the other is one of conflict' (1999: 195). Instead, we should conclude from early developmental psychology that our 'original relation with others' is cooperative and 'involves self-discovery and possibly even self-creation, rather than alienation' (1999: 195, 203).

Conversely, findings of animal psychology have been cited in support of the view attributed to Sartre that relations between people are fundamentally conflictual. George Stack and Robert Plant have argued that 'human responses to being stared at' should be understood as 'a replication of the prey–predator relationship in simpler life forms' (1982: 365). They describe a continuum across the animal kingdom of responses to being looked at. The presence of eyes, or even fake eyes, is enough to induce in some creatures a tonic immobility response that is designed to prevent predators from gaining further information about the animal's location from its movement. The eye-like patterns on some insects, fish, birds, and animals seem to ward off predators by inducing a similar fear response in them. Primates and other large animals tend to respond to a fixed stare with fear, which in turn leads either to aggression or to a submissive aversion to the gaze. Fighting among children is often preceded by staring. In this context, argue Stack and Plant, the conflict that Sartre sees as the basis of human relations is simply a further elaboration of this fundamentally aggressive nature of eye contact.

Sartre does not hold, however, that conflict is a fundamental feature of human existence. If he did, he would be contradicting the basic tenet of his existentialism. For the slogan 'existence precedes essence' means that an individual's behaviour is ultimately driven by the values, or projects, that they pursue and that they can abandon. The desire that other people affirm one's own self-image cannot be a basic feature of an individual's outlook, on Sartre's theory, for as we have seen in Chapter 5 the idea that all desires express underlying projects is central to his existentialism. The relevant project here is the bad faith of seeing oneself as having a particular fixed nature, which in Garcin's case is the nature of being essentially macho. For this reason, the developmental psychology that Wider cites does not conflict with Sartre's theory. It rather presents an account of the development of the capacity to view other people as having perspectives on the world, and on oneself, that differ from one's own perspective. This is consistent with the idea that this capacity generates a specific kind of desire in the context of the project of bad faith, the desire that one's preferred self-image is affirmed by other people from their perspectives.

For the same reason, Stack and Plant are mistaken to think that the theory of conflict that Sartre elaborates in *Being and Nothingness* and dramatizes in *Huis Clos* could be supported by the findings of animal psychology. However, this is not yet to say that the findings they summarize are irrelevant. For these could rather be interpreted as threatening Sartre's theory that the conflict he describes results from a pervasive project that people need not pursue. The continuum of animal fear responses to the gaze of others might rather suggest that the conflict is a feature of human nature, an inbuilt feature of our evolutionary inheritance. The evidence Stack and Plant mistakenly take to support Sartre, that is to say, might instead present a challenge to the fundamental tenet of his existentialism.

In a further irony, however, the reason why this challenge to Sartre's theory would fail is itself indicated by Stack and Plant in their own criticism of the theory that they mistakenly attribute to Sartre. They argue that Sartre overlooks the transformation of the primordial animal fear response in human contexts of attention, interest, and attraction. In these contexts, they argue, our animal response to the gaze of others is not experienced in its raw form, but grounds very different emotional feelings (1982: 370–2). Sartre's actual view, however, is that a bodily response owed to our animal ancestry can never be experienced raw. It can only be experienced as transformed into a particular emotion by the individual's projects and situation. The conflict engendered by the views that other people have of oneself is not primordial or independent of one's own projects, according to Sartre's initial form of existentialism, but is a transformation by the project of bad faith of our basic bodily response to the gaze of others.

7

Sedimentation and the Grounds of Cultural Values

At the time of the existentialist offensive in 1945, as we have seen, Beauvoir and Sartre agreed on a complicated set of claims summarized in the slogan 'existence precedes essence'. They agreed that there is no human nature, no fixed set of qualities that explain human behaviour in general, and no such fixed qualities of any group of people, such as a gender or a race. They agreed that this is because no individual has a fixed personality. Rather, on their view, an individual's behaviour is explained by their 'projects', the values they pursue even though they could choose to do otherwise. Beauvoir and Sartre further agreed that someone's social context can shape their behaviour only through forming the detailed content of these projects.

They disagreed, however, on a point so fundamental that it led them to importantly different varieties of existentialism. Beauvoir held that projects become progressively sedimented, increasing in influence over cognition and experience and becoming more difficult to alter. Sartre held that projects carry no such inertia, but are sustained only by the individual continuing to pursue them. This causes two immediate problems for Sartre's theory. One concerns his insistence that 'radical freedom' allows us to abandon any project without needing any reason to do so. This seems inconsistent with the very idea of pursuing a project at all. As we saw in Chapter 3, however, the rest of Sartre's existentialism remains intact if we replace this claim with the idea that any project can be abandoned for reasons grounded in another project.

Sartre's second problem is more significant. Beauvoir holds that commitment to a project consists in progressive sedimentation through reaffirmation in action. Sartre's theory has no resources to substantiate the idea of commitment to a project. Beauvoir and Sartre agree that projects structure our experience, so that the world is experienced as a set of reasons for action that reflect our values. But where Beauvoir explains this as an effect of the sedimentation, Sartre leaves entirely mysterious how choosing a value, which need not even be a conscious decision, could have this effect on our experience. This might be considered merely an incompleteness in Sartre's phenomenology of motivation, one that could perhaps be remedied without the idea of sedimentation. However, as we will see in this chapter, Sartre's initial form of existentialism requires his cultural theory to assume a widespread and entirely unexplainable coincidence. Sartre eventually came to accept the idea of sedimentation, as we will see, and the development of his cultural theory suggests that this is why he did so.

7.1 Two Varieties of Existentialism

We can see clearly the difference between Beauvoir's variety of existentialism and Sartre's variety in *Being and Nothingness* in the ways they each adapt the idea of an inferiority complex. This is central to Beauvoir's account of the origins of gender in *The Second Sex*, as we saw in Chapter 5. The idea that boys are superior to girls, men superior to women, is instilled in boys and girls by their being offered different opportunities, encouraged to do different things, praised for different things, and discouraged from different things. The resulting difference in physical abilities is an aspect of Beauvoir's theory that has since been emphasized and developed (Young 1980; Chisholm 2008). Beauvoir's emphasis, however, is on the ambitions, interests, preferences, values, and self-image that are fostered in girls. It is this socialization that, on her view, results in women having a sense of inferiority to men. Sartre, on the other hand, treats the inferiority complex entirely as a project that some individuals freely choose: the project of attempting to establish that one is by nature inferior structures one's experience, as we saw in Chapter 5, so that one seems genuinely to be pursuing goals that one is in fact aiming to fail to achieve.

It might seem that this contrast merely reflects the fact that Beauvoir focuses on explaining the origins of a set of characteristics common to a group of people, whereas Sartre is focused here on the origins of an individual's character. It might seem that these differing theoretical contexts produce different conceptions of the inferiority complex.

But this would miss the deeper point that Sartre's initial form of existentialism could not accommodate Beauvoir's analysis of the origins of common characteristics of social groups. On his view, social meanings can shape one's outlook only through being internalized into the projects one has freely chosen and can abandon. If you are categorized as a member of an inferior group, for example, then this social context needs to be taken into account in the ways you pursue your values, but it cannot shape those values themselves. For you have absolute freedom to adopt projects that accept your purported inferior status, or that attempt to disprove it, or that attempt to ignore it.

This is because the values one freely chooses, according to Sartre's initial form of existentialism, are ontologically prior to any reasons that might be presented by other people's views of one, which is a consequence of his more general view that it is the values at the heart of one's projects that transform the social and physical structure of one's environment into a field of reasons. Garcin and Estelle are tortured by other people's views of them only because these views conflict with their projects of seeing themselves as macho or feminine by nature. However, as we saw at the end of the last chapter, Sartre also thinks that most of us are committed to the project of bad faith. This is the project of identifying oneself with a particular set of characteristics as though these are a fixed essence that causes one's behaviour. Garcin and Estelle have this bad faith in common, even though they do not ascribe to themselves the same fixed essence.

Sartre's initial form of existentialism ascribes to this common bad faith two roles that Beauvoir ascribes to sedimentation: to explain why we are unaware of the origins of some of our motivations in our own values and to explain why we sometimes feel constrained by the reasons we experience in the world. Through the lens of bad faith, according to Sartre, reflection on our own motivations portrays them as manifestations of a fixed nature rather than expressions of our chosen projects. According to Beauvoir's existentialism, by contrast, a sedimented value can produce desires that conflict with our more recently endorsed values, leaving us puzzled about the origins of the desire. And we can become genuinely constrained by the reasons we experience in the world, at least in the absence of a concerted effort at changing through counter-conditioning the sedimented projects that shape those reasons. Beauvoir can explain by sedimentation features of experience that Sartre can explain only by bad faith. This is why Beauvoir and Sartre develop, as we saw in Chapter 5, different varieties of existentialist psychoanalysis.

Beauvoir's reliance on sedimentation makes her form of existentialism preferable to Sartre's for a reason that seems to explain why Sartre went on to adopt Beauvoir's conception of sedimentation and revise his existentialism accordingly. The issue is not one of internal coherence. Sartre's reliance on bad faith does not threaten the philosophical integrity of his theory of the structures of motivation. Rather, the problem arises because Sartre wants to ground an account of cultural characteristics in this phenomenology of motivation. How could his initial existentialism explain why members of a social category, such as a gender or ethnic group, often have characteristic values in common? Sartre does not want to deny the apparent empirical reality of such cultural values. But his attempt to explain them rests on bad faith being a widespread characteristic, which simply pushes the question back one step. How can Sartre explain this common feature of people's outlook? Sartre's initial form of existentialism precludes there being any answer to this question, as we will see. This is the unexplainable coincidence that Sartre's cultural theory must postulate and that Beauvoir's theory avoids.

7.2 Cultural Values Without Sedimentation

We can isolate the problem with Sartre's initial form of existentialism by analysing his attempt to account for the origin of cultural values within its framework, the essay on the place of Jewish culture in French society that he wrote in the immediate aftermath of the liberation of Paris in 1944. He published its first chapter in *Les Temps Modernes* during the existentialist offensive towards the end of 1945, then the whole essay as a small book in 1946. The book analyses the relationship between anti-Semitism and Jewish culture without drawing on the empirical studies and historical analyses available at the time and without much attention to the atrocities that had just been committed against Jewish people (Baert 2015: 123–4, 130–1). Despite these features, or perhaps partly because of them, Sartre's book set the agenda for analyses of anti-Semitism and Jewish identity in post-war French culture (Rybalka 1999). But this book is also a significant moment in Sartre's philosophical development. For it demonstrates the inadequacy of his initial form of existentialism to ground a cultural theory, an inadequacy which, as we shall see, Sartre may soon have recognized.

Sartre presents his analysis of Jewish identity in opposition to two other views. One is the view that there is some fixed essence, some ethnic nature, shared by Jewish people. Understanding people as having fixed natures, of course, is the core of bad faith. Sartre ascribes this view to anti-Semitism, which he argues is the project of seeing oneself as having a fixed nature in virtue of one's ethnicity, a nature which is superior to the nature of Jewish people, who are consequently cast as refusing to accept their supposedly natural inferior position (A&J: 17, 25-7). Sartre focused his analysis of the idea of ethnic nature on this anti-Semitism because he thought that, as a matter of fact, this anti-Semitism was strongly influential in French society at the time. The idea that there are ethnic natures does not itself entail racial supremacism of any kind, for there is no contradiction in the idea that ethnic groups have different essential natures of equal value. But all forms of ethnic essentialism would be instances of bad faith, according to Sartre's initial form of existentialism, precisely because they ascribe fixed natures to people.

Sartre's second opponent is 'the democrat', who denies that there are any significant differences between ethnic groups. Sartre argues that this is simply a different form of the tendency 'to suppress the Jew' (A&J: 144). Whereas the anti-Semite wants us to see the Jewish person entirely as Jewish and not as a person, the democrat wants us to see the Jewish person entirely as a person and not as Jewish (A&J: 57). Sartre argues that it is rather the whole Jewish person 'with his character, his customs, his tastes, his religion if he has one, his name', not just his abstract humanity, that 'we must accept' (A&J: 147). If there is no Jewish essence, then what is it that Sartre wants us to accept beyond the common humanity of each person? It is clear that Sartre is here committed to the idea that there are cultural characteristics of Jewish people. This does not require any particular values had by every Jewish person, only that there are values that are characteristic of Jewish people in general.

This cultural identity is grounded, Sartre argues, not in any ethnic essence, but in the situation that, he claims, is common to all Jewish people. This is the situation of living in a broader society that contains substantial hostility towards Jewish people. Because each Jewish person has to formulate and pursue their projects against this common background, there are likely to be features in common across those projects

(A&J: 60, 67, 72, 89, 90, 145). This is what Sartre means when he argues that anti-Semitism cannot be a reaction to any characteristics of Jewish people, as anti-Semites themselves claim it to be, but rather any such cultural characteristics come about as a result of anti-Semitism (A&J: 143). He has taken his inspiration here from Richard Wright, whom he cites as having recently argued that 'there is no Negro problem in the United States, there is only a White problem' (A&J: 152). Likewise, argues Sartre, there is no 'Jewish question' facing France at the end of the war, no question of the proper place of Jewish people in French society, but only a question of how anti-Semitism is to be defeated (A&J: 151–3).

It might seem, therefore, that Sartre's declaration that Jewish culture is grounded in the context of anti-Semitism is merely a rhetorical overstatement of his central claim that anti-Semitism is not a response to Jewish culture. The notable absence throughout the book of any reference to stories, histories, aphorisms, poetry, music, humour, festivals, rituals, and other cultural items that shape families and communities, apart from his occasional use of the word 'customs', might similarly seem merely an effect of Sartre's desire to emphasize that anti-Semitism is not a response to Jewish culture. But these features of his analysis are required by his initial form of existentialism. For according to that existentialism, the significance of an individual's cultural context depends on their projects, so this cultural context cannot itself shape those projects. If there are values common among members of a cultural group, therefore, these must be explained primarily by features common to the projects they have each freely chosen. But why should these people each choose projects that have these common features? It is to answer this question that Sartre needs to appeal to the anti-Semitism common to the situations of Jewish people.

7.3 Bad Faith as the Ground of Cultural Values

In itself, however, this appeal to the wider culture suffused with anti-Semitism is not sufficient to explain any cultural characteristics of Jewish identity within the framework of Sartre's initial form of existentialism. For this wider social context in which Jewish people pursue their projects, like the narrower social context of Jewish culture itself, can be constituted for the individual as a field of reasons only in the light of that individual's freely chosen projects. The significance of the anti-Semitism that an individual encounters results from that individual's projects, on

Sartre's initial view, so cannot constrain the choice of those projects any more than the fabric of Jewish culture could. If there are to be features common to the ways in which Jewish individuals respond to this wider cultural climate, therefore, these need to be explained in terms of common features of the projects that shape this wider climate as a field of reasons for those individuals. This is why Sartre appeals, at this stage of his cultural theory, to his conception of bad faith.

More specifically, he appeals to the form of bad faith that he here labels 'inauthenticity', which he describes as the attempt by an individual 'to deal with their situation by running away from it' (A&J: 92). This does not mean that the Jewish person taking this attitude denies that there is a climate of anti-Semitism, or even denies that they are a member of the group of people that anti-Semitism categorizes together as inferior. Rather, this project incorporates the anti-Semite's idea that there are such things as ethnic essences. The person pursuing this project attempts to prove through their behaviour and outlook that they have an essence other than the one the anti-Semite ascribes to them and that the anti-Semite is therefore wrong about the nature of Jewish people in general (A&J: 94–5). This is a project of 'running away from' an essence ascribed to one by asserting a contrary essence.[1] Just as Garcin attempts, in *Huis Clos*, to establish that his nature is not what other people think it is, Sartre thinks that Jewish people pursuing this project attempt to prove that the nature of Jewish people is not as the anti-Semite portrays it.

In contrast to this response to anti-Semitism, the attitude of authenticity accepts that there are no fixed natures and recognizes that the anti-Semitism pervading the wider society ascribes to oneself a fixed nature nonetheless, one of ethnic inferiority. In adopting this attitude, the individual becomes 'a man, a whole man, with the metaphysical horizons that go with the condition of man' (A&J: 137–8). The authentic individual recognizes that they are pursuing freely chosen projects in their particular situation. There is nothing more to be said about authentic people in general or more specifically about authentic Jewish people, according to Sartre; the authentic individual 'is what he makes himself, that is all that can be said' (A&J: 137). There is nothing generally true of authentic people apart from their affirmation that there are no fixed

---

[1] For an analysis of the varieties of bad faith that Sartre outlines in *Being and Nothingness*, see Webber 2009: chs. 6 and 7.

natures, even when there are significant features of their situations in common. For there is nothing generally true of the projects they pursue, except that these embody 'a true and lucid consciousness of the situation' and assume 'the responsibilities and risks that it involves' (A&J: 90).

It follows from this that if there are cultural characteristics of Jewish identity, if there are values common to many Jewish people in virtue of their being Jewish people, then these are not grounded in authentic responses to the climate of anti-Semitism, but must rather result from inauthentic responses to it. Sartre argues that the inauthentic response to being ascribed some negative fixed characteristic, such as being untrustworthy or avaricious, is to attempt to demonstrate the contrary fixed property, such as honesty or generosity (A&J: 73–4, 95–6). Because anti-Semites are motivated by an idea of their own superiority, however, not by a particular image of Jewish identity, anti-Semites can admit that Jewish people may be honest or generous by adding the qualification that these are somehow inferior forms of honesty and generosity (A&J: 74–5; see also A&J: 82). A more general feature of inauthenticity, argues Sartre, is the valuing of critical introspection, initially aimed at ensuring that one's behaviour repudiates the anti-Semitic stereotype. The resulting tendency to self-analysis is then cited by the anti-Semite as itself a feature of Jewish inferiority (A&J: 94–5).

This theory of cultural characteristics, however, fails to establish what Sartre claims to want to establish. It fails to establish that society at large should respect Jewish people not only as people, but specifically as Jewish people. The priority given to anti-Semitism in the construction of Jewish culture and the recommendation that French society work to undermine anti-Semitism together imply that Jewish culture itself should be undermined. The role accorded to bad faith in the theory implies that widespread recognition of the reality of the human condition would result in the disappearance of Jewish culture. Sartre comes close to admitting this when he points out that the erosion of anti-Semitism would 'make easier' an authentic response to the Jewish condition and 'make possible, without violence and by the very course of history, that assimilation' that he had earlier described as the goal of 'the democrat' (A&J: 147). This erosion of Jewish culture would not be forced, but the very fact that Sartre's theory entails that it ought to occur looks rather less respectful of Jewish culture than Sartre proclaims himself to be, as various prominent critics of Sartre have pointed out (Silverman 2005: 117; Haddour 2011: 76–8).

7.4 The Project of Bad Faith

Sartre's theory of cultural characteristics in *Anti-Semite and Jew* relies on his concept of bad faith to explain not only why a particular individual adopts the values common in their cultural group, but also why there already are prevailing values among that cultural group. This cultural question cannot be answered with reference only to that group's wider situation, such as the climate of anti-Semitism, within Sartre's initial form of existentialism, because that wider situation would not itself constitute a field of reasons for behaving in one way or another. Any field of reasons is constituted by the physical and social world in relation to the values of the individual for whom they are reasons. A group of people making a common response to a common situation, therefore, can be explained only by a common project or set of projects. This is what led Sartre to argue that Jewish culture is grounded in a very general project that he considered prevalent across his society, the project of bad faith.

But this does not yet explain the origin of cultural characteristics. For we can ask why bad faith should be prevalent across this wide cultural group. Indeed, even if it were prevalent across the whole of humanity, we could ask why. Sartre cannot hold that bad faith is an innate or necessary part of human existence, since this would contradict the basic claim of his existentialism, that existence precedes essence. For bad faith is a project that values the attribution of fixed essences to oneself and to people in general. If this value can be innate and necessary, then why not other values? Sartre clearly does not think that it is essential to human existence, however, for he claims that there are authentic individuals, although these are rare (A&J: 90, 138). But why should they be rare? 'There is no doubt that authenticity demands much courage and more than courage', Sartre proclaims, telling us that authenticity involves accepting 'risks and responsibilities' and inauthenticity is a response to the situation seeming 'intolerable' (A&J: 90, 92). His philosophy, however, requires that these reasons are grounded in prior projects of the individuals. What could the relevant projects be?

If one is already committed to the project of bad faith, to seeing oneself as having a particular fixed essence, then one would find the continual attribution of a different essence to oneself intolerable, would need courage to overcome this project that is fundamental to one's outlook and self-image, and the risks and responsibilities that come with doing so would seem to be reasons against overcoming it. But bad faith is precisely the project that we are trying to explain. Sartre does describe the awareness that we have no fixed natures as 'anguish' (B&N: 54–7). This cannot be the claim that we are by nature inclined against embracing our freedom over our projects, that it is part of the essence of our existence that awareness of this freedom induces anguish, and that we are thus naturally inclined towards bad faith, for this clearly would contradict the basic claim of Sartre's existentialism. Sartre must rather view anguish as a symptom of bad faith, a reason present in our experience as a result of our project of affirming that we have a fixed nature (Webber 2009: 111–16; Webber 2011: 185–6).

There are passages in *Being and Nothingness* where Sartre suggests that it is social pressure that leads us to adopt the project of bad faith. The customers in the café expect the waiter to behave as nothing more than the embodiment of the essence of waiterhood. 'Society demands that he limit himself to his function', Sartre writes, 'as if we live in perpetual fear that he might escape from it' (B&N: 82–3; see also A&J: 73–4). More generally, the person in bad faith will exert pressure on those around them not to exhibit behaviour that threatens the idea that people have fixed natures. Being raised and continuing to live in a climate of bad faith, it might be argued, therefore explains why an individual is likely to adopt this project oneself: to do otherwise requires them to resist that social pressure (Webber 2009: 112; Webber 2011: 187). Authenticity does not itself exert a contrary pressure, moreover. The authentic person's belief that there are no fixed natures could not be threatened by other people behaving as if there are, since the authentic person could put that down to those people's bad faith.

However, this explanation of the widespread adoption of the project of bad faith overlooks one of the central claims of Sartre's initial form of existentialism, which we considered in Chapter 3. This is the claim that one experiences the world as a field of reasons to be considered, compared, accepted, rejected, or revised, rather than as a nexus of causes that simply force one to behave in a particular way. Each individual therefore has strong continuous evidence that they do not have a fixed nature that produces their behaviour through causal interaction with their environment (see especially 3.4 above). This continuous evidence constitutes internal pressure against the project of bad faith. In order to explain why the individual adopts the project of bad faith, therefore, the social pressure to do so must constitute a reason to value having a particular fixed nature, a reason strong enough to outweigh the contrary evidence of one's own experience. But one would only see it this way, according to Sartre's initial form of existentialism, if one already had some relevant project. What is that project and why is it widespread? This is essentially the question we started with: what explains the prevalence of bad faith?

7.5 An Unexplainable Coincidence

Ultimately, this question cannot be answered within Sartre's initial form of existentialism. This is due to its combination of two claims. One is that features of the individual's physical and social environment constitute reasons for that person only in the light of projects that person is already pursuing. The other is that projects have no inertia of their own, but influence our experience and behaviour only if we continue to endorse them. The features of the wider environment within which Jewish culture develops, therefore, cannot constitute reasons for that culture to develop in one way or another, except in the light of some prior project common to the members of that community. Sartre identifies this project as bad faith. But the problem does not rest on this claim. Whatever that prior project is claimed to be, we can ask why it is common to those people. This could be answered only with reference to another project, about which the same question could be raised. In the end, we must reach a project whose adoption by each individual is unmotivated. Sartre's cultural theory therefore rests on the unexplainable coincidence of the widespread adoption of that project.

Beauvoir's variety of existentialism does not face this problem, even though it agrees that features of the physical and social environment constitute reasons for the individual only in the light of that person's projects. For on Beauvoir's view, the opportunities, encouragements, and discouragements that shape childhood direct the individual towards projects that incorporate the meanings of their surrounding culture. Because projects become sedimented, these cultural meanings become sedimented. Once the individual has matured and is able to adopt projects on the basis of their own critical reflection, their thought will be influenced by these sedimented meanings. If new projects are formed that contradict these meanings despite their influence, moreover, it would take considerable pursuit of these projects for them to become sedimented sufficiently to counteract or remove the old ones. Beauvoir's focus on the limitations imposed on women by the sedimentation of gender should not be taken to imply that acculturation is itself ethically problematic. On her variety of existentialism, this cultural transmission is simply a feature of human existence, whatever the ethical status of the meanings transmitted in this way.

Beauvoir's existentialism can therefore account for values being common to the outlooks of members of a social group. If there are any values characteristic of Jewish people, or of some particular group of Jewish people, then these would be explained by the sedimentation of the cultural climate in which those people grew up and which they perpetuate in adulthood as a result. The set of social meanings transmitted in upbringing not only constitutes a cultural group's shared outlook, but in being sedimented constrains the range of possible values likely to be adopted by members of that cultural group. There is no need for any underlying existential project like bad faith whose adoption could not be explained. This variety of existentialism, moreover, can provide a more sophisticated analysis of prejudice. Sartre's initial variety of existentialism constrained him to understanding anti-Semitism as a project of claiming a natural superiority over Jewish people. As well as resting on the unexplainable coincidence of a widespread adoption of bad faith, Sartre's view excludes subtle forms of anti-Semitism that might infect the outlooks of people who do not endorse such a project of racial superiority, as George Orwell pointed out in response (1948). Beauvoir's form of existentialism allows that anti-Semitism present in one's surrounding culture can become sedimented in one's outlook, such that it can influence one's thought and behaviour even if one explicitly rejects anti-Semitism.

Sartre's initial form of existentialism cannot account for the transmission of culture in this way, because sedimentation is ruled out by his claim that projects, having no inertia of their own, persist only by the individual upholding them. Childhood plays no special role in the formation of the individual, according to Sartre's initial form of existentialism. The adult chooses projects in relation to their physical and cultural surroundings. Although they may continue with projects first chosen in childhood, their upbringing does not constrain them. They might choose to uphold the values of their families or immediate communities, but they are just as able to choose not to. Although he does not mention this possibility in *Anti-Semite and Jew*, Sartre's initial form of existentialism allows that an inauthentic person might uphold the values of their family or community precisely in order to identify with these as their own essence. If a theory of cultural transmission were developed from this idea, then it too would rest on the unexplainable coincidence of widespread bad faith.

Bad faith therefore plays a crucial role in Sartre's initial variety of existentialism. He portrays it as a social malady responsible not only for the idiosyncratic difficulties people face and the basic conflicts between people, but also for the very existence of common values largely shared across a cultural group. Unlike his claim that projects can be abandoned for no reason, therefore, his idea that bad faith is a widespread project cannot simply be denied while accepting the rest of his initial existentialism. Yet this reliance on bad faith to explain cultural characteristics requires us to accept a theory that rests on a large scale coincidence that is not just unexplained, but is in principle unexplainable. This problem is generated by combining the claim that projects have no inertia of their own with the claim that the reasons we encounter are dependent on our chosen projects. The second of these is the core of the claim that our existence precedes our essence. To avoid the problem without abandoning existentialism, therefore, Sartre needs to replace his claim that projects have no inertia with Beauvoir's idea of sedimentation.[2]

7.6 Sedimentation in the Formation of Saint Genet

By the time he wrote his biography of Genet, published in 1952, Sartre had revised his conception of human existence to include the sedimentation of values central to Beauvoir's form of existentialism. The biography analyses the literary works, lifestyle, and character of Jean Genet as expressions of a single complex project rooted in his childhood. In his

---

[2] We saw in Chapter 3 that Merleau-Ponty was right to object to Sartre's theory that one could modify or abandon a project for no reason, since this is incompatible with the commitment required to have a project at all (3.6). We saw in Chapter 4 that Beauvoir's theory of sedimentation offers an account of commitment to a project where Sartre's theory of radical freedom cannot (4.4, 4.6). But if the argument of this chapter is right, Sartre's rejection of his earlier theory of radical freedom in favour of Beauvoir's theory of the sedimentation of projects was not motivated by either of these arguments, but instead by his recognition that his idea of radical freedom ultimately precludes the development of a cultural theory.

early years, a moral outlook was instilled into him. 'Work, family, country, honesty, property' are central to this moral outlook and even though he grows up to flout these values in his actions and writings, he does so precisely because the idea of their goodness remains 'graven forever upon his heart' (SG: 6; see also SG: 21–2). His project is born of the tension between this outlook and his own status as a poor peasant child and an adoptee. He imaginatively attains the good of owning property through occasional petty thefts. In doing this, 'he is unaware that he is forging his destiny' (SG: 16).

For he is repeatedly caught in these little acts of theft and condemned severely for them. 'In all probability, there were offenses and then punishment, solemn oaths and then relapses', writes Sartre, but the significance of these events can be summarized in the instantaneous judgment, 'You're a thief' (SG: 17). Over this period of time, he comes to accept that this judgment correctly identifies his essential nature, that this 'dizzying word' makes sense of his life as an outsider in this pious community, the offspring of dishonest reprobates who would abandon their own son (SG: 17–19). Sartre describes this stage of Genet's life as his first 'metamorphosis', adopting the term that Beauvoir used in *The Second Sex* to describe a gradual change in outlook (SG: 1, 18; SS: 780). Through instilling the meanings that constitute their morality in him and then bringing him to accept their moral judgment of him, his society 'have penetrated to the very bottom of his heart and installed a permanent delegate there which is himself' (SG: 21). Much like the 'superego' described by Freud, this sedimentation of society's moral code will continue to condemn Genet for desires and actions that violate that code.

Unlike the Freudian superego, however, this representative of society's judgments is partly responsible for Genet continuing to violate that moral code. For this sedimentation is only the first stage of Genet's 'progressively internalising the sentence imposed by adults' (SG: 37). The second is his decision to embrace this essence, rather than resist its influence. Sartre describes this as a 'conversion', but does not mean the instantaneous reorientation of values that he had called 'radical conversion' in *Being and Nothingness* and that we contrasted with Beauvoir's idea of 'metamorphosis' in Chapter 5. Sartre is clear that Genet's 'conversion' to being a thief is a form of sedimentation. 'Again and again the child pledged himself to Evil in a state of rage, and then one of his judges only had to smile at him and the decision melted in the fire of love', he writes, but 'then, one day, he found himself converted, exactly as one finds oneself cured of a passion that has caused long suffering' (SG: 50). What makes this a conversion is that it is based on conscious decision, rather than an unnoticed development. But it is sedimentation: Genet's evaluative outlook is gradually transformed by his repeatedly deciding to embrace his supposed evil nature.

Sartre has adopted Beauvoir's conception of commitment to a project. What commits Genet to being a thief is this sedimentation, which transforms his outlook in the same way that his earlier repeated endorsement of his society's morality left him 'unable to liquidate a system of values that denies him his place in the sun' (SG: 16). 'To adopt a mental attitude is to place oneself in a prison without bars', Sartre claims; one can reason to 'a new point of view entailing new commitments', but this does not in itself displace the original attitude, which continues to influence thought and action (SG: 69). This sedimentation, however, does not prevent us from being free. 'We are not lumps of clay, and what is important is not what people make of us but what we ourselves make of what they have made of us' (SG: 49). We choose the projects that become sedimented in our outlooks and we can erode them through new projects. It is by facing the givens of life 'and digesting them little by little' into its own projects that 'freedom alone can account for a person in his totality' (SG: 584).

Sartre therefore no longer needs his theory of bad faith to explain how we can be unaware of some of our motivations or why we sometimes feel constrained by the reasons we find in the world. He can agree with Beauvoir that these phenomena arise when our deeply sedimented meanings and values are at odds with our more recently endorsed values. Sedimented meanings and values are the prison without bars. Moreover, he no longer needs to rest his cultural theory on bad faith. The meanings of one's surrounding culture can become sedimented in one's outlook just as the Morvan peasant morality becomes sedimented in Genet's and an idea of male superiority becomes sedimented according to Beauvoir's theory of gender. Sartre does retain his theory of bad faith, however, including his claim that it is widespread (SG: 33–4). He retains his theory that our experience of the world as a field of reasons conflicts with the idea that we have fixed natures and that anxiety is the experience of this conflict (SG: 60, 591–2). But he now has the resources to explain the widespread adoption of bad faith in terms of its sedimentation as a cultural value (SG: 34–6).

7.7 Existence Precedes Sedimentation

Sartre's mature form of existentialism in *Saint Genet* thus retains some of the distinctive features of his initial existentialism. But in abandoning the idea of radical freedom in favour of sedimentation, he transforms his philosophy. Sartre criticized Freud's theory of mind for its explanatory incompleteness, yet his own alternative articulated in *Being and Nothingness* left entirely unexplained what undertaking a project amounts to and how such commitment shapes one's experience, and left entirely unexplainable the claimed widespread adoption of the project of bad faith. These explanatory deficiencies are remedied by adopting the idea of sedimentation. This is the development of Sartre's philosophy that Beauvoir mentions in her response to Merleau-Ponty a few years after *Saint Genet* was published: Sartre came to see freedom as inherently engaged in its social context through the sedimentation that gave projects their 'temporal thickness' (MPPS: 242–3). 'Genet the child emerges in a world filled with meanings which impose themselves upon him' (MPPS: 211; see also MPPS: 252 and Chapter 3.7 above). He therefore came to accept the version of existentialism that Beauvoir had first articulated in *She Came To Stay*. Her first detailed philosophical elaboration of it, however, was *The Second Sex*, to which Sartre acknowledges his debt in *Saint Genet* (SG: 37, 57, 291).

As a result of this transformation of his existentialism, Sartre is able to explain not only the social prevalence of bad faith, but also the transmission of cultural values generally in terms of sedimentation. He had argued that values characteristic of Jewish culture resulted from a form of bad faith, as we have seen. His initial form of existentialism denied that there are any 'innate qualities' of individuals, and therefore of any groups of individuals, and denied that sedimentation was possible, so he had no other option than to explain cultural values in terms of projects, or 'ventures in behaviour' (A&J: 93). Bad faith was simply the project that could ground such an explanation. Once he had accepted the idea of sedimentation, he could describe Genet as imbued with the morality of the people who raised him without attributing to him any prior project of bad faith. Sedimented meanings and values can be overcome through new projects, on Sartre's mature view, but when great social pressure is exerted in childhood the resulting meanings and values are deeply sedimented by the time the individual is sufficiently mature to formulate their own projects, so will strongly influence these projects (SG: 21).³

Although his focus is on a specific individual, Sartre does hold in *Saint Genet* that sedimentation of meanings under social pressure in childhood explains more generally why members of a social group have values in common. In particular, he argues that it explains how a particular social meaning can be deeply embedded in the self-image of each member of a cultural group (SG: 34, 54–5). This echoes his essay 'Black Orpheus', published in 1948, where he first describes the sedimentation of cultural meanings. There he argues that black people share a common 'basic experience' of the human condition as filtered through 'the still fresh memory of a historical past' of slavery (BO: 312). A century after its abolition, a 'collective memory', 'the most vivid of memories', 'an enormous nightmare' haunts the descendants of the victims of this slavery (BO: 311–12). This shapes the relative values that a black person places on black and white people, argues Sartre, including the evaluative dimension of the black person's self-image. This aspect of the individual's self-image resembles an essence that is discovered as much as it resembles a project freely created (BO: 317–19). The black man 'finds race'—a cultural meaning—'at the bottom of his heart' (BO: 323; see Haddour 2011: 82).

The contrast between this theory of an ongoing cultural effect of slavery and his analysis of Jewish culture written only a few years earlier is striking. He no longer thinks such characteristics could be explained only by projects, instead gesturing towards a quality of the individual's outlook that is neither innate nor chosen, but received through upbringing. At its basis is 'an original sin', but this is not bad faith, for 'the black

³ In an interview in 1982, Beauvoir seems to deny that Sartre's extensive analysis of Genet's childhood marks a theoretical departure from his earlier form of existentialism, saying that this was rather due to his intention to write comprehensively about Genet and to respond to Genet's own interest in childhood (Simons 1999: 57). However, this stands in tension with an earlier interview in which she accepts that her own interest in child development, especially her focus on this in *The Second Sex*, may well have influenced Sartre to consider more carefully how childhood shapes the individual's outlook (Simons 1999: 10). Sartre's two descriptions of childhoods in works before Saint Genet, first in his short story 'The Childhood of a Leader' and then in his biography of Baudelaire, only describe the circumstances that the child is responding to when deciding to undertake the fundamental project that will shape their life. There is no suggestion in either text of the sedimentation of values that drives his account of Genet's childhood. Indeed, the biography of Baudelaire, published three years before *The Second Sex*, briefly comments that gender characteristics are created and sustained entirely by the individual's present situation (B: 152–3).

man is its innocent victim' rather than its perpetrator (BO: 313). Where he had analysed Jewish culture as a product of bad faith, Sartre now argues that the black person is 'forced into authenticity' by being visibly a member of the group that was the victim of slavery (BO: 268). This authenticity is the recognition of a value that Sartre describes as 'a pledge and passion at one and the same time', that 'makes you and you make it' (BO: 319). The black person who wants to identify just as human cannot simply reject this sedimented value and embrace a new outlook; 'a bitter regret shows through' (BO: 322). Instead, this value can be overcome only through a gradual process (BO: 323).

Sartre's acceptance of sedimentation in 'Black Orpheus' allows him to explore cultural effects of the violence of slavery, which contrasts with his emphasis on anti-Semitic opinion rather than anti-Semitic violence in his earlier analysis of Jewish culture. It also allows that racist values have an insidious influence on the thought and action of people who do not knowingly endorse those values. Sartre does not explore this implication, but it is precisely the form of racial prejudice that Orwell complained was missing from Sartre's analysis of anti-Semitism. That he first embraced sedimentation in 'Black Orpheus', written as a preface to an anthology of poetry by black authors and published as Beauvoir was finalizing *The Second Sex*, however, does suggest that this transformation of his existentialism was motivated by his recognition of the inadequacy of his analysis of anti-Semitism and Jewish culture, and perhaps its indication of a more general inability of his initial form of existentialism to ground a cultural theory. But while he was rethinking his existentialism through writing his biography of Genet, an analysis of racism and its cultural effects far more sophisticated than Sartre's own was being developed by Frantz Fanon. In the next chapter, we will see that this too is a canonical work of existentialism that incorporates the idea of sedimentation.

8

Black Skin, White Masks

Fanon initially intended his now seminal work *Black Skin, White Masks* as the final year dissertation for his medical degree at the University of Lyon. Having been born and raised in Martinique, he had served in the Martinican Corps of the French army during the Second World War, then moved to Paris to study dentistry on a scholarship for war veterans, but soon transferred to Lyon to study medicine, specializing in psychiatry. His intended dissertation, 'Essai sur la désalienation du Noir', drew on his analyses of psychiatric theory, his interests in philosophy and literature, and his personal experience of the differing racisms he had experienced in Martinique, in the army, and in France after the war, to describe a specific psychiatric condition that he claimed affected black people in French society, and to diagnose its causes. His supervisors advised against submitting such an unusual work, so he wrote a new dissertation on a neurophysiological disorder of the spinal column and qualified as a psychiatrist in 1951.

Fanon sought to publish his essay on the 'disalienation' of black colonized people. His manuscript was enthusiastically received by Francis Jeanson in his role as an editor at Éditions du Seuil. It was Jeanson who suggested the title *Peau noire, masques blancs*, which Fanon accepted, and the book was published in 1952 when Fanon was twenty-seven years old. It carried a preface by Jeanson praising the book for disrupting the white intellectual elite's confidence in the adequacy of their own perspective on social reality and lauding the implication of Fanon's work that a revolutionary transformation of the social order is required, rather than individual revolt against it (Jeanson 1952). This was around the time that Jeanson wrote his review of *The Rebel* that, as we saw in Chapter 2, ignited the infamous row that ended the friendship between Camus and Sartre.

The contrast is revealing. Jeanson's preface does not explicitly classify *Black Skin, White Masks* as a work of existentialism, but it does make regular reference to Sartre. By drawing attention to the difference between revolution and revolt, an implication of Fanon's thought to which the book does not devote much space, Jeanson implicitly contrasts Fanon with Camus. Where his review of *The Rebel* is a decisive rejection of Camus by the existentialist establishment, his preface to *Black Skin, White Masks* subtly situates Fanon within their movement. It was nine years later that Sartre first met Fanon and agreed to write a preface to his new book, *The Wretched of the Earth*. But this only cemented an intellectual affinity that Jeanson had already seen in the manuscript he had been sent. It is impossible to tell, however, quite how much of Fanon's existentialism Jeanson had recognized, for *Black Skin, White Masks* is a thoroughly existentialist work, as we will see, but its existentialism is distinctive in both its theoretical details and in their application.

8.1 Eclecticism and Theoretical Unity

The most striking features of *Black Skin, White Masks* on first reading are its wide range of reference points and its apparently chaotic literary style. Fanon presents critical analyses of the novels of Mayotte Capécia and Richard Wright and the poetry of Leopold Senghor and Aimé Césaire, among many other works, alongside his theoretical responses to highly influential works of European anthropology, philosophy, and psychoanalysis. His writing is often lyrical, but regularly adopts the drier voice of standard academic prose. He switches between the detached, objective perspective of abstract theorizing and the engaged, first-personal perspective of confessional or meditative literature. This eclecticism of both substance and style makes the book a very challenging read. It is difficult to discern the logical progression or any underlying theoretical unity to the various claims made in the book.

Indeed, the book has been read as intending to demonstrate the impossibility of capturing the social structures of colonialism in any unified way. Homi Bhabha argues that its haphazard progression represents 'a desperate, doomed search for a dialectic of deliverance' from colonial subjection, one that explores different perspectives on colonialism largely through the interactions between them and finds them all wanting (Bhabha 1986: x–xi). Such a reading might seem to ascribe to Fanon only a relatively shallow intellectual contribution as a comparative critic of other people's thought, or as raising important questions, rather than as an originator of valuable ideas (see also Lee 2015: 76). But to draw this conclusion would be to forget that Fanon is a psychiatrist. For it would prioritize philosophy's ambition of formulating internally consistent and robust theories over psychiatry's ambitions of treating psychological distress and safeguarding against people suffering that distress. Since the goals of psychiatry are treatment and prevention, what matters is what works. If we read Fanon as eschewing theoretical unity, therefore, we should see his original contribution as the development of a pragmatic eclecticism for psychiatry in place of what were then its traditional attempts at more systematic conceptual frameworks.

If we read Fanon in this way, then we can accept his eclecticism as fundamental to his theoretical outlook without ascribing to him what Lewis Gordon calls 'a subordinated theoretical identity' (2015: 5). For we would be reading his critical reflections on other thinkers as his vehicle for developing and articulating his own thought, as Stuart Hall recommends (1996: 30–1). However, this reading might be criticized for committing a different error that Gordon finds in the literature on Fanon, the 'disciplinary decadence' of prioritizing one of Fanon's intellectual concerns to the exclusion of others (2015: 17). Bhabha can be accused of losing sight of the psychiatric ambition of *Black Skin, White Masks* by reading it exclusively through its concern with the sociological analysis of colonialism. But conversely, if we read the book as fundamentally advocating pragmatic eclecticism in psychiatry and demonstrating its use through diagnoses of psychiatric problems generated by colonialism, then we risk occluding the ethical, social, and political dimensions of the book.

Should we conclude that there are simply distinct lenses through which we can read *Black Skin, White Masks* and ourselves renounce any ambition to resolve the apparent disagreements that arise from comparing readings taken through these different lenses? If we do this, we risk losing some of the most valuable intellectual contributions that this book has to offer. We would be filtering Fanon's thought through our understanding of the relations between his intellectual concerns and through our understanding of the relations between his influences, rather than aiming to uncover his own views of these relations. If we instead read the book as having the more ambitious aim of developing a unified theory addressing Fanon's various intellectual interests, then we stand to gain significant insights into the deep structural relations between these interests. To get the most out of this work, then, we should accept Gordon's description of the book as offering a 'metatheoretical' analysis of how its various theoretical concerns and influences fit together, as well as pursuing those concerns through analyses of those influences (2015: 17). We should ascribe fragmentation or incompleteness only where we cannot explain how this aim has been achieved.

One of the reasons Bhabha gives for his reading of *Black Skin, White Masks* as conceptually disunified is that Fanon draws on both existentialism and psychoanalysis, or both 'a phenomenological affirmation of Self and Other and the psychoanalytic ambivalence of the Unconscious' as he puts it (1986: x). We have already seen in Chapter 5 that existentialism is not in fact antagonistic towards psychoanalysis, since Beauvoir and Sartre developed their forms of existentialism as grounding a kind of psychoanalysis that retained many of Freud's insights. In this chapter, we will see that Fanon's use of psychoanalysis similarly aims to integrate its insights into an existentialist theory. Indeed, we will see that the fundamental theoretical purpose of *Black Skin, White Masks* is to argue for a form of existentialism that provides a conceptual framework for psychiatry and an ethical, social, and political outlook. The book's progression is unified as a single line of argument for this existentialism and its literary style exemplifies this existentialism. This is not to deny that Fanon employs an eclectic approach to psychiatry, but to uncover his deeper idea that motivates and constrains that eclecticism. To see exactly what this means, we need first to trace the book's line of argument for Fanon's form of existentialism.

8.2 The Dilemma of White Masks

One aspect of the book where we must acknowledge an incompleteness is Fanon's use of the terms 'black' and 'white' to refer to groups of people. He often treats these terms as synonymous with 'colonized' and 'colonizer', suggesting that he intends his analysis to apply specifically within a colonial context. This is not to say that he considers it to apply equally to all colonial systems. His analysis rests on details of the French colonial rule in the Caribbean, as we will see in section 8.4, though he does consider it to apply to relations between people in mainland France as a result of this colonial rule. But he does not seem to intend his analysis to be wholly restricted to this context. At one point, he refers to resistance to French colonial rule in Southeast Asia (BSWM: 201). In an article published in the same year as *Black Skin, White Masks*, he describes a behavioural syndrome among Arabic men in the French colonies of north Africa, briefly suggesting a diagnosis similar to his analysis of life under French colonialism in the Caribbean (NAS: 15).

Who, then, are the 'black' and 'white' people he describes in the book? His text does not provide a complete answer to this question. We should read his use of these terms primarily as applying within French culture, in mainland France and in its colonies, at the time when Fanon was writing, to people classified as 'black' and 'white'. Unless we keep that specific meaning in view, Fanon will seem to be generalizing too broadly from a narrow evidential base. But we should also bear in mind his intention that this analysis has broader application, especially given that its deep structure is a form of existentialism and therefore rests on an understanding of human existence itself. Translating his thought out of the specific colonial context he details is therefore legitimate, but requires careful attention to the differences between that context and the time and place to which his thought is then applied (see BSWM: xviii, 2).

With that specific context in mind, the opening chapters of the book present a puzzle. These present an initial description of an inferiority felt by the colonized black people and analyse the attempt to overcome this feeling by identifying with the white colonizers. Perhaps because of the prominence of Fanon's analysis of this strategy in his book, readers have often taken the book's title to refer entirely to this strategy. The book's title refers, on this understanding, to the attempt by black colonized people metaphorically to wear a mask that identifies them with the white colonizers (e.g. Caute 1970: 11; Bhabha 1986: xv–xvi; Nayar 2013: 50). This strategy is doomed to failure, according to Fanon. The colonized black person cannot escape their feeling of inferiority in this way because they cannot fully identify with the white colonizer. At best, their behaviour can be mere impersonation of the white person (BSWM: 18–19, 21–3). But why should this be so? We might continue with the metaphor and say that it is because the mask occasionally slips, or the mask is ill-fitting. But why should these metaphors necessarily apply?

One response to this question might be to suggest that there are essential differences between the black colonized people and their white colonizers that prevent the former from behaving exactly like the latter. But this is precisely what Fanon is going to reject. As we will see in more detail in section 8.5, Fanon is an existentialist. Another response would be to suggest that the black colonized people have deeply internalized a cultural identification through their upbringing that is distinct from the culture of the white colonizers. But this cannot be Fanon's answer either. For, as we will see in more detail in section 8.4, Fanon argues that the root of the inferiority complex that the colonized black person suffers from is in part that they have deeply internalized a cultural identification with the white Europeans. As the book's title suggests, the reason why the colonized cannot wear perfectly the mask presenting them as white is not that they have some innate or acquired psychological properties, but because they have 'black skin'. How does 'black skin' itself have this effect?

To answer this, we need first to recognize that the adjective 'white' in the phrase 'white masks' indicates not a visible feature of the masks, but rather their origin. White masks are white in the same way that French philosophy is French. White masks are masks produced by white colonizers and their features manifest the cultural background of those creators, just as works of French philosophy have features that manifest the French cultural background of their creation. The confusion arises because a subset of these white masks are indeed designed for the white colonizers to wear and Fanon does describe the attempt by people of 'black skin' to wear these masks. But to see clearly why this can never be more than impersonation, we need to contrast this set of white masks, which we will call (w), with the set that the white colonizers have designed for the black colonized to wear, which we will call (b). 'Making him speak pidgin', for example, is 'tying him to an image, snaring him, imprisoning him as the eternal victim of his own essence, of a *visible appearance* for which he is not responsible' (BSWM: 18).

The difference between the two kinds of masks lies in the kind of control that the white colonizers have over them: the features of (w) are defined simply by the behaviour of the white colonizers, so that when the behaviour of that category of people changes the features of (w) change with it; but the features of (b) are defined by the view that the white colonizers have of the black colonized people. Somebody classified as black in this system can adopt masks of kind (w), but they cannot stand in the same relation to (w) as the colonizer stands. This is why their wearing of this kind of mask can only be a kind of impersonation. It is both subjection and alienation for the same reason: it requires the colonized black person to follow behavioural norms over which they are denied any influence. The other option is to wear masks of kind (b). But these too are controlled by the white colonizers, whose outlook belittles and dehumanizes the colonized black people. This, therefore, is the initial form of the dilemma of white masks: the colonized black person is forced to choose between wearing (w) and wearing (b), both of which are forms of subjection and alienation.

8.3 The Strategy of Negritude

It is in the context of this dilemma that we should read Fanon's critical response to the Negritude movement, which aimed to explore and enrich the cultural identities of black people through historical investigations of African cultures and through art, literature, and music embodying African aesthetic forms. This movement had developed in the 1930s and had brought the margins of the French Empire to the heart of Parisian culture (Haddour 2005: 287–9; Lee 2015: 47–51). One of its leading lights, the poet Aimé Césaire, became one of the teachers at the high school Fanon attended as a student and Fanon had then worked on Césaire's successful campaign to be elected mayor of Fort-de-France in 1945 (Gordon 2015: 13, 52). Fanon even opens his book with a quotation from Césaire that encapsulates one important part of the analysis developed in the book. But by the time of writing *Black Skin, White Masks*, Fanon had come to see the Negritude movement as a response to the dilemma of white masks that ultimately cannot succeed in overcoming the problem.

Within the context of that dilemma, Negritude is a strategy that exploits the difference in the power the colonizer has over the two kinds of mask. Since masks of kind (w) are defined by the behaviour of the colonizer, there is nothing the colonized can do to alter those masks. But if (b) are defined only by the colonizers' expectations of the colonized, then the colonized can confound those expectations and thereby shape (b) by their own behaviour. To confound those expectations by behaving like the colonizer, of course, is to adopt masks of kind (w), so is not a way of escaping the dilemma. But by emphasizing aspects of their pre-colonial history and culture, the colonized can change the features of masks (b). By identifying as black people and then defining what that means independently of the expectations of the white colonizers, the colonized can take control of masks (b) without subjection to the colonizers' expectations and therefore without the alienation of being forced to live up to those expectations.

Fanon deepens his conception of the dilemma of white masks through his critical analysis of this strategy of responding to it. Ultimately the problem with wearing masks (b), he argues, is not that the colonizer controls the features of those masks, but that the colonizer classifies as inferior whatever features those masks have. They do this at first by defining the features of masks (b) in a way that belittles the colonized. But faced with the independent assertion of a black identity by the colonized, faced with a loss of control over the features of (b), the white colonizer simply classifies the new set of features as representing 'the childhood of the world', as exemplifying humanity's pre-scientific, pre-industrial sensitivity, a 'naive, ingenuous, and spontaneous' outlook that has been lost to the formal, polite, civilized European colonizer (BSWM: 111). Indeed, this relationship to the colonized is justified in the mind of the colonizer by the very fact of colonization: the superior social and technological sophistication of the Europeans is evidenced, they think, by their conquest and rule of these colonies (BSWM: 161-3). Negritude cannot overcome the subjection and alienation of wearing masks (b), because that subjection and alienation are ultimately caused by the colonizers' belittlement of the colonized, rather than by their control of the features of those masks (BSWM: 14; compare Sartre A&J: 74-5, 82; see 7.3 above).

It is with this understanding of the motivation and prospects of Negritude that Fanon turns to his famous critique of Sartre's 'Black Orpheus', his preface to a poetry anthology edited by Leopold Senghor, another leading light on the Negritude movement, that we considered in the last chapter (7.7). In this essay, Sartre characterizes Negritude as unable to establish the superiority or equality of a black culture, but nonetheless as paving the way to dissolving the distinction between the white colonizers and the black colonized (BO: 320). Fanon's response is very subtle. He argues that in describing Negritude as an inevitable stage in the unfolding of a logical historical process, Sartre has undermined the status of the Negritude movement as an achievement of black people. 'I did not create a meaning for myself; the meaning was already there, waiting', if Sartre is right (BSWM: 113). What is more, according to Fanon, Sartre effectively belittles Negritude by characterizing it as a developmental phase on the way to the mature position that he must himself already occupy in order to recognize this development (BSWM: 114). To this, we may add that in addressing 'Black Orpheus' to a white readership, Sartre inadvertently belittles black colonized people by talking about them without talking to them.

And yet Fanon does not think that what Sartre says is wrong. Sartre, he tells us, 'by naming me shattered my last illusion' (BSWM: 116). By correctly describing this project of Negritude, that is, Sartre has made it impossible for black colonized people to attempt to wrest control over the meaning of masks (b) through establishing a richer and more positive image of black culture. Fanon agrees with Sartre that Negritude cannot liberate the black colonized simply through control of masks (b), as we have seen, and that Negritude has an important role to play in dissolving racial categories, as we will see in section 8.5. Sartre has undermined, however, the possibility of Negritude playing that role through aiming to take control of masks (b), in Fanon's view. For this strategy could be pursued only under the illusion that establishing the equality of black people independently of the power of the white colonizers, taking control of masks (b), is something that the black colonized can themselves achieve. This is the illusion that Sartre has shattered, by pointing out the historical inevitability of the Negritude movement and its inability to achieve control over the meaning of masks (b).[1] But why does Fanon consider this belief, this 'illusion', necessary for the strategy of wresting control over masks (b)? The answer to this question lies in Fanon's theory of the inferiority complex.

8.4 The Inferiority Complex

Fanon's criticism of Sartre's characterization of the Negritude movement rests fundamentally on his claim that 'Sartre forgets that the black man suffers in his body quite differently from the white man' (BSWM: 117).

---

[1] Fanon's objection, therefore, is not that Sartre, as a white man pronouncing on the significance of Negritude, has tacitly asserted the right of the colonizer to determine the meaning and value of the cultural expressions of the colonized (Bernasconi 2005: 107–8; Silverman 2005: 117–18). For that objection would simply classify Sartre's essay on Negritude alongside countless other works that assume the same right. It would merely cast Sartre's work on this topic as just another part of the problem that Fanon had hoped the Negritude movement would help to overcome. Fanon's concern is rather that the specific content of Sartre's analysis directly undermines the prospects of Negritude as a strategy for overcoming that problem.

Fanon adds in a footnote that this is because Sartre's basic model of antagonism between people is his account of 'the look', which assumes that the two antagonists see one another as equals and that the antagonism is driven by bad faith. Within contexts that fit this assumption, Fanon is happy to accept Sartre's theory of the look. But its 'application to a black consciousness proves fallacious' because here that assumption is false; 'the white man is not only "the Other", but also the master, whether real or imaginary' (BSWM: 117 n24; see also BSWM: 24).[2] Fanon immediately goes on to describe this suffering of the black colonized, this relationship to the white colonizer as to a real or imaginary master, as a deep feeling of inferiority to the point of not fully existing, and of being guilty of some profound sin without knowing what the sin is (BSWM: 118). Fanon then turns, in the next chapter, to analysing the origins of this suffering.

He develops his view in critical dialogue with the psychoanalytic tradition, though this is distorted by his limited knowledge of it. Fanon mistakenly takes Freud's early theory that neuroses are rooted in childhood traumas to be characteristic of Freud's mature work and of classical psychoanalysis generally (Macey 2000: 133, 190–2; 2005: 23–4). Fanon takes Freud to look for originary traumas within each patient's family upbringing in part because Freud aims to explain neuroses that are abnormal in his society. Fanon's central points are that the inferiority complex that he diagnoses is normal among black colonized people and that its causes are to be found in the wider social context that they share rather than in details of childhood that will differ from person to person. Fanon thus reads Freud as holding that a 'normal child brought up in a normal family will become a normal adult', and then argues that this does not apply in the colonial context: a 'normal black child, having grown up with a normal family, will become abnormal at the slightest contact with the white world' (BSWM: 121–2; see also BSWM: xv).

To explain this, Fanon appropriates the idea of a 'collective unconscious' common to all members of society. Rather than agree with Carl

---

[2] Fanon has here assumed that Sartre's 'Black Orpheus' is philosophically continuous with his *Being and Nothingness*, but as we saw in the last chapter this essay is the first place where Sartre adopts the idea of sedimentation in place of the radical freedom of his earlier works. We will not consider here, however, whether Sartre's adoption of sedimentation entails a transformation of his theory of 'the look' that would invalidate Fanon's criticism.

Jung that this collective unconscious is innate, internal, and invariable, an inescapable basic content of the mind, Fanon argues that 'it is cultural, i.e., it is acquired'; the cause of the inferiority complex is a 'habit', not an 'instinct' (BSWM: 165). All children in the French-speaking world at the time, he points out, are raised on European storybooks, comics, and films, in which the heroes are white and the only black characters are belittled and dehumanized (BSWM: 124–33; see also BSWM: 17). This view of black people as inferior then pervades the culture through adult life, most especially in the continual use of blackness to symbolize evil and death (BSWM: 165–7; compare Sartre BO: 282). Black colonized children are raised on these same stories and positively encouraged to identify with the conquering, civilizing, white explorers of their stories and to see the real historical colonizers of their region as their true ancestors (BSWM: 126, 168–9). The view of black colonized people as inferior is a collective unconscious because it is encoded in the cultural fabric, from which each individual acquires it through continual habituation to the point at which it shapes their outlook.

This is why the black colonized person suffers trauma, in Fanon's view, on contact with the wider white world. The black colonized person has internalized a view of black people as inferior to the white colonizers, with whom the colonized person identifies. But 'at the first white gaze, he feels the weight of his melanin' (BSWM: 128). For the white colonizers too view people of 'black skin' as inferior, since they share in the same collective unconscious, and this means that they view the black colonized as inferior even though the colonized identify with the white colonizers. The inferiority complex is this combination of being racialized as black by the white colonizers while also having internalized the shared cultural classification of black people as inferior. Because this classification is part of the collective unconscious, deeply engrained and continually reaffirmed in myriad subtle ways in the wider culture, this inferiority complex cannot be overcome simply by rational thought that denies the inferiority of black people. This is what Fanon means by the term 'negrophobia' (BSWM: 138, 168–9). Like a phobia, this collective unconscious classification of black people shapes the outlook and behaviour of each individual without being responsive to their own rational thought. 'In the phobic, affect has a priority that defies all rational thinking' (BSWM: 133).

We can now see why Fanon thought that the strategy of Negritude as a response to the dilemma of white masks required the illusion that the black colonized people could reconfigure the meaning and value of masks (b) by their own agency. By emphasizing the sophisticated belief systems, social organizations, and aesthetic forms of pre-colonial black cultures, the Negritude movement can change the representation of black people in the collective unconscious. But addressing the inferiority complex requires more than a change in the particular forms of behaviour expected of black people. It requires that the expected behaviour is not classed as inferior to the ways of white people. If the Negritude movement could substantially change the collective unconscious through research, scholarship, and linguistic and aesthetic articulation achieved by black people, then this very achievement would itself help to efface the idea of black inferiority. But if this is seen as an historical inevitability, rather than as the achievement of black people, then it will lack this performative aspect. To overcome the inferiority complex, the strategy of Negritude would have to be understood as clearly produced by the agency of black people, rather than merely as a historical process.

8.5 Black Skin and the Dilemma of White Masks

Through his analysis of this inferiority complex, Fanon again deepens his conception of the dilemma of white masks. 'I have two ways of experiencing the problem' of the inferiority complex, he writes. 'Either I ask people not to pay attention to the colour of my skin; or else, on the contrary, I want people to notice it' (BSWM: 174). The first of these is an attempt to escape the feeling of inferiority by wearing masks (w), which by its nature is a form of subjection and alienation. The second is an attempt to wear masks (b) while taking control of their features. But 'I then try to esteem what is bad—since, without thinking, I admitted that the black man was evil' (BSWM: 174). The inferiority complex cannot be overcome this way, not simply because the white colonizers insist on associating blackness with evil, but more deeply because the wearers of those masks have themselves internalized that association. This association in the collective unconscious is 'phobic' in the sense that it is not responsive to the individual's rational rejection of it, so an attempt to value positively a mask of kind (b) is effectively an attempt to esteem something associated with evil.

The dilemma of white masks is therefore generated by a prior division of people into two categories, those of 'white skin' and those of 'black skin'. The association between the latter category and inferiority is not incidental. Rather, the relation between superiority and inferiority is the essence of this categorization. Fanon is clear that there is no unity to the category of 'black person' other than this construction in the collective unconscious by the white colonizer (BSWM: 149–50). Indeed, there is no unity to the category of 'white person' either beyond this construction (BSWM: 204). 'The black man is not. No more than the white man' (BSWM: 206). The strategy of Negritude is mistaken ultimately because it operates within this categorization; 'what is called the black soul is a construction of white folk' (BSWM: xviii). 'In order to put an end to this neurotic situation' of the dilemma of white masks, therefore, 'there is but one answer', which is to 'rule out these two elements that are equally unacceptable', to refuse the initial categorization of black skin and white skin that produces and governs the dilemma (BSWM: 174).

Fanon encapsulates this problem in the claim that 'there is but one destiny for the black man. And it is white' (BSWM: xiv; echoed at BSWM: 202). Once one has accepted the categorization of being a black person, one is trapped in a dilemma controlled by those categorized as white. 'The black man is a toy in the hands of the white man' for the same reason (BSWM: 119). Because these categorizations are part of the shared collective unconscious, they also constrain those categorized as white. This is why Fanon is confident that the Negritude movement will only be understood by the white colonizers as exploring 'the childhood of the world': the belittlement of black people is deeply instilled in their outlook through cultural habituation. White people who do not want to treat black people as inferior are caught in a dilemma that parallels the dilemma of white masks. Although the book is focused on the problem faced by those racialized as black, Fanon is clear that he thinks the dissolution of these categories will liberate everyone (BSWM: xvi, 12; Bernasconi 2005: 103, 108–10).

How are these categories of 'black skin' and 'white skin' to be removed from the collective unconscious? Fanon says very little about this in *Black Skin, White Masks*. He does say that 'through the particular' we should 'reach for the universal' (BSWM: 174). We should recognize our own specific situation, but define ourselves in terms of our common humanity. We should each see ourselves as heirs to all the aspects of human history that have shaped our upbringing and cultural surroundings, not just to the achievements of people of our own skin colour. Fanon thus lays equal claim to each of the Peloponnesian War, the invention of the compass, and the slave revolt in Saint Domingue. The importance of the Negritude movement, in this perspective, lies in its countering the Eurocentric bias that colonialism has introduced to the historical and cultural record of humanity (BSWM: 200–1). But this liberation from the classifications of black skin and white skin is not something that can be achieved instantly simply by deciding on it. 'Before embarking on a positive voice', Fanon tells us at the end of the book, 'freedom needs to make an effort at disalienation', because 'man is always congested, drowned in contingency' (BSWM: 206). The classifications of white skin and black skin are deeply engrained in the collective unconscious. They can be removed only gradually through 'a permanent tension' (BSWM: 206).[3]

Fanon ends the book without giving any more detail about how this is to be achieved. This is hardly surprising. There can be no simple formula to be applied across all of the situations in which the collective unconscious divides people into the superior and the inferior, the white and the black, the colonizer and the colonized. Strategies that work for the medical doctor from Martinique are unlikely to liberate the construction worker in Abidjan or the children working in the sugar fields of Guadeloupe (BSWM: 198–9, 205). Not only are these situations different, but the people suffering in them are not suffering precisely the same problems. Whether his diagnosis of an inferiority complex can be applied to a person or group of people will depend on the degree to which the collective unconscious in which they participate resembles the French

---

[3] It is sometimes argued that Fanon here contradicts his argument earlier in the book that Sartre's abstract, schematic, intellectualized characterization of Negritude fails to recognize its true nature and emancipatory potential. If the Negritude movement 'has a profound psycho-existential significance that Sartre should not have cut short', argues Kruks, 'then neither should Fanon have finally abandoned it' at the end of *Black Skin, White Masks* (1996: 132; see also Parry 1999: 236–9; Haddour 2005: 291–3; Silverman 2005: 121; Vergès 2005: 34–5). Fanon does not, however, criticize Sartre's characterization of Negritude, but explains that Sartre inadvertently brought him to realize that liberation could not be achieved through taking control of masks (b). Neither does he 'abandon' Negritude; he accords it a new role in a struggle for liberation through dissolving the racial categories underlying the dilemma of white masks. In this sense, Sartre's description of Negritude as a moment in a historical dialectic is itself a moment in the dialectical development of Fanon's thought (Judy 1996: 64).

colonial context that Fanon has described. There may even be, as Fanon acknowledges, people racialized as black from our perspective who suffer no such problem at all (BSWM: xvi). Even so, the question remains: how is the collective unconscious to be changed? This is a central theme of his later book *The Wretched of the Earth*, though it is a further question how far Fanon retains the analysis of *Black Skin, White Masks* in that book.

8.6 Why Fanon is an Existentialist

We have seen that *Black Skin, White Masks* is structured as a unified argument concluding that the dilemma of white masks can be resolved only by overcoming the inferiority complex that grounds it, which requires gradually changing the cultural collective unconscious so that people are no longer classified as black or white. This argument makes extensive use of the psychoanalytic tradition, especially through its focus on the manifestation of psychic problems in sexual desire. Fanon criticizes Sartre's theory of social relations for failing to take account of cases like the inferiority complex he diagnoses through this psychoanalysis. Rather than being driven by the individual's bad faith, the problems that arise for the black colonized person under the gaze of the white colonizer are rooted in a deeply internalized negrophobia that cannot be removed simply by a change in the sufferer's projects. Because his appropriation of ideas from the psychoanalytic tradition allows Fanon to articulate a form of social alienation that contrasts sharply with the theory of 'the look' in Sartre's initial form of existentialism, it can seem that Fanon here opposes the existentialism that he draws on elsewhere in the book.

Fanon's overall position, however, is profoundly existentialist. He does not simply adopt psychoanalytic concepts as they already are, but translates them into his paradigmatically existentialist conception of the human individual. This conception rejects the idea that an individual's past simply determines their present outlook. 'I can also revise my past, prize it, or condemn it, depending on what I choose', he writes, referring to Sartre approvingly (BSWM: 203). His conception of the individual similarly denies that there can be any essential difference, any difference in fixed nature, between black people and white people, as we have seen. 'There are from one end of the world to the other men who are searching' (BSWM: 204). This is an application of his deeper rejection of any human nature at all. 'In the world I am heading for', he tells us, 'I am endlessly creating myself' (BSWM: 204). This is an endorsement of the idea that existence precedes essence, the tenet that Beauvoir and Sartre both identified as the core claim of existentialism when they gave that term its definition, as we saw in Chapter 1. It is because Fanon holds this existentialist conception of the human individual that he cannot accept Jung's idea of the collective unconscious as an innate, internal, invariable instinct. Since there are no such instincts, according to existentialism, any collective unconscious must be encoded in the cultural situation.

Fanon's disagreement with Sartre, therefore, is not grounded in his endorsing aspects of psychoanalysis inconsistent with existentialism. His disagreement is rather within the ambit of existentialism itself. Fanon sees this cultural collective unconscious as operating through the sedimentation of a cultural representation of black people that becomes so engrained that it is not responsive to rational decision. Sartre, in *Being and Nothingness*, cannot accept this idea of sedimentation. For it is inconsistent with his idea of radical freedom as the ability to overthrow any project, or any value, so long as one is willing to pay the price of doing so. This is why, in Fanon's view, Sartre's theory of social relations cannot explain the problems faced by the black colonized. This is also why Fanon thinks that these problems can be resolved only gradually through social change, rather than through the kind of 'radical conversion' that Sartre describes as an outcome of existentialist psychoanalysis. Fanon does not hold that one can 'through sheer commitment, leap beyond the bounds of historical situation', as Kruks claims (1996: 132; see also Vergès 2005: 34–5). Rather, he develops a form of existentialism that explains the constraints that historical situations place on the individual's freedom to change their own outlook and that recognizes the necessity of an ongoing critical engagement with the legacy of the past.

At the time Fanon was writing *Black Skin, White Masks*, Sartre was writing *Saint Genet*, in which his existentialism is transformed by the inclusion of the idea of sedimentation. The only work of Sartre's available to Fanon that indicated this transformation was 'Black Orpheus', as we saw in Chapter 7, but read only against the backdrop of Sartre's preceding works this essay's indications of this development are perhaps too slight to be noticed. In the two contemporaneous books, Fanon and Sartre both articulate a form of existentialism that at its core matches Beauvoir's in *She Came To Stay* and *The Second Sex*. This is why Fanon's prescription of social change resembles Beauvoir's recommendation that changes to the cultural representation of women are required for their 'metamorphosis' away from inferiority and subjection.

Fanon does not cite Beauvoir anywhere in *Black Skin, White Masks* and has been accused of 'epistemic sexism' in failing to acknowledge his debt to her (Gordon 2015: 32). However, such a debt would be very difficult to establish, given their many influences in common. The appearance of the phrase *'l'expérience vécue'* ('lived experience') in the titles of both the second volume of *The Second Sex* and the pivotal chapter 5 of *Black Skin, White Masks*, for example, is hardly surprising, given that it had been coined by Beauvoir's good friend Merleau-Ponty, whose lectures Fanon had attended while studying for the degree for which *Black Skin, White Masks* was intended as the final dissertation (Judy 1996: 53–4; Gordon 2015: 13, 47). The emphasis on sedimentation in Merleau-Ponty's work, especially in *Phenomenology of Perception* which Fanon cites (BSWM: 200 n2), likewise accounts for this similarity between Beauvoir's thought and Fanon's thought, irrespective of the direction of influence between Beauvoir and Merleau-Ponty here.

Focusing on the agreement of Fanon with Beauvoir, moreover, risks occluding important differences between them. Fanon is not primarily advancing a theory of racial identity that parallels Beauvoir's theory of gender. He is a psychiatrist with clinical experience of distress analysing what he sees as a widespread neurosis. Beauvoir does suggest that her theory of gender can have this kind of application (SS: 779). But as she has no experience as a psychiatrist or a psychoanalyst, this is not the focus of her concerns. Fanon and Beauvoir do have in common the idea of the inferiority complex as a culturally transmitted feature of a social group rather than simply an individual's problem. But only Fanon links it to cultural representations of evil and death, analysing it as a kind of irrational phobia as well as a representation of lesser abilities. This exemplifies a profound difference between their uses of the idea of symbolism. Beauvoir argues that social meanings are symbolized in desires and behaviour that embody them, but Fanon argues that symbolism is already part of the structure of those social meanings.

To ensure that we do not overlook significant differences between these two thinkers, we should not focus on the similarities between them. We should accept the ambiguity of influence here, as we should for different reasons in the case of Beauvoir, Merleau-Ponty, and Sartre (see 4.7, above). Critical engagement with Sartre's initial form of existentialism has clearly shaped Fanon's theory, as we have seen in this chapter.[4] But in the absence of compelling evidence that Fanon was directly influenced by Beauvoir, we should place *Black Skin, White Masks* and *The Second Sex* side by side as independent primary exponents of the mature form of existentialism.

8.7 An Existentialist Eclecticism

Existentialism is more than a theory of the nature of human existence. It is the theory that all value is grounded in the structure of what it is to be human, as we saw in Chapter 1. It is the attempt to enshrine in an ethical, social, and political outlook the existential premise that existence precedes essence. Fanon devotes *Black Skin, White Masks* to arguing for this premise through an analysis of the roots of deep existential problems faced by colonized black people. The form of existentialism that he develops understands the individual's perspective as fundamentally shaped through the sedimentation of culturally mediated ideas, which form the collective unconscious of that individual's wider society. At the end of the book, it becomes clear that Fanon intends this insight not only to inform psychiatric practice, but also to have profound ethical, social, and political implications. Far from being a 'banal' moral coda written 'as if Fanon is fearful of his most radical insights' concerning the impossibility of an integrated and complete theory, as Bhabha (1986: xx–xxi) claims, Fanon's form of existentialist humanism is the conclusion that his whole book is designed to establish.

This is not to prioritize Fanon's concern with the structure of human existence to the exclusion of his sociological, political, ethical, and psychiatric concerns. It is rather to claim that he aims in this book to establish his existentialism as the fundamental perspective in which we need to approach those issues. Bhabha is right that Fanon's sociological

---

[4] Peter Hudis argues that Fanon analyses racism as having the structure that Sartre finds in human relations more generally, but departs from Sartre in seeing this structure as a product of history rather than a fixed aspect of the ontology of human existence (2015: 30–2). Sartre does not, however, understand the conflictual structure of human relations that he analyses in *Being and Nothingness* and dramatizes in *Huis Clos* as a fixed feature of human ontology, but rather as a product of bad faith, which is socially pervasive but can be overcome both individually and socially (see 6.7 above; see also Webber 2009: ch. 9; Webber 2011). What is more, Fanon explicitly recognizes that Sartre's theory of the look is internal to his theory of bad faith (BSWM: 24, 117 n24).

analyses of colonialism and racism and his political programme remain incomplete in this work, which is also true of his psychiatric analysis (Macey 2000: 196), but none of these are left entirely open-ended and there is no claim that they cannot be completed. Neither is the book itself incomplete. For its central methodological point is that these sociological, political, ethical, and psychiatric concerns are to be addressed through an analysis of what it is to be human (see Hall 1996: 34–5). And its central substantive point is that the correct analysis of human existence that should frame these concerns is the form of existentialism that emerges across the book.

It is this existentialism that both motivates and constrains Fanon's eclecticism. For it requires Fanon, as he points out, to see himself as equally heir to all the intellectual and literary traditions that shaped his cultural background (BSWM: 200–6). To restrict himself to drawing only on those traditions associated with the colonized or only on those associated with the colonizer would be to fail to live up to this existentialist ideal in the development of his own thought. This is why he analyses African and Caribbean poetry alongside European phenomenology and psychoanalysis. And by presenting these analyses through a juxtaposition of distinct literary registers, including both lyric poetry and standard academic prose, in both the objective voice of detached analysis and the subjective autobiographical voice, Fanon manages to exemplify this existentialism in the very textual form of the book.

Fanon's writing has been described as 'creolized', as synthesizing elements of disparate literary and intellectual traditions in a way that inaugurates a new form of distinctively Caribbean literature (Gordon 2015: 73–4, 166 n56). We should recognize, however, that he sees this not as a literary project distinct from the content of the thought that it expresses, but as demanded of him by his existentialism, which would demand a different literature from a writer with different cultural influences. In particular, we should recognize that Fanon's existentialism constrains the ways in which he can draw on his influences. To look for insights into an aspect of human life exclusively in one tradition could be justified only by some feature of that tradition's cultural context that is lacking in the cultural contexts of his other influences. And conversely, the claims made by a thinker cannot be accepted without consideration of their relation to mistaken ideas in the collective unconscious of that thinker's cultural context. This is why a concern with a writer's cultural background is a prominent feature of Fanon's critical analyses: his existentialism requires that appropriation of the ideas of other thinkers takes account of this.

We should see the eclecticism of Fanon's approach to psychiatry in the same way. It is an application of his existentialism, rather than simply the pragmatism of a practitioner who will deploy any tool that will get the job done. His existentialism entails that many authors from different backgrounds, writing with different aims and in different literary genres, will all provide insights into the fundamental human condition through the condition of people in their cultural context. For according to Fanon's existentialism, whatever claims his sources make, they have arrived at their views in response to the universal human condition as it is expressed in their own cultural context. Fanon does not read Capécia or Freud, for example, simply for their ideas about race or the mind. He derives insights useful to his psychiatric goal from the facts that these people, from their cultural contexts, have developed these ideas. That is what helps him to diagnose an inferiority complex among black colonized people and to trace its origins to a cultural collective unconscious.

Fanon's eclecticism of styles and sources is therefore a demonstration of the existentialism that it is deployed to articulate and substantiate. The performative implication that psychiatry should eschew adherence to any specific theoretical tradition of writing is underwritten by that same existentialism, which determines not the range of admissible sources of insight but the approach for uncovering useful insights from any source. Sartre looked forward to the time when existentialist psychoanalysis had a theoretician of equal stature to Freud, as we saw in Chapter 5, and hoped himself to become that figure. Fanon, by contrast, recognizes that his existentialism entails that psychiatry neither needs nor could have a single central theoretician of the forms of psychiatric distress. For the psychological difficulties that people suffer are not simply produced by the basic structure of the mind. They are grounded in the collective unconscious, so they can be uncovered by analysing literature from the relevant cultural context. But no individual thinker could hope to understand all cultural realities.

9

From Absurdity to Authenticity

Classical existentialism is an ethical theory. It is an attempt to answer the question of how one should live. The theory that existence precedes essence is intended as a framework for answering this question. The existentialist concerns with the ontology of human existence and with the fundamental origins of desires and behaviour, that is to say, are classically motivated by the idea that in order to identify how to live well, we must first understand how our lives work. We should take the canonical form of the existentialist theory of human existence to be the theory common to Beauvoir's *She Came To Stay* and *The Second Sex*, Fanon's *Black Skin, White Masks*, and Sartre's *Saint Genet*. We should take this as canonical precisely because it overcomes the explanatory deficiencies of Sartre's initial form of existentialism that incorporated his idea of radical freedom.

In this canonical form, existentialism is the theory that individuals do not have innate personalities that explain their outlook and behaviour, from which it follows that there is no human nature and there are no essential features of gender or ethnicity, but rather the individual's own projects exert a degree of influence over their outlook and behaviour that is proportionate to the degree to which that individual has previously deployed them in thought and action. It is through this sedimentation that the social meanings of one's environment become embedded in one's outlook, along with the values at the core of one's projects. This does not mean, however, that we are simply the products of our cultural surroundings. We retain the freedom to reconsider these projects and to alter or displace them through the same process of sedimentation. We will consider the prospects for this view of human existence in Chapter 11.

How could an ethical theory be grounded in this theory of human existence? Beauvoir, Fanon, and Sartre agree that we ought to recognize and respect the structure of human existence. This is the existentialist virtue of authenticity, which they see as the basis of ethics. But their own theory presents a challenge to this prescription. If the reasons we encounter are dependent on the values at the heart of our projects, then how can any reasons constrain which projects we should adopt? How could anything be truly valuable beyond our free project of treating it as valuable? This is the existentialist problem of absurdity. In relation to authenticity, the problem is that the dependence of values and reasons on our freely chosen projects seems to undercut any claim that we ought to adopt the project of valuing human freedom. In this chapter, we will first sharpen this problem, before considering the ways in which Fanon and Sartre argue for authenticity on grounds of human well-being. We will find these arguments insufficient, however, to establish that we all ought to embrace authenticity. In the next chapter, we will turn to Beauvoir's more promising argument for authenticity.

9.1 The Origins of Absurdity

If there are no values beyond those enshrined in the projects that the individual freely chooses, then there are no reasons that ultimately govern the choice of projects. This would mean not only that everything is permitted, but equally that nothing is justified. For if there is no objective reason to reject any project, so that lives of murder or tyranny are ethically equivalent to any other, then neither can there be any reason to adopt any particular project. There would simply be no reason to prefer any project to any other. The result would be not only nihilism, but also absurdity. None of our commitments or accomplishments could really matter, since there would be no reason why we should not have valued something else instead. We can identify more precisely the problem this poses for existentialist ethics by considering the development of the problem of absurdity across the works leading up to the existentialist offensive.

For when Sartre first used the term, in his 1938 novel *Nausea*, it was to describe the lack of structure in the world beyond our experience of it. 'The word Absurdity is now born beneath my pen', writes the diarist narrator Roquentin, a word to name what has already been revealed in his wordless and formless experiences of his own body and other objects in the world (N: 185). Roquentin also describes this lack of structure, and therefore lack of meaning or reason, in the world as contingency and as superfluity (N: 188). These terms are intended to capture the revelation that 'the world of explanations and reasons is not that of existence' (N: 185). Roquentin has these experiences because the only projects that have given his life meaning, his relationship with Anny and his work on a biography of an obscure historical figure, have come to an end. Sartre's idea here, as we have seen in Chapter 3, is that the meanings we find in the world are dependent on our projects.

It is this idea of absurdity that Camus develops in *The Myth of Sisyphus* and *The Outsider*, but for him absurdity is not simply a property of the world beyond our experience. Rather, absurdity is presented in those works as the tension between the lack of any objective meaning in the world and our innate and inescapable drive to find objective meaning in the world. One of the central concerns of these works is with the implications of this idea for ethical value. But his argument, as we saw in Chapter 2, is that absurdity does not entail nihilism. Ethical value is grounded, according to Camus, in our natural emotional fraternity. This theory of an innate drive for objective meaning and an innate emotional concern for other people sets Camus apart from the existentialists. But the distinction he implicitly draws here between meanings and values is one that is also central to existentialism. Where he has used this to confine absurdity to the realm of meaning, however, Beauvoir and Sartre see the problem of absurdity as threatening the realm of value.

By the time of writing *Being and Nothingness*, as we saw in Chapter 3, Sartre no longer held the view articulated in *Nausea* that the meanings of things are dependent on our projects. His view had evolved into the idea that structures of meaning are already present as a result of our physically and socially determined relations with our surroundings, but we experience these meanings as presenting us with reasons and these reasons reflect the values enshrined in our projects. Thus, in *Being and Nothingness*, his first statement of his initial form of existentialism, it is the field of reasons, not the field of meanings, that is dependent on our freely chosen projects. Although some projects may be chosen for reasons grounded in other projects, Sartre argues, fundamentally our overall choice of projects 'is absurd in this sense—that the choice is that by which all foundations and all reasons come into being' (B&N: 501).

Because it is the ground of all reasons, the initial choice of projects 'is absurd as being beyond all reasons' (B&N: 501).

Beauvoir argues in *Pyrrhus and Cineas*, published the year after *Being and Nothingness*, for the similar view that although our unreflective engagement in life is shaped by values that matter to us, we can see on reflection that these values matter to us only because we are pursuing them. This is particularly clear when we have achieved some goal: it ceases to be valuable to us and we set a new goal, a new value, in its place. We seem to be faced with the absurdity of being aware that the things we treat as valuable only matter to us because we treat them as valuable (P&C: 90–1, 99–100). We cannot avoid this, moreover, simply by concluding that nothing really matters. Camus held that we cannot respond to his version of the problem of absurdity by renouncing the search for objective meaning because he considered that search to be essential to human nature (see 2.2 above). Beauvoir and Sartre likewise hold that the pursuit of projects that enshrine values is the very structure of our existence, so we cannot live as though nothing matters. 'I live, even if I judge that life is absurd', argues Beauvoir, 'like Achilles always catching up with the tortoise' despite Zeno's reasoning (P&C: 100).

9.2 Why Irony is not the Answer

The problem of absurdity for existentialism, therefore, is not simply the tension between the unreflective commitment to values and the reflective judgment that these values depend on our commitment to them. It is that, given our form of existence, we are necessarily committed to values while also being aware that we generate these values by our commitment to them. 'The paradox of the human condition is that every end can be surpassed', as Beauvoir puts it, 'and yet, the project defines the end as the end' (P&C: 113). When we each 'step back' from the 'highly specific and idiosyncratic' set of concerns that shape our lives, as Thomas Nagel puts it, we can see these concerns 'with the detached amazement which comes from watching an ant struggle up a heap of sand', a perspective on ourselves 'that is at once sobering and comical' (1971: 720). We cannot justify our set of commitments, argues Nagel, because 'the whole system of justification and criticism, which controls our choices and supports our claims to rationality', rests on this set of commitments (1971: 720).

Nagel's solution is to embrace absurdity, to live with our commitments 'laced with irony': we should simply accept that our lives rest on 'the inertial force of taking the world and life for granted', which includes the evaluative commitments that we rely on to give reasoned justifications, so that those commitments cannot be given any ultimate justification (1971: 724). He compares the problem of absurdity with epistemological scepticism. We justify our factual beliefs in terms of experience and reason, but if we cannot justify that practice itself then we should not conclude that all beliefs are equally unjustified. We should rather accept the irony that our practices of justification rest on 'natural responses' that cannot themselves be justified (1971: 723–4). It is a structural feature of the mind that beliefs are formed and justified by experience and rational connections with other beliefs. We cannot do otherwise, so must accept this process even though we cannot justify it. The problem with this response to absurdity, however, becomes clear when we ask what provides the analogous ground of our evaluative commitments.

If the existentialists are right, it is a structural feature of human existence that we endorse values. This exerts pressure towards the individual having a coherent set of values, because one cannot consistently act in accordance with contrary values and because situations may require one to decide the relative importance of some of one's values. But there seems to be nothing analogous to the role that experience plays in forming and justifying factual beliefs, nothing external to an individual's values that they must measure up to. Although we can evaluate someone's factual beliefs against the world we all live in, there seems to be no shared reality against which to evaluate an individual's evaluative outlook. If murder, oppression, and exploitation conflict with my values, then from my evaluative stance I would reject the outlook and behaviour of anyone who positively values these. But on reflection, I would have to accept that this rejection is merely a subjective preference, with no more claim to authority over other people than their rejection of my outlook has over me. Indeed, if my evaluative commitments ought to be coherent, then I should integrate this reflection on the value of my values into my basic evaluative outlook itself. My unreflective engagement in the world ought to respect any coherent evaluative outlook no matter how different it is from my own.

Nagel's response to the problem of absurdity is therefore incompatible with the ethical theory of existentialism that we ought to recognize and respect the basic structure of human existence, which is that our motivations are ultimately rooted in our chosen and revisable projects. If we were to agree with Nagel's response to absurdity, then we should view this project of authenticity as one among many equally justified, and equally unjustified, evaluative outlooks. It might be objected that irony requires only respect for coherent ethical outlooks, so inauthenticity might be ruled out by being incoherent. 'I can bring a moral judgment to bear' on bad faith, argued Sartre in *Existentialism Is a Humanism*, because 'it is a contradiction'; authenticity is required by 'a strictly consistent attitude' (EH: 48). Indeed, as we will see in the next chapter, the most promising argument for authenticity in the classical works of existentialism proclaims that an imperative of authenticity is logically entailed by our own evaluative commitments. But to accept any argument that inauthenticity is incoherent is to reject the absurdity that grounds Nagel's irony. For it is to accept that one evaluative outlook can be justified objectively.

If we understand ethics broadly as the concern with how we should live, then we can distinguish three ethical questions posed by the problem of absurdity. What attitude towards our own evaluative outlook would it be reasonable to adopt? How can we avoid or overcome the anxiety or distress that might be caused by the reflection that we have built our lives around commitments that do not really matter, around values that might just as well have been entirely different? Are there any objective reasons why we ought to adopt some particular attitude or behaviour, or at least why we ought not to have some particular values or act in some particular ways? The first of these three questions is motivated by a concern to organize our lives rationally. The second is motivated by the psychoanalytic concern to diagnose any beliefs, desires, or values that are causing distress. The third is the metaethical concern with the grounding of normativity. Nagel's recommendation of irony is designed to answer only the first two questions. But it entails an answer to the third, as we have seen, which is the permissibility of any coherent value system.

9.3 Eudaimonism and the Renunciation of Racial Essence

Fanon and Sartre both offer arguments for the virtue of authenticity that are grounded in the psychoanalytic concern with diagnosing sources of distress. These are eudaimonistic arguments. They aim to ground the normativity of ethics in the best life for the individual to lead, the life of happiness or well-being. Anxiety, despair, and other forms of distress detract from the quality of an individual's life. It is therefore better for the individual, other things being equal, not to have any attitudes that generate such suffering. Fanon and Sartre both aim to show that inauthenticity inevitably leads to distress. Sartre's argument is in part that experiencing the problem of absurdity through the lens of inauthenticity produces depair. Fanon's argument is not concerned with the experience of absurdity, but with the distress that he considers to be caused more directly by inauthenticity. Both arguments, as we will see, fail to ground robust ethical constraints of the kind that the metaethical concern about absurdity seems to demand.

Fanon presents his argument very briefly in the final chapter of *Black Skin, White Masks*, but this draws on the existentialist theory of the structure of human existence and the diagnosis of the psychological difficulties faced by black colonized people that he has developed across the whole book. Fanon dramatizes the problem that he sees at the heart of these difficulties with an autobiographical anecdote. A child pointed him out on a train. 'Maman, look, a *nègre*; I'm scared!' (BSWM: 91). The term '*nègre*' does not translate easily into English: in some contexts it is a classificatory term akin to 'Negro', but in others, particularly when accompanied by negative adjectives, it is deeply derogatory and offensive (Judy 1996: 60–1). This ambiguity is central to the child's use of the term in this incident. In response to the child's exclamation, Fanon writes, 'I cast an objective gaze over myself, discovered my blackness, my ethnic features' and felt immediately 'deafened by cannibalism, backwardness, fetishism, racial stigmas, slave traders' (BSWM: 92).

Being identified as a '*nègre*' in this incident caused Fanon to have an intense experience of the connotations of the term that had been sedimented into his outlook through his colonial upbringing. Fanon argued that these sedimented ideas of the inferiority of the colonized have a pervasive influence on the individual's thought and behaviour, particularly on their self-image and their perspective on black people and white people, as we saw in Chapter 8. Occasional incidents bring these ideas into sharp focus, but their wider influence is generally unnoticed by the individual. This 'historical-racial schema' is woven 'out of a thousand details, anecdotes, and stories' provided 'by the Other, by the white man' (BSWM: 91).

The threat posed by other people, therefore, is not the one that Sartre describes in *Being and Nothingness* and dramatizes in *Huis Clos*, that other people interpret behaviour as manifesting essential characteristics that differ from the individual's self-image. Neither is it analogous to the problem of anti-Semitism as Sartre analysed it, that the wider society has a particular stereotype of Jewish people. 'I am a slave not to the "idea" others have of me', Fanon writes, 'but to my appearance' (BSWM: 95).

Underlying the problem, according to Fanon's diagnosis, is the sedimented idea of blackness itself as associated with inferiority, with the childhood of humanity before civilization, and ultimately with evil and death. This does not describe any particular behaviour of black people. It is not ultimately that black people are expected by their wider society to wear masks with particular features. It is rather that whatever the features of those masks are, they will be understood as features of inferiority and will be found aversive. The solution to the psychological difficulties faced by black people, Fanon argues in the final chapter, is therefore to erode the deeply instilled classification of people into black and white, colonized and colonizer, inferior and superior. Although his emphasis in *Black Skin, White Masks* is on the problems faced by black people, he is clear that he thinks the erosion of this classification will liberate everyone (BSWM: xvi, 12; Bernasconi 2005: 103, 108–9). 'It is through self-consciousness', an awareness of the true structure of human existence, he tells us, and consequent 'renunciation' of the idea of race, 'that man can create the ideal conditions of existence for a human world' (BSWM: 206).

Fanon has therefore argued for the virtue of authenticity on eudaimonist grounds. Our lives will be better, in his view, if we recognize and respect that our existence precedes our essence. This conclusion is threatened by the problem of absurdity: if the values that shape a person's thought and behaviour are ultimately rooted in their projects, then what can ground the objective value Fanon places on a world without racialization? Fanon does not address this metaethical question. As a psychiatrist, he is concerned with diagnosing causes of suffering and recommending ways to treat and prevent it. This takes for granted the value of overcoming distress. This value is likely to be shared by anyone suffering this distress to the extent that it significantly reduces their ability to achieve goals they value. But even if racialization causes some problems for everyone, it would not follow that we ought to overcome it. For the process of doing so would come at the cost of ruling out the pursuit of other achievable goals whose value for us might outweigh the disvalue of racialization. What consideration, then, could ground the demand to embrace authenticity regardless of our goals? This question takes us beyond the purview of Fanon's book.

9.4 Eudaimonism and the Threat of Despair

This strategy of arguing for authenticity through the problems caused by inauthenticity can also be found in Sartre's initial form of existentialism. The final section of *Being and Nothingness* proclaims that the book so far has not indicated any ethical imperatives. 'It is concerned solely with what is', he writes, 'and we cannot possibly derive imperatives from ontology's indicatives' (B&N: 645). The book does allow us, however, 'to catch a glimpse' of the ethics of authenticity: the existentialist psychoanalysis outlined in the book 'is moral description, for it releases to us the ethical meaning of various projects' (B&N: 645). It shows the falsity of any ethical theory that relies on either egoism or altruism being intrinsic to human nature, precisely because it shows human behaviour to be grounded in the individual's freely chosen projects, of which egoism and altruism are mere possibilities among others (B&N: 646). Sartre ends this section by raising the question of exactly what constraints an ethics of authenticity would impose, what its imperatives would be, and promises to devote a future work to this issue (B&N: 647).

What he does not address, or even raise, in this section is the question of why we should adopt the project of authenticity in the first place. He indicates that it is a recognition of the true structure of our existence, but does not give any reason why we should value living in recognition of that structure. Bad faith is the project of valuing an image of ourselves as having a particular fixed nature, which entails viewing people generally as having fixed natures. Why should we abandon this value? To put the question another way, why should we prefer the truth, of which we have always been somewhat aware, according to Sartre, instead of continuing to prefer the denial of that truth and the illusion of having a personal essence? These questions are implicitly answered, however, through Sartre's emphasis on the role of existentialist psychoanalysis in the ethical conversion from bad faith to authenticity. For the very idea of psychoanalysis presupposes that the individual is suffering a problem that they want to solve. It presupposes, that is to say, that their life conflicts in some way with their own values.

Sartre outlines, in *Being and Nothingness*, two ways in which the project of bad faith conflicts with the values that the individual pursues. These are general eudaimonist arguments. Their conclusion is that we are all, each of us, better off without the project of bad faith. Such an argument needs to apply to everyone who pursues the project of bad faith irrespective of which other projects they pursue with it. The arguments that Sartre outlines in *Being and Nothingness* to this effect therefore focus on the interaction between bad faith and the individual's other projects whatever they are. The shortest and simplest of these arguments is presented in the final section of the book. It is that bad faith leads to despair. It leads, that is, to the view 'that all human activities are equivalent' and 'that all are on principle doomed to failure' (B&N: 646). From this perspective, it makes more sense to be a 'solitary drunkard' than to be 'a leader of nations', because the latter mistakenly thinks their projects matter whereas the former does not (B&N: 647).

This passage is often misunderstood. Sartre claims here that this 'despair' (*désespoir*), which is the evaluative demotivation characteristic of depression, arises from realizing that people pursue their projects with the impossible aim of establishing that they have some particular essence (B&N: 646). He argues here that the impossibility of achieving this aim is made clear by existentialist psychoanalysis. But according to his phenomenology of motivation, this is not the only way we can become aware of it. For, as we saw in Chapter 3, he holds that we experience the world as reasons that can be resisted, not simply as causes to which our behaviour automatically responds, and this experience implies that we do not have any fixed nature. This is why seeing ourselves as having such a nature is bad faith, or self-deception, rather than an honest mistake. We are already aware that people have no fixed nature. Sartre agrees that all projects aimed at establishing a fixed essence are doomed to fail, which is why he can seem to agree with the despairing view that it does not matter at all whether one strives to achieve anything or not.

This misreading relies on the assumption that aiming to demonstrate a fixed nature, which he here describes as establishing oneself as 'in-itself-for-itself' and earlier called the 'desire to be God' (B&N: 586–7), is a necessary feature of human existence. This is a project, however, with an evaluative structure. The idea that existence precedes essence, the core claim of

Sartre's existentialism, entails that it cannot be necessary. Moreover, it is built on the same value as the project of bad faith. The passages where Sartre seems to imply that it is fixed, therefore, are better read as expressing his view that bad faith is a widespread project (Webber 2009: 106–11). Recognizing that this project is futile leads to despair only if one does not also recognize that it is merely an optional project rather than an essential feature of human existence. Only people who 'believe that their mission' of establishing that they have a particular nature 'is written in things' are 'condemned to despair' (B&N: 646). The threat of despair is therefore ubiquitous in bad faith, but removed by conversion to the project of authenticity.

9.5 Eudaimonism and the Trouble with Other People

Sartre's more complicated eudaimonist argument for authenticity in *Being and Nothingness* concerns the effect he considers bad faith to have on our relationships with one another. This analysis is also often misunderstood as a theory of essential structures of human existence, a misreading encouraged by some of Sartre's less careful statements. 'Conflict is the original meaning of being-for-others', he writes at one point (B&N: 386). This might seem to indicate that he considers the interpersonal conflict summarized in Garcin's declaration in *Huis Clos* that 'Hell is . . . other people!' is an intrinsic part of the human condition (HC: 223). But, as we saw in Chapter 6, his view is rather that our relations with one another are distorted by the project of bad faith in such a way that inevitably produces conflict. The extended analysis in *Being and Nothingness* of the forms that this conflict can take is developed within the framework of bad faith outlined much earlier in the book.

His core argument in this analysis is that the project of seeing oneself as having some particular fixed essence is threatened in two ways by other people. One threat arises from the fact that their projects shape their perceptions of one's behaviour, leading them to formulate views of one's character that do not fully coincide with one's own. This is the problem that drives the narrative of *Huis Clos*, as we saw in Chapter 6. Garcin's view of himself as essentially macho is threatened by other people's views of some of his actions as cowardly. But bad faith is also threatened by other people affirming one's self-image. For that affirmation does not seem valuable if it is merely the mechanical output of their own fixed essence.[1] The pride in having one's self-image affirmed thus implies the other person's freedom, which threatens one's project of seeing people as having fixed essences. It threatens one's bad faith in the same way that the waiter would threaten the bad faith of his clientele if he did not accede to their demands to behave in accordance with the essence of being a waiter.

Sartre details this argument through analyses of possible attitudes towards other people (B&N: 383–434; Webber 2009: 137–42). He concludes with a footnote reminding us that he has described only interpersonal relations in the context of bad faith. 'These considerations do not exclude the possibility of an ethics of deliverance and salvation', he writes, but 'this can be achieved only after a radical conversion which we cannot discuss here' (B&N: 434 n13). The theory of interpersonal conflict in *Being and Nothingness* is thus intended to ground an eudaimonist argument for abandoning the project of bad faith that underlies this conflict and thereby converting to authenticity. This eudaimonist argument is not developed in *Being and Nothingness*, presumably because it is beyond the book's purview as a work of ontology restricted to describing how things are. But we can immediately see the shape such an argument would have to take. It would not be enough to point out that bad faith causes conflict. For the basic premise of existentialism entails that whether overcoming this conflict would be valuable for an individual depends on that individual's projects.

We can raise a similar point about Sartre's shorter eudaimonist argument for authenticity. Why should someone who has become aware that people are generally trying to demonstrate some particular fixed essence that they do not in fact possess thereby fall into despair? This despair assumes that such projects are inevitable and that their futility is disvaluable. It is bad faith, according to Sartre, that causes the assumption that such projects are inevitable as part of human nature. But we might

---

[1] This point echoes a thought experiment devised by the seventeenth-century French philosophers Antoine Arnauld and Pierre Nicole, in which a lone person who knows that all the other apparent people in the world are merely automata can amuse himself by getting these automata to display admiration for him, but will never be able to nourish his self-esteem by doing so (James 2003: 153).

still ask why the futility of these projects must be valued negatively, why the person in bad faith cannot instead pursue projects that value this futility positively or neutrally (compare Landau 2012). The answer to this question must also lie in the project of bad faith itself. It is because this person still values a fixed nature that they disvalue the futility of trying to demonstrate it. This is why the conversion to authenticity is necessary to avoid despair. From the perspective of bad faith, the project of trying to demonstrate a fixed essence must seem inevitable and its futility disvaluable.

Likewise, the argument from interpersonal conflict is that this conflict is necessarily disvaluable to the person in bad faith. For the conflict is nothing more than the threat other people pose to one's self-image as having a particular fixed essence and the futility of the only possible strategies for preventing that threat. Bad faith thus generates its own frustrations, which are valued negatively precisely because they frustrate the project of bad faith. This implies the value of a solution to these frustrations. But the only solution is to abandon the project of bad faith, which inevitably produces them, and embrace instead the idea that people do not have fixed natures, that existence precedes essence. The project of bad faith, therefore, provides the individual with reason to abandon it in favour of authenticity (Webber 2009: 142). Although values are grounded in our projects, the project of authenticity is valuable for everyone irrespective of their current projects. It is valuable for those in bad faith, whether they understand this or not, just as it is valuable, and already valued, by those who embrace authenticity.

9.6 Why Eudaimonism is not the Answer

Neither of the eudaimonistic arguments that Sartre outlines in *Being and Nothingness*, however, can fully resolve the problem of absurdity. For neither of these arguments can provide a satisfactory solution to the metaethical problem of the grounding of normativity. Within the general framework of existentialism, they face the same problem as Nagel's recommendation that we respond to the problem of absurdity by tempering our values with irony. The problem is that they do not provide reason to reject any internally coherent system of values. This problem for Sartre's eudaimonist arguments has two parts. One is that these arguments do not provide considerations in favour of authenticity strong enough to require that everyone adopt the project of authenticity. The other is that the project of authenticity that they recommend does not set constraints on behaviour that distinguish it in practice from the nihilism it is intended to overcome. These eudaimonistic considerations in favour of authenticity, therefore, are not sufficient to ground the moral and political outlook that Sartre develops.

The first part of the problem arises from Sartre's aim of showing that the project of bad faith, which is the opposite of authenticity, has consequences of negative value to the person in bad faith. Arguments of this kind cannot show that this negative value must outweigh the positive value of remaining in bad faith. The person in bad faith has many strong reasons against embracing authenticity. The project of bad faith itself enshrines a value that grounds reasons to continue the project. If it is indeed, as Sartre claims, spread and reinforced by social pressure, then authenticity would carry a social cost to the individual. If bad faith shapes one's other projects, relationships, and self-image, as Sartre claims, then conversion to authenticity would require substantial revision of one's life. Sartre's theory of bad faith requires that we accept the idea of sedimentation (see 7.5 above), so overcoming bad faith would be a difficult long-term task, taking time and effort away from other valued goals. Sartre's eudaimonist arguments cannot show that these reasons to remain in bad faith are necessarily outweighed by reasons for authenticity grounded in the threat of despair and difficult interpersonal relations.

The second part of the problem arises because Sartre's strategy is to argue against an evaluative attachment to the idea that people have a fixed essence. Even if the argument succeeded, it would not show that we should positively value the freedom that, according to existentialism, structures human existence. All that is required to abandon the project of bad faith, that is to say, is the recognition that people do not in fact have fixed natures. This recognition does not entail any significant restrictions on one's behaviour towards other people. It does not rule out projects that disvalue other people's freedom and therefore does not rule out subjugating the lives and freedoms of other people to the pursuit of one's goals. We can see this problem in Sartre's brief remarks on play, which he considers a temporary respite from bad faith (B&N: 601–2; Pitt 2013). Play is here defined by an attitude. It is in intending one's actions to express one's free creativity that play exemplifies authenticity. This sets no limits on the actions themselves. One can see oneself as freely, creatively, even playfully suppressing other people in order to achieve one's goals.

Sartre's eudaimonistic arguments do overcome two of the three ethical problems of absurdity. Once we realize that the values that structure our lives depend on our projects, it is rational to adopt a playful attitude to our lives and the values we pursue. The anguish that comes from the recognition of absurdity is grounded, according to Sartre, in bad faith itself: it is because we deny that our values are enshrined in freely chosen projects that we are averse to any evidence that they are (see 7.4 above). Authenticity replaces this anguish with play (B&N: 601). But these eudaimonistic arguments cannot resolve the metaethical problem of absurdity. For they do not rule out any coherent value system. They merely argue that in order to be coherent, any value system that included bad faith would have to generate reasons to continue in bad faith that outweighed the reasons in favour of authenticity that bad faith generates. It seems perfectly plausible that this condition could be fulfilled in many ways. Conversion to authenticity, moreover, seems not to restrict the content of the individual's value system either, except to require a playful attitude towards it.

In the context of existentialism, eudaimonistic arguments cannot establish an imperative that applies to everyone irrespective of their projects. For according to existentialism, the structure of human existence is one that we cannot fail to express equally in all of our thought and action. There can be no question here of the idea, which motivates Aristotle and other naturalist eudaimonist philosophers, that to flourish we need to act in accordance with our nature rather than against it, or should develop our defining natural capacity to its fullest extent. It is thus existentialism itself that constrains this eudaimonistic approach to merely indicating that authenticity has some value to be weighed among the individual's other values. And it is thus existentialism itself that constrains this eudaimonistic approach to showing that authenticity is valuable for everyone in bad faith. This requires that the argument is based on the problems caused by the denial of the true structure of human existence, which constrains these eudaimonistic arguments to concluding only that we should recognize that structure. They cannot show that we should value it.

9.7 From Eudaimonism to Existentialist Humanism

It may be that Sartre accepted these shortcomings of his eudaimonist approach at the time of writing *Being and Nothingness*. Indeed, his book on anti-Semitism and Jewish culture, written the year after *Being and Nothingness* was published, introduces his conception of inauthenticity with this qualification: 'the term "inauthenticity" implying no moral blame, of course' (A&J: 93). In his lecture *Existentialism Is a Humanism*, delivered as part of the existentialist offensive a year after the book on Jewish culture was written, however, Sartre declares that 'I am able to bring a moral judgment to bear' against inauthenticity (EH: 48). In this lecture, Sartre proclaims that there is a universal form of morality, which Kant accurately described as the imperative to will the freedom of oneself and of others (EH: 49). Sartre disagrees with Kant only over the specificity of morality: Kant thought that this universal form was sufficient to ground precise moral imperatives, argues Sartre, whereas in fact it merely circumscribes an arena of acceptable behaviour within which one is free to invent. 'The only thing that counts is whether or not invention is made in the name of freedom' (EH: 50).

In this lecture, therefore, Sartre clearly holds that authenticity is imperative for everyone irrespective of their projects and that this authenticity requires not only recognizing but also valuing the true structure of human existence. The 'existentialist humanism' that Sartre describes in this lecture is an ethical outlook that he argues we are all required to adopt (EH: 53). But because this is a popular lecture, Sartre does not provide much detail of how his argument for this categorical imperative to respect human freedom is supposed to work. He does say that 'once a man realizes, in his state of abandonment, that it is he who imposes values, he can will but one thing: freedom as the foundation of all values' (EH: 48). And he adds that 'as soon as there is commitment, I am obliged to will the freedom of others at the same time as I will my own' (EH: 48–9). But these comments are puzzling. Just what argument does he have in mind here? We have already seen that the eudaimonist considerations in favour of authenticity found in *Being and Nothingness* cannot establish these conclusions.

One way to resolve the puzzle is to read this passage in the lecture as developing a new argument for the imperative of authenticity. On this reading, Sartre's comments here claim simply that it is incoherent to respond to reasons that we encounter in experience, to treat as valuable the values that those reasons manifest, without also treating as valuable the ground of those reasons in our own freedom over our projects (Poellner 2015: 238). This reading seems supported by Sartre's claim that 'a strictly consistent attitude' requires that we embrace authenticity (EH: 48). In response, we might wonder what reason somebody in bad faith could have to respect this consideration of consistency rather than act on the reasons they have to preserve their bad faith. Perhaps more importantly, the idea that the reasons we encounter in experience are grounded in our projects is distinct from the idea that we are free to change our projects, so the most that this argument could show is that we should value our projects, not that we should value freedom. Indeed, the person in bad faith will anyway value their own projects as manifestations of their supposed fixed essence.

An alternative way to solve the puzzle is to deny that these comments are really intended to support an imperative of authenticity. On this reading, this passage of *Existentialism Is a Humanism* simply sketches the moral outlook entailed by the abandonment of bad faith in favour of authenticity, an outlook that Sartre intended to detail in later work (Gardner 2005: 349–50). This reading seems supported by Sartre's emphasis on authenticity as a recognition of the truth and bad faith as in error (EH: 47–8). But this would leave us with no solution to the metaethical problem of absurdity. For it provides us with no reason why we ought to recognize the truth. The eudaimonist arguments that Sartre indicates in *Being and Nothingness* are intended to provide such a reason, but as we have seen these cannot provide a reason that would necessarily outweigh the reasons to remain in bad faith. If it were not his intention in *Existentialism Is a Humanism* to replace those arguments with a stronger one, then it is difficult to see why he did not simply state his eudaimonist arguments in this lecture. He might have recognized their shortcomings, but they do at least provide some universal motivation for authenticity.

It can seem, therefore, that we must choose between reading this passage of *Existentialism Is a Humanism* as a failure to demonstrate that everyone ought to value human freedom irrespective of their other projects and reading it as not even attempting to argue for any grounding of normativity beyond the projects individuals choose. Sartre's existentialist writings generally can seem to vacillate between an objective morality of freedom and a theory of human existence that precludes any objective morality (Thody 1981: 433–4). Indeed, there seem to be no resources in Sartre's works preceding or following *Existentialism Is a Humanism* that could be used to formulate a robust argument that authenticity is morally required of everyone and entails valuing the freedom of everyone. But we need not read the lecture purely with reference to his own writings. For it was presented as part of the existentialist offensive, a joint project to promote the shared philosophy of Beauvoir and Sartre. So we can read its comments on authenticity as summarizing the argument for a categorical imperative to value human freedom in Beauvoir's essay *Pyrrhus and Cineas*, published the previous year. The next chapter is devoted to explicating that argument.

10
The Imperative of Authenticity

Existentialism is the theory that we ought to recognize and respect the human freedom encapsulated in the slogan 'existence precedes essence'. It is, as Sartre points out, a form of humanism that grounds all moral value in the structure of human existence, rather than in human achievements or potential for achievement (EH: 51–3). But this ethical theory stands in tension with the theory of human existence that it refers to. For to say that existence precedes essence is, as we have seen, to say that the reasons we encounter in the world reflect the values at the core of our projects, which we have chosen and can change. What reason could there be, therefore, that requires us to endorse any particular value? How could there be reason for everyone, irrespective of their existing commitments, to undertake any particular project, such as the project of authenticity?

One strategy for answering this question is to argue that inauthenticity has implications that are disvalued by the inauthentic individual no matter what their other projects are. Fanon and Sartre pursue this strategy primarily with the psychoanalytic aim of uncovering and countering sources of distress. In this context, they aim only to derive what Kant describes as a 'hypothetical imperative', an imperative to undertake some means to an end that one already has. The goal is to overcome the distress, the means is conversion to the project of authenticity. Sartre wants to derive a moral conclusion from the same considerations, because he thinks that the distress he diagnoses is a necessary consequence of inauthenticity. But this strategy cannot succeed, as we saw in Chapter 9. For it can at best provide reasons for authenticity that might be outweighed for an individual by contrary reasons that are grounded in their projects. And its conclusion only rules out commitment to the idea that people have fixed natures, which does not seem to set much constraint on permissible behaviour.

Existentialist eudaimonism therefore fails as a moral position. The imperialist entrepreneur who subjugates thousands of people in pursuit of their own goals, for example, might reasonably conclude that the benefits from continuing this practice outweigh any benefits of giving it up out of respect for human freedom, or might conclude that authenticity only requires that they are aware that the people they subjugate have no fixed natures. Beauvoir offers an alternative route to the imperative of authenticity. She aims to derive it not from the internal contradictions of the project of inauthenticity, but rather from the structure of human existence itself. If this argument succeeds, the imperative will be not hypothetical but categorical. It will apply to all creatures whose existence precedes their essence, irrespective of their existing projects. And it will require them to value human freedom, not merely to recognize it.

10.1 A Kantian Moral Cogito

In her works of the 1940s, Beauvoir rests her moral philosophy on this claim that the imperative of authenticity follows from the nature of human existence. More precisely, she argues that the fact that we freely adopt values that shape our experience entails that we ought to treat this feature of human existence as objectively valuable. She occasionally asserts this entailment without explanation (MIPR: 189; EA: 57–8). She does sketch an argument for it in her essay *The Ethics of Ambiguity*, but so briefly that she can seem to be offering nothing more than a series of unsupported assertions (EA: 71–2). This explains why Iris Murdoch, in her review of *The Ethics of Ambiguity*, criticized Beauvoir for providing no argument for the claim that the imperative of authenticity follows from the existentialist conception of human existence (1950: 127). Beauvoir does clearly indicate, however, that these remarks in *The Ethics of Ambiguity* are intended to summarize the argument of her earlier work *Pyrrhus and Cineas* (EA: 71).[1] To identify her argument for authenticity, we need to turn to that work.

---

[1] It is thus mistaken to claim that 'a constitutive premise in Beauvoir's moral philosophy' across her career is that 'no values are given' (Pettersen 2015: 84). At this stage of her career

If the summary in *The Ethics of Ambiguity* obscures the argument by being too concise, its full statement in *Pyrrhus and Cineas* obscures it by being nowhere near concise enough. This short book, first published in 1944 and unavailable in English until 2004, is written in the style of the classical French essay pioneered by Michel de Montaigne. Her argument is regularly illustrated and substantiated by references to literature and examples from medieval European politics, the development of Western art, the postulates of classical physics, and the tensions in Christian theology. There is no clear summary of the overall sequence of thought to ensure that its message is properly conveyed, though there is a liberal sprinkling of anecdotes, witticisms, and aphorisms to keep the reader entertained. It can read like an iteratively digressive stream of consciousness. It can seem, that is to say, like a breathless rush to expound a host of novel ideas without the editorial discipline required to ensure coherence and clear overall direction (Sandford 2006: 12, 18).

Yet we should take seriously Beauvoir's claim in *The Ethics of Ambiguity*, published only three years later, that this essay presents an argument for the imperative of authenticity on the basis of the idea that existence precedes essence. We can indeed find such an argument in *Pyrrhus and Cineas*, one that deserves serious attention in moral philosophy. This argument parallels in the moral domain the structure of the argument Descartes develops for the possibility of knowledge. It begins from a premise that the reasoning subject must accept. Descartes begins his argument with the claim 'I think', which he argues cannot be doubted by the thinker (1984: 16–17). It is a common criticism of Descartes that he is only really entitled at this point to the premise 'there is thinking' or 'there are thoughts' (e.g. Nietzsche 1998: § 17). Beauvoir's parallel opening premise could not be subjected to a similar objection, since her argument begins not with the thought that I value things, but with the thought that some things are valuable.

I have to accept this premise, according to Beauvoir, because it is an essential structure of human existence that the individual values the ends they pursue. This is, as we have seen throughout this book, the basic ontological claim of existentialism: existence precedes essence; the individual's behaviour is ultimately explained by their pursuit of values that

at least, Beauvoir's moral philosophy was grounded in an imperative to respect the objective value of the structure of human existence.

they have set for themselves. From the first-person perspective, those ends appear phenomenologically to be valuable and are treated in practice as valuable. If staying alive is one of my projects, then it seems to me in my unreflective experience that my life is valuable and I treat it as such. Just as Descartes does not need to specify what it is that I think, or what those thoughts are about, Beauvoir does not need to specify what values I accept in the initial premise. All that is required is that I accept that my ends are valuable. And I do accept this, she thinks. Although I can reflectively decide that nothing is valuable, my unreflective experience and action cannot embody this nihilism. 'I live, even if I judge that life is absurd, like Achilles always catching up with the tortoise despite Zeno' (P&C: 100; compare EA: 55–6).

Just as Descartes aims to derive an objective conclusion from his subjective starting place, so Beauvoir aims to derive the conclusion that I ought to treat the basic ontological structure of human agency as objectively valuable. Descartes does not merely want to establish that knowledge is possible, however. He wants to show *how* it is possible, thereby establishing which beliefs are knowledge. Beauvoir's conclusion sets similar constraints in the realm of value. The imperative of authenticity requires that we do not treat as valuable any ends that conflict with the value we ought to place on human agency (P&C: 137–8; MIPR: 189; EA: 71).

This outcome closely resembles one of Kant's formulations of the categorical imperative, the injunction to treat humanity, or rational agency, 'whether in your own person or in the person of any other, always at the same time as an end, never merely as a means' (1997: 4:429). Kant defines an 'end' as something valued for itself, a 'means' as something valued for its contribution to an end. Some ends are subjective, on Kant's view, having their value only because they are pursued as ends. But humanity is an 'objective' end, having its value irrespective of whether anyone recognizes it (1997: 4:428). Beauvoir does not indicate this similarity in *Pyrrhus and Cineas*, where her only comments on Kant's ethics argue that it is incapable of providing practical advice in a world where people are opposed to one another's ends (P&C: 127, 131, 138). However, she soon comes to acknowledge the similarity between her underlying theory and Kant's formula of humanity (MIPR: 189; EA: 17, 33). But before reconstructing her argument for this Kantian conclusion, it is worth seeing why her argument itself is Cartesian rather than Kantian.

10.2 From Subjective Ends to Objective Value

Kant has been read as arguing in *Groundwork for the Metaphysics of Morals* that the imperative to treat rational agency as an end in itself can be derived directly from the idea of rational agency as the capacity to pursue ends. As a reading of Kant, this is mistaken. He is clear that he does not intend to establish any moral imperative in the part of the book containing these comments (1997: 4:444–5). The first section of the *Groundwork* analyses the concept of moral goodness to show that it is the concept of obedience to a categorical imperative. The second analyses this concept of a categorical imperative in order to show what such an imperative would be if there were any. The statement of the formula of humanity occurs in this second section. His argument there is intended to show that if there is any categorical imperative, then it can be stated as the formula of humanity. It is not an argument that there is any such imperative. The argument that we are subject to the categorical imperative is in the third section of the book and does not explicitly refer to the formula of humanity.

Despite this, it is worth considering an argument for the formula of humanity that has been assembled from Kant's comments in the paragraphs surrounding it in the second section of the *Groundwork*. For this argument resembles Beauvoir's: both begin from the idea of rational agency or human existence as the capacity to set and pursue ends; both aim to establish the objective value of that capacity. The argument derived from Kant's comments, however, does not succeed. The reasons for its failure will help us to see the strengths of Beauvoir's argument. Rather than consider every variation of the neo-Kantian argument, we will focus on the version that has received the most attention, the one propounded by Christine Korsgaard. Her initial statement of it argues that the value my ends have depends on my setting them as ends, which entails the value of my capacity to do so, and since this value does not depend on any subject's attitude towards that capacity it is an objective value rather than a subjective value (1986: 196–7; see also 1997: xxii).[2]

---

[2] Sartre's comments on the inconsistency of bad faith in *Existentialism Is a Humanism* have been read as suggesting an argument like this (Poellner 2015: 238). But, as we saw in the last chapter (9.7), the most this kind of argument could show within the framework of Sartre's initial form of existentialism is that we ought to value our own projects, not that we ought even to recognize our freedom over those projects.

Various objections have been raised against this argument. For our purposes, the most important is that it cannot establish the objective value of rational agency in general. If I accept that the foundation of the value of my ends must itself be valuable, then I am led only to the value of my own rational agency, my own capacity to set and pursue ends. Korsgaard claims that it is incoherent to value one's own rational agency but not other people's (1986: 196). She does not say why, but perhaps her thought is that the capacity to set ends is the same in everyone and it is incoherent to treat cases differently that are in fact the same. However, it is incoherent to treat cases differently only when they are the same in the relevant respect. If the value of my rational agency is established on the basis that it grounds the value of my subjective ends, then my rational agency is different from everyone else's in the relevant respect. Nobody else's capacity to set ends grounds the value of my subjective ends. It is perfectly coherent to value my rational agency as the ground of my subjective ends without valuing other people's rational agency.

Alternatively, perhaps Korsgaard intends to be arguing that if I recognize the grounding of the value of my own subjective ends in my own rational agency, then I must also recognize that the value of other people's subjective ends is grounded in their rational agency (see Korsgaard 1996: 123; 1997: xxii). But this would assume that I recognize the value of other people's subjective ends. This assumption fails to recognize the subjectivity of subjective ends. Korsgaard treats subjective ends simply as conditional values, so that what makes a subjective end subjective is that its value is conditional on it being willed (see 1996: 123–4). But this is not what it is for value to be subjective. Kant rightly defines a subjective end as something that 'has a worth *for us*' (1997: 4:428). My subjective ends are valuable to me, so their value can be used in an argument intended to lead me to some conclusion. But other people's subjective ends are only valuable to them. (They may coincide with my subjective ends, but that does not mean that I value them as other people's ends.) So I do not need to accept the value of other people's subjective ends as a premise.

Any attempt to derive the value of rational agency directly from its structure as setting the value of ends will be caught in this dilemma. Either the premise refers only to the value my own ends have for me, in which case the most it can establish is the value of my own capacity to set that value. Or the premise refers to the value of all subjective ends, in which case I can reject its claim that other people's subjective ends are valuable. Kant himself does not fall foul of this dilemma, because he does not try to derive the objective value of rational agency directly from the capacity to set ends. His argument for the objective value of rational agency rests on the argument in the third section of the *Groundwork* that we are subject to moral imperatives.[3] We are not concerned here with identifying which interpretation of Kant is correct, but we are now in a position to see clearly the problem that Beauvoir's argument in *Pyrrhus and Cineas* is trying to solve: how can an argument reach the conclusion that rational agency, rather than simply my own rational agency, is objectively valuable, if the only starting premise that I must accept is the value of my own subjective ends?

10.3 A Reconstruction of Beauvoir's Argument

Beauvoir aims to establish the imperative of authenticity on the basis of the structure of human existence. Her argument is therefore distinct from Kant's, which combines an argument that any categorical imperative must be expressible in the formula of humanity with an argument that we are subject to a categorical imperative. But it is also distinct from Korsgaard's, for two reasons. One is that it begins from a proper recognition of the subjectivity of the individual's subjective ends. This is what makes Beauvoir's argument distinctively Cartesian: it starts from a premise that the reasoning individual must accept, according to her theory of human existence. The second is that Beauvoir's argument does not aim to derive the objective value of human existence directly from this premise. Rather, she proceeds via the axiological concept that Kant deploys in his formula of humanity but which Korsgaard ignores in formulating her argument: the idea of a means. Something is valuable as a means, according to Kant, if it is required for some valuable end (1997: 4:428). I might value exercise as something required for good health, for example, or value a free press as an essential constituent of democracy.

More precisely, Beauvoir's argument proceeds via her concept of a 'point of departure' (*point de départ*), something that is valuable as a

---

[3] In her most recent paper on the formula of humanity, Korsgaard no longer attempts to derive it directly from the value of subjective ends. Instead, she develops a reconstruction of Kant's argument that rests on the third section of the *Groundwork*. Specifically, she rests it on the claim in that section that I am rationally committed to treating my own rational agency as legislating value in a shared kingdom of ends (Korsgaard forthcoming, § III).

potential means irrespective of whether it is ever actually deployed as a means. This idea is required, she argues, in order to make sense of the value that we accord our ends. For in pursuing our ends we accord that value to those ends, not to our pursuit of them. This means that we value the end being achieved. Once the end is achieved, argues Beauvoir, any value it has must reside in its being a potential means, a 'point of departure', for further ends. This value as a potential means rests on the capacity to use it as a means, which is the capacity to set and pursue ends, but it does not rest on any particular instance of this capacity. An achieved end is a potential means for anyone pursuing a relevant end. The value of a potential means therefore derives from the value of rational agency or human existence in general, a value that human existence therefore has irrespective of whether anyone recognizes that value.

This reasoning can be clarified by setting it out as a sequence of numbered propositions. The opening premise is:

(1) Some ends are valuable.

Beauvoir considers each of us to be committed to accepting this premise, whether we are aware of it or not, because we do in fact treat some ends as valuable in action. This is the nature of the projects that shape our experience. The second premise clarifies that to treat an end as valuable is to treat its value as attaching to that end, rather than to my pursuit of it:

(2) It is incoherent to treat an end as *valuable* and as *valuable only because I treat it as valuable*.

To try to bring something about is to treat it as valuable. It may be valued as a means to an end or as an end. But nothing could be valued as a means unless something is valued as an end (P&C: 112). On reflection, it can seem to us that our ends seem valuable to us only because we pursue them as ends. But this reflective thought threatens our commitment to those ends. It does not clarify the kind of value the end has, but rather makes the end seem arbitrary and unjustified. It is this reflective threat to our values that Beauvoir considers to be the experienced problem of absurdity, as we saw in the last chapter. The third premise draws out an implication of this point that we treat our ends themselves as valuable:

(3) To treat an end as valuable is to treat the achievement of it as valuable.

To treat the achievement of an end as valuable is to treat the achieved end as having some property that makes it valuable. This cannot be that it is an end, since once it is achieved it is no longer pursued. If there is to be something valuable about this end, then it must be that adding it to the world would be valuable. What could make this valuable?

(4) An achieved end is a 'point of departure' for other ends; a potential means.

(5) The existence of a potential means is necessary for a subjective end that requires that means.

(6) An achieved end, therefore, is valuable.

If the reasoning up to this point is correct, then it shows that to treat an end as valuable commits one to treating the achievement of that end as valuable, which commits one to the idea that its value lies in its being a potential means for other ends. But this value, Beauvoir argues, requires that the capacity to use the achieved end as a means is itself valuable.

(7) This value of an achieved end depends on the capacity to set ends for which it is a means.

(8) The capacity to set ends (human agency) is thus valuable.

Since proposition (8) is intended to follow logically from the commitment to the value of one's ends, a commitment that according to existentialism we cannot avoid, the argument this far aims to show that we ought to treat human agency as valuable. Finally, the argument then concludes that this value of the structure of human existence must be an objective value, rather than a subjective one:

(9) This value does not depend on human agency being pursued as an end.

(10) Therefore, human agency is objectively valuable.

From the fact that we do treat our own ends as valuable, then, Beauvoir has argued to the conclusion that we ought to treat human existence, or human agency, as objectively valuable. If this reasoning is right, then the imperative of authenticity, the requirement that we all value the basic structure of human existence, follows logically from the very structure of human existence itself. This ambitious argument is very subtle, however, and its commitments have not all been elucidated in this reconstruction, so the next three sections of this chapter will clarify it further.

10.4 The Commitments of Beauvoir's Argument

We are likely to misunderstand the implications of Beauvoir's argument if we fail to keep in mind that it is only an argument, which Monty Python rightly defined as a connected series of statements intended to establish a definite proposition (Chapman et al. 1989: 87). Beauvoir's argument, that is, is an epistemic device. It is intended to lead the individual from the value they place on their own ends to the imperative to treat human existence as objectively valuable. It is not an attempt to trace the contours of the metaphysics of value. The step from one proposition to the next is intended to articulate a relation of logical implication, not a relation of metaphysical dependence. The argument does not claim, therefore, that any end that can become a potential means is thereby valuable. For this reason, the argument is not subject to the objection that some morally disvaluable ends can become potential means.

Rather, the argument's conclusion sets a constraint on the value of ends. It entails that we ought not treat an end as valuable if it is incompatible with the objective value of human existence. This rules out ends that involve killing people, because this is the destruction of something objectively valuable. It also rules out the suppression of what is objectively valuable in people, their capacity to set and pursue their own ends. Slavery is an extreme form of this suppression, but any form of coercion or subordination is a failure to respect this objective value. Beauvoir's argument, therefore, entails that our ends must respect the existence and autonomy of any human agents affected by them. Yet this does not restrict the range of subjective ends that the reasoning subject can treat as valuable in order to accept the opening premise. At that stage of the argument, all that matters is that the reasoning subject takes some end to be valuable. If doing so leads to the conclusion that this same end ought not be taken as valuable, then it is the end that needs to be rejected, not the argument's conclusion.

Similarly, the argument does not claim that the value of an end depends on its availability as a potential means once it has been achieved. For this reason, it is not subject to the objection that some ends seem valuable entirely independently of any potential means that their achievement might produce. I value listening to music as an end, but the value of my pursuit and achievement of this end on some occasion does not depend on its availability as a potential means. The achievement of the end is a potential means: it is an experience that can be built on in the ongoing trajectory of my enjoyment of music, either by myself or by other people involved in writing and performing music. But the value of the experience seems to outstrip its potential for such future use. Beauvoir is not committed to the idea that this seeming value is not truly valuable, or is absurd. For the conclusion that we must treat the structure of human existence as objectively valuable is consistent with the idea that the ends we pursue within that constraint derive genuine value from being expressions of the structure of human existence. The argument is consistent, that is, with the metaphysical dependence of the value of ends on the value of the capacity to set and pursue them.

Although the argument's conclusion thus sets a constraint on which of our ends are truly valuable, it should not be read as the conclusion that I should respect the value of humanity, or rational agency, in order that my ends will be truly valuable. Because the problem of absurdity plays a significant role in Beauvoir's articulation of her argument, she can seem to be recommending morality as an antidote to absurdity. Read in this way, her argument aims to establish the hypothetical imperative 'to avoid absurdity, respect the value of humanity'. This would seem an objectionably egotistical basis for morality (Sandford 2006: 19). It would also allow one to evade the constraints of morality by taking up the ironic attitude that it does not matter whether one's own ends are truly valuable. But this reading mistakes the logic of the argument. The conclusion is the categorical imperative that you ought, irrespective of your own aims, to respect the value of human agency. This is not argued to be a means to establishing the value of your own ends. It is simply a consequence of the argument that ends that are ruled out by this imperative are absurd. The argument itself is that this categorical imperative is logically entailed by the value that you do in fact place on your ends.[4]

---

[4] Beauvoir seems to have read her own argument in this mistaken way. In two volumes of her autobiography, written more than a decade and a half after *Pyrrhus and Cineas*, she chastises her younger self for thinking that the individual 'should hammer out his "project" in solitary state, and only then ask the mass of mankind to endorse its validity' and for placing 'a search for the meaning of life' at the core of her ethics, adding that 'to look for reasons why one should not stamp on a man's face is to accept stamping on it' (PL: 549–50; FC: 77). These criticisms, which target the argument of *Pyrrhus and Cineas* both directly and indirectly as the philosophical basis of the moral essays she published soon after it, read *Pyrrhus and Cineas* as recommending a respect for humanity on the grounds that it gives

The argument can, however, be stated as a conditional: if you are an agent that pursues ends and treats them as valuable, then you ought to treat this kind of agency (whether in your own person or in anyone else) as objectively valuable. But this conditional statement is not a hypothetical imperative. In a hypothetical imperative, the antecedent refers to some end that you might or might not pursue, such as 'if you value your health, then you should take regular exercise'. In the conditional statement of Beauvoir's argument, the antecedent refers only to the kind of creature that is subject to the imperative. The fact that the argument can be expressed in this way simply reflects the fact that the imperative of authenticity applies only to agents that value their own subjective ends. Only things that exist in the way that we exist, only things whose ontological structure is our form of agency, are required to treat that form of agency as objectively valuable. For those subject to the requirement, however, the imperative is categorical.

It might seem, therefore, that one can reject the argument by rejecting the ontology of human existence that motivates it. Beauvoir's aim in this argument is indeed to show that the existentialist theory that the reasons we find in experience are shaped by the values we freely adopt and can replace entails the imperative to treat the capacity to set ends as objectively valuable. But the existentialist theory of the origins of reasons does not appear among the premises of the argument. The reasoning subject led through the argument is not asked at any point to accept the existentialist theory of agency. Rather, the role of that theory is to substantiate the claim that the reasoning subject must accept the opening premise. But this does not mean that the best way to persuade someone that they do in fact have ends, goals that they value in themselves, is to argue for the full existentialist conception of human agency. The best way might rather be for that person to reflect on what they care about. If the existentialists are right, this person should see that they do have ends that they consider valuable in themselves and thus accept the first premise.

---

one's own life meaning. If we read it more sympathetically, however, her argument seems intended to establish not that stamping on people's faces threatens the meaning of one's own actions, but that stamping on people's faces is categorically wrong.

10.5 The Value of a Potential Means

Beauvoir's argument aims to establish the objective value of a potential means as a step on the way to the value of humanity. We should treat a potential means as having objective value, rather than subjective value, because we should see its value as dependent only on its possibility of being deployed as a means, not on the actuality of anyone in particular deploying it as a means. The argument holds this objective value to be implied by the value of my achievable ends: because I am committed to these being valuable once achieved, I must accept their being valuable as potential means. At this point, however, an objection might be raised that would parallel the objection against Korsgaard's argument that we considered in section 10.2. Why should I accept that an achieved end is valuable as a potential means in general, rather than simply as a potential means for me? If the value of my achieved end were dependent only on it being a potential means for my own subjective ends, then a potential means would have only subjective value and the most the argument could establish would be that I ought to treat my own humanity or agency, rather than humanity or agency in general, as objectively valuable.

To accept this alternative, however, would be to undermine the argument's opening premise that some ends are valuable. For this conclusion would set only minimal constraint on the ends that I could adopt. It would preclude there being any value in ends that killed me, enslaved me, or impaired my ability to set and pursue my own ends. But within that constraint, anything that I willed would be equally valuable. The problem here parallels one horn of the famous Euthyphro dilemma, which points out that if there are no constraints on what God can proclaim to be good, then God's proclamations are arbitrary rather than valuable (EA: 41). Perhaps that problem can be resolved by appeal to features of God, but the parallel problem for existential ethics could not be solved in that way. The idea that just about any end would be valuable if I were to pursue it as my end seems incoherent. For it would not matter whether I achieved any particular end, because I could instead simply replace it with just about any other possible end. This is not to treat my ends as valuable, but to accept that they are arbitrary.

In itself, this does not show that my ends are indeed valuable rather than arbitrary. If accepting the value of my ends in the initial premise could be shown to entail that my ends are in fact arbitrary, then we would have to accept that the initial premise was mistaken. If we indeed cannot live except by treating our ends as valuable, then we would have to conclude that life is absurd. Beauvoir's argument shows, however, that the initial premise does not entail this conclusion that undermines it. For we do not need to account for the value of the potential means in terms of our own agency. We can instead understand it as valuable as a public potential means. Beauvoir's argument leads from here to a conclusion that is consistent with the premise that some ends are valuable. If her argument is successful, therefore, the reasoning subject working through the argument should accept at that stage of the argument that the value of their own achieved ends consists in these ends being potential means for rational agency, or human existence, in general.

It might be objected, however, that the value of my achieved end as a potential means for other people does not require the value of human agency in general. For the value of a potential means might instead consist in the possibility of its being deployed by other people as a means towards ends that I foresee and value. Perhaps, that is to say, its value might be conferred by my subjective ends, but imply the value of other people's agency in bringing about those ends. The most we could conclude from this would be that other people's agency is valuable when it might be deployed to further my own subjective ends. I would be required to value the agency only of people in a position to further my subjective ends. Indeed, if the value of other people is determined by their role in bringing about my own subjective ends in this way, then their value would not rule out killing, enslaving, coercing, or subordinating them whenever doing so would be expedient to furthering my own ends.

Beauvoir obviates this objection by pointing out that a potential means can be used for purposes incongruent with my ends. 'Everything that comes from the hands of man is immediately taken away by the ebb and flow of history', she writes, 'and gives rise around it to a thousand unexpected eddies' (P&C: 109; see also P&C: 117, 135). An achieved end cannot be valuable only as a potential means to my ends, since its potential to defeat my ends would cancel out this value. But this does not mean that its value is conferred by the ends to which it is put by other people. For this would lead to an infinite regress: if a necessary condition of the value of some end is that it be used as a means to some further valuable end, then the same necessary condition applies to this further end, and so on. An infinite chain of necessary conditions could not be fulfilled, so no ends or means could be valuable; our 'transcendence', or pursuit of ends, 'would be dissipated in time's elusive flight' (P&C: 106; see also P&C: 112). For these reasons, according to Beauvoir's argument, the value of an achieved end must consist in its *possibility* of being deployed as a means, which entails the value of the capacity to use it as a means.

10.6 Why the Argument could not be Shorter

Two interpretations of *Pyrrhus and Cineas* attribute to Beauvoir shorter arguments for the objective value of human agency in general. Both are grounded in comments that she makes in *Pyrrhus and Cineas* and both are encouraged by her rather ambiguous summary in *The Ethics of Ambiguity* (EA: 71–2). One is the argument that my ends can be valuable only if they are carried forward by other people (Arp 2001: 25; Moser 2008: 55–8; Sandford 2006: 17–18). This is primarily based on Beauvoir's claim towards the end of her essay that my actions will 'fall back on themselves, inert and useless if they have not been carried off toward a new future by new projects' pursued by other people (P&C: 135). However, she is not here contradicting her earlier rejection of this idea as requiring an infinity of necessary conditions. Rather, this statement is the opening stage of a brief dialectical argument that draws together points already made with the aim of establishing that to treat an achievable end as valuable is to treat its achievement as the creation of a potential means for other people (P&C: 135–6).

The second shorter argument that has been attributed to Beauvoir is focused not on the potential of my own ends to be deployed as means by other people, but on the role that other people already play in my pursuit of my own ends. There are two parts to this interpretation. One is that the world is already replete with the products of other people's projects, which I can deploy as means to my ends (Arp 2001: 64). 'The house that I did not build becomes mine because I live in it', as Beauvoir puts it (P&C: 94). The other is that the ends I pursue are inherently social: their meaning is conferred on them by other people (Arp 2001: 64; Tidd 2004: 35). 'The writer does not want only to be read; he wants to have influence', Beauvoir writes, and the 'inventor asks that the tool he invented be used' (P&C: 132). According to this interpretation, other people's capacity to pursue ends is valuable because it provides means and meaning for my own ends. However, as we have already seen, an argument that holds humanity to be valuable only in the pursuit of my own ends would not rule out killing, enslaving, coercing, or subordinating other people whenever doing so would be expedient to furthering my own ends. It would not rule out, as Beauvoir points out, a selective respect for only those who do further my ends (P&C: 130–1). It therefore would not reach the conclusion that Beauvoir is trying to establish.

A third shorter argument would combine elements of Korsgaard's argument for the formula of humanity with one of the considerations against accounting for the value of a potential means in terms of one's own subjective ends. This hybrid argument would not be concerned with the value of a potential means, but would instead proceed from the value of subjective ends directly to the objective value of humanity. If the value of my end depends on my pursuit of that end, this argument would run, then my end is valuable either because it is willed by a rational human agent or because it is willed specifically by this rational human agent. But the foundation of the value of the end cannot be specifically my agency, since this would lead to the conclusion that my ends are arbitrary rather than valuable, for reasons that parallel one horn of the Euthyphro dilemma. So my subjective end is valuable only because it is pursued by a rational human agent, which establishes the objective value of rational human agency in general.

However, we should not accept the opening premise of this hybrid argument. Beauvoir's argument itself provides reason not to accept that my subjective end is valuable only because I pursue it as an end. For her argument rests on the claim that it is incoherent, from the first-person perspective of the reasoning subject, to consider an end valuable and to consider its value to consist in my pursuing it as an end. The intuitive plausibility of this claim, which forms premise (2) in the reconstruction of her argument in section 10.3, is substantiated by the point that parallels one horn of the Euthyphro dilemma: if the value of an end is not constrained by anything other than my pursuit of it as an end, then the end is arbitrary rather than valuable. Beauvoir's argument begins from the recognition that I must accept, indeed do accept, that some ends are valuable in themselves. I cannot accept, therefore, that the value of these ends consists solely in my pursuing them.

This point does not contradict the idea that subjective ends can be valuable as expressions of human agency, because this idea is compatible with there being other constraints on the value of subjective ends. If we accept the conclusion of Beauvoir's argument, then we must accept that subjective ends incompatible with the value of humanity, ends that involve killing, enslaving, or coercing people, for example, are disvaluable. It follows from this that the value of an end does not consist in it being willed by the person pursuing it. For some ends that people pursue are disvaluable. But we can still hold that ends compatible with the value of human agency are themselves valuable as expressions of human agency. If Beauvoir's argument as reconstructed in section 10.3 is sound, then we can accept that our ends can be valuable in precisely this way. All of this is also consistent with the further claim that some of our ends are valuable as providing potential means for expressions of human agency.

10.7 An Existentialist Kantian Ethics

The core claim of existentialism is that the values that shape our experience and behaviour are ones that we have freely chosen and can replace. This is what the slogan 'existence precedes essence' means, as we have seen throughout this book. It can seem to entail that there are no objective moral values that restrict the permissible choice of projects. Beauvoir's argument in *Pyrrhus and Cineas* is a particularly sophisticated response to this reading of existentialism. This argument aims to establish not merely that existentialism is consistent with a moral imperative that can both constrain and ground the value of our own ends, but that such a moral imperative is entailed by the claim that existence precedes essence. It aims to establish this by a chain of logical implications from a premise that, according to existentialism, the reasoning subject must accept. It therefore aims to establish the imperative of authenticity on the grounds of the same subjective valuing that the critics of existentialism interpret as precluding any objective value.

Beauvoir's argument thus presents a sophisticated solution to the problem of establishing the objective value of human agency when the only opening premise that the reasoning subject must accept is the value of their own subjective ends. Her strategy is to argue that this opening commitment entails that I must think of my subjective ends as having an objective value once achieved. It is this value as a potential means, rather than as an actual means, that provides the bridge from the subjectivity of the value of my own ends to the objective value of human agency in general. The categorical imperative of authenticity, that we must value the structure of human agency as the setting and pursuing of ends, is claimed to be established not as something external to my projects that I must respect, but as an implication of my projects, whatever those happen to be. If the argument is successful, Beauvoir has shown that the imperative of authenticity is 'self-legislated', meaning that its authority derives from the agency of the individual who is subject to it, even though it does so irrespective of that individual's choices.

It is therefore no threat to the individual's autonomy. Rather, as Kant argued, if an imperative is legislated by the structure of agency, then the individual is not truly autonomous, not fully self-governed, unless they accept the authority of that imperative (1997: 4:440–1; see Reath 1994: §§ 3–5). Against the idea that an individual's authenticity consists in their pursuit of whatever ends they set for themselves, Beauvoir's argument is that authenticity requires one's ends to be constrained by the imperative to respect human agency. Failure to obey this categorical imperative is inauthentic, because it is a failure to act in a way that is consistent with one's own structure as an agent. This is not to say, however, that there is some prior imperative that we must behave in ways that are consistent with our structure as an agent. The conclusion of Beauvoir's argument is not the hypothetical imperative that we should respect other people's agency if we want to be consistent, or that we should do so if we want to be authentic. The argument's conclusion is a categorical imperative: we ought to respect human agency. If the argument is right, this imperative is implied by the structure of our agency, so we cannot be authentic or consistent unless we obey it.

Beauvoir argued in *Pyrrhus and Cineas* that this imperative requires us to strive for the conditions people need in order to exercise their agency fully. Respecting the value of humanity requires aiming to ensure 'health, knowledge, well-being, and leisure' for everyone 'so that their freedom is not consumed in fighting sickness, ignorance, and misery' (P&C: 137). She accepted that this moral outlook is limited by dilemmas in which one cannot respect the agency of everyone concerned, arguing that sometimes we are 'condemned to violence' (P&C: 138). There are situations, therefore, in which it is not possible to keep our hands clean and our conscience clear (P&C: 127; MIPR: 189–90). But later she saw this problem as a decisive objection to the ethics she had built on the value of human agency. She described *Pyrrhus and Cineas* as containing 'a streak of idealism that deprived my speculations of all, or nearly all, their significance' (PL: 550). She wrote that of all her books, *The Ethics of Ambiguity* 'is the one that irritates me the most today', in part because the morality it articulates is 'as hollow as the Kantian maxims' (FC: 75–6).

It is unclear, however, whether these comments concern the foundation of her earlier moral philosophy or the specific practical ethical claims that she built directly on that foundation. 'I was in error', she writes, 'when I thought that I could define a morality independent of social context' (FC: 76). This could be a rejection of the idea of an abstract categorical imperative of authenticity defined and established independently of the agent's historical situation. Or it could be the claim that the practical implications of that imperative cannot be defined independently of the agent's historical situation. Rather than take her own later rejection of her moral philosophy at this stage of her career as a reason to reject it ourselves, therefore, we should assess the structure and implications of her argument for the imperative of authenticity ourselves. We have seen that it is a distinctive argument that withstands the analysis we have subjected it to. It promises to establish the categorical imperative of authenticity, perhaps with the further implication that we should treat as valuable any human endeavours within the constraints of that imperative. For these reasons, the argument deserves careful attention in contemporary moral philosophy.

11

The Future of Existentialism

We should classify the version of the idea that existence precedes essence articulated most fully in Beauvoir's *The Second Sex*, Fanon's *Black Skin, White Masks*, and Sartre's *Saint Genet* as the canonical form of existentialism. This is the theory that the reasons we each respond to in our thought and behaviour reflect the values enshrined in our own projects, which we can change but which become progressively sedimented as they are deployed in cognition and action. As a result of this sedimentation, values can continue to shape our thought and action even if we no longer explicitly endorse them, indeed even if we now reject them, at least until contrary values have become equally sedimented. Socialization in childhood therefore has a profound and lasting influence, but one that can be reduced over time through action expressing more recently endorsed values.

This theory of the structure of human existence grounds an ethical theory that has two dimensions. One dimension is the psychoanalytic theory that some forms of distress can be traced to the mistaken idea that people have fixed personalities, an idea that can become sedimented as part of the project of valuing oneself as having some particular fixed nature. Fanon and Sartre both argue that we should overcome this false idea in favour of recognizing that our existence precedes our essence. This eudaimonist kind of argument, however, cannot ground the second dimension of existentialist ethics, which is a moral requirement to value the structure of human existence. This is supported by Beauvoir's argument that agents whose freedom consists in the fact that their existence precedes their essence are thereby obliged to value that freedom generally. If these arguments are right, the virtue of authenticity is morally required and has therapeutic value.

This is the canonical version of existentialism. Other theories of human behaviour can be classed as forms of existentialism only if, or only to the extent that, they agree that our existence precedes our essence, that human individuals have no fixed natures and their motivations are rooted in projects that they have chosen and can revise. Likewise, other eudaimonist ethical theories and other proposed moral obligations can be classified as existentialist only if, or to the extent that, they recommend or require recognition that our existence precedes our essence. What are the prospects for this canonical existentialism? What contributions can it make to current thinking about the roots of motivation, about the sources of anxiety and other forms of distress, and about how we ought to behave? How should this existentialism develop in response to the advances made in philosophy and psychology across the two-thirds of a century since these works were published? This final chapter sketches contributions that this renewed understanding of existentialism could make to moral philosophy, empirical psychology, psychotherapy, and literary criticism through analyses that would, reciprocally, test and develop this existentialism.

11.1 Authenticity and Social Conditioning

One question posed by Beauvoir's argument for the categorical imperative of authenticity, her argument in *Pyrrhus and Cineas* that we are obliged to respect the objective value of human freedom, is whether it succeeds in establishing its conclusion. One issue here is whether we should accept that it is incoherent to value an end and to see this value as dependent solely on oneself treating the end as valuable. Beauvoir's argument relies on this being incoherent, as we saw in Chapter 10. A second issue is whether we can explain the value of an achieved end without identifying it with the value of a potential means and without presupposing the objective value of human agency. A third is whether we can account for the value of a potential means without accepting the objective value of the structure of human existence as the free pursuit of projects. These complicated issues, however, will not be addressed here. For there is a prior question to ask about the argument. Does the conclusion even set substantive moral constraints on behaviour anyway? If the answer to that question is negative, then the concern with whether the argument is logically sound loses its interest.

One of the weaknesses of the eudaimonist argument for authenticity is that it can conclude only that we should recognize the true structure of reality, as we saw in Chapter 9. This style of argument cannot recommend valuing that structure positively, rather than disvaluing it or treating it as neutral in value. As a result, it cannot set restrictions on acceptable behaviour. Beauvoir's argument does conclude that we should value human freedom. But it is not immediately clear that this would restrict behaviour either. For according to existentialism, the freedom we have to set our projects, to change the values that animate the field of reasons we experience, is an inalienable metaphysical structure of our experience. Even 'the slave in chains', Sartre proclaims at one point, 'is as free as his master' in this sense (B&N: 570). But this entails that freedom cannot be increased or diminished. 'If freedom is indeed equal in all of our actions', writes Merleau-Ponty in response to Sartre, 'if the slave displays as much freedom by living in fear as he does in breaking his chains, then it cannot be said that there is such a thing as free action' in contrast to unfree action (PP: 461).

If freedom cannot be increased or diminished, then it might seem that the imperative to respect the objective value of freedom is only a requirement not to extinguish any instance of it by killing someone. How else could valuing that metaphysical freedom limit our behaviour? Beauvoir argues in *The Second Sex*, however, that freedom can be constrained by the individual's circumstances. To identify this argument, we need first to solve a puzzle about Beauvoir's use of the term 'transcendence' in that book. Within the space of a few sentences in the Introduction, she identifies 'transcendence' as the structure of 'every subject', but then talks of its 'degradation' as 'transcendence lapses into immanence', a degradation which one ought not cause in oneself or in others (SS: 17). How can transcendence be the structure of human existence and yet vary between individuals? The answer cannot be that Beauvoir is here using the term 'transcendence' in two different senses. For the whole argument of the book is that there is a contradiction between the humanity of woman and the conditioning imposed by her situation (Young 1980: 141). Woman 'is denied transcendence' (SS: 677). This contradiction is felt as frustration, which engenders resentment and recrimination (SS: 661–4, 770).

Yet the term 'transcendence' does have two aspects in Beauvoir's book. For it can be opposed either to 'facticity' or to 'immanence', which are not equivalent to one another. Facticity is the set of one's own physical features and the physical and social features of one's situation, the facts that one has to deal with. But our situation comprises more than our facticity. The structure of human existence is that we pursue projects, we endorse values, through which we experience our facticity as a field of reasons. This is the ontological aspect of our transcendence (P&C: 97–9). The projects we pursue can either transform that facticity or can simply maintain it. A sense of powerlessness is engendered in women through being denied the education and skills available to boys and men, Beauvoir argues. In response, women tend to value obedience to men and their own confinement to cyclical repetitive tasks like housework (SS: 654–60). This leaves women with the task of maintaining their facticity rather than transforming it, absorbing their ontological transcendence in immanence. Only through paid employment, argues Beauvoir, can women escape this life of immanence and regain the kind of transcendence that transforms facticity (SS: 737).

Sedimentation is what unifies the two aspects of transcendence. Because girls are raised for a life of immanence, sedimentation of the requisite values through upbringing narrows the range of projects they are equipped to formulate and pursue in adult life. Social pressure to conform to gender norms reinforces this sedimentation in adult life. The woman's ontological transcendence is directed to formulating fields of reasons that reflect the sedimented value of maintaining, rather than transforming, facticity. The demands of facticity thus come to shape experience, thought, and behaviour, leaving little role for the freedom to imagine that facticity transformed. Thus, 'degradation' into immanence is also one 'of freedom into facticity' (SS: 17).[1] But being degraded is not the same as being reduced: woman's ontological transcendence, her metaphysical freedom, remains entirely (SS: 680). This is why its degradation is felt as frustration, which implies an eudaimonist reason to

---

[1] This point seems to undercut Alison Stone's contention that *The Second Sex* is 'deeply biased against the female body' in that Beauvoir assumes that women have a general tendency towards immanence rooted in their experience of their bodies as potential obstacles to their transcendence (2017: 128–9). The potential for any kind of body, male or female, to frustrate the pursuit of goals is a feature of the relation between transcendence and facticity, not of the relation between transcendence and immanence. 'The same drama of flesh and spirit, and of finitude and transcendence, plays out in both sexes; both are eaten away by time, stalked by death' (SS: 780). That there are some ways of impeding projects that are unique to the female body does not specifically encourage 'degradation' of female transcendence into immanence. That degradation is better explained, within Beauvoir's analysis, by the sedimentation of social values during upbringing.

oppose the conditioning of femininity (SS: 776–7, 780). Beauvoir's argument for the imperative of authenticity, moreover, applies here too. For the objective value of transcendence is violated by constraining it to a subset of possible projects. It is, however, a further question whether the imperative to respect transcendence requires us to secure conditions that allow its wider exercise beyond maintaining current facticity, as Beauvoir claims (P&C: 137), or whether it requires only that we do not preclude those conditions.

11.2 Sedimentation as Character Formation

Whatever the practical implications of the moral imperative of authenticity, the idea that we are subject to that imperative rests on the core idea of the canonical form of existentialism. This is the idea that the human individual is neither to be identified with the radical freedom that Sartre had earlier endorsed, which is currently often thought to be central to existentialism, nor to be understood as merely the product of social forces, as has been a prevalent view in European philosophy since the heyday of existentialism, but rather combines the freedom to revise the values that shape one's outlook with the sedimentation of one's projects over time. These are not two distinct components, but are unified in the structure of human existence as the pursuit of projects. For the existentialist idea of a project is a commitment to valuing some end that informs one's thought and action. Through repeated endorsement, the value becomes progressively sedimented into the individual's outlook, increasing its influence in shaping the reasons that person encounters in the world. Yet the individual can reject that value and work to sediment some contrary project to overcome it. Is this a coherent theory of human existence?

It certainly has a strong philosophical pedigree. For it is essentially the idea of character that animates the tradition of Western ethical thought that emphazises virtue, an idea stretching back to ancient Greece and still most thoroughly developed by Aristotle. The existentialists articulate this theory in a distinctive way. They place great emphasis on the individual's ability to critically reflect on the values that shape their characters and to develop new sedimented values in their place. And they pay greater attention than is usual in the virtue ethical tradition to the role of society in shaping the individual's character through childhood and through social pressure in adult life. These have been features of the virtue tradition since Aristotle, as has the idea that one's character traits shape one's perception of the world, but in existentialism these ideas become the focus of attention. This facilitates the two innovations of existentialism within this tradition. One is the use of this theory of character to develop a form of psychoanalysis that traces anxiety and other forms of distress to the individual's sedimented values. The other is to adapt Kantian ideas of morality to argue for a categorical imperative to respect this structure of human existence.

Empirical social psychology is converging on a similar conception of motivation. Disparate research traditions concerned with the psychological functioning of goals, values, schemas, and attitudes have each developed towards the conclusion that the mental item in question gradually increases its influence over the individual's cognition and behaviour whenever it is deployed in reasoning or affirmed in action. This idea is presently best supported and explored in the social psychology of attitudes, where it is generally agreed that any evaluative attitude has a dimension of 'strength' as well as a dimension of 'content'. The strength of an attitude is not the degree to which the individual approves or disapproves of the attitude's object, which is part of the content, but is rather the degree of influence it has over their cognition and behaviour. If you think that democracy is a very good thing, for example, then this attitude has the content that democracy is a very good thing. How strong the attitude is depends on how quickly it comes to mind in connection with relevant matters, which determines the degree of influence it has over your thought and behaviour (Webber 2015, 2016a).

It is difficult to draw such general conclusions from social psychology in much detail, because this research is currently fragmented into investigations of distinct constructs without much disciplinary pressure towards integrating these findings into a general framework. But one concept that has become well established on the basis of this research is accessibility. Mental items are generally thought to have a degree of accessibility that increases every time they are deployed in cognition and action. The more accessible an item is, the more quickly it comes to influence some cognitive process. The high-speed cognition characteristic of spontaneous, engaged, unreflective behaviour tends to be influenced by only the most highly accessible mental items, the ones that are most sedimented by previous deployment in thought and action. Slower cognitive processes, such as careful thought and planning, draw on these same items and on less accessible items, in proportion to the time taken to make the decision. This idea of a distribution of accessibility is well modelled by the 'cognitive–affective system' theory of personality, which integrates a wide range of experimental findings (Mischel and Shoda 1995).

This model can account for both the social conditioning and the freedom over our values that existentialists describe. Social pressure to formulate and act in accordance with specific values, particularly in childhood but also throughout adult life, produces a tendency for those values to become highly accessible mental items, well connected with the rest of one's mind and highly influential over one's thought and behaviour. But this operation of social pressure is through a cognitive system that can just as well embed the values formulated by the individual through critical reflection. In so doing, the influence of social conditioning can be overcome. This critical reflection will not simply repeat and reinforce the values sedimented through social conditioning, for two reasons. One is that this is the slower form of cognition, which draws on one's less accessible ideas, attitudes, goals, values, and so on, as well as on the ones that have been made highly accessible through repeated use. The other is that this can involve critical reflection on those more accessible mental items, reflection that will itself be informed by the less accessible ones, which may have their own roots in all manner of sources other than the prevailing culture of one's social context.

11.3 Empirical Psychology and the Philosophy of Mind

Although this convergence in empirical psychology supports the core claims of existentialism, psychology is an ongoing science. Its current findings cannot be taken as the final word. Further empirical work may change this understanding of the mind significantly and further conceptual work on integrating the range of constructs that psychologists have developed may provide reason to revise this picture. The cognitive–affective system model of personality, for example, stands empirically supported by the wide range of empirical research that it incorporates, but its ability to accommodate new findings would strengthen and perhaps refine it further, while it would be challenged by experimental data that it could not accommodate. However, we should not think of existentialism simply as a philosophical theory that must be passively informed by developments in the empirical study of the mind. We should not take every experimental result at face value, still less the interpretation of that result offered by the experimenters. Existentialism should rather evolve through critical engagement with the empirical study of the mind, contributing its own conceptual integrative perspective and consequent critical evaluations of experimental data.

Indeed, the classical works of existentialism that we have considered in this book all have this dimension. They are works in the philosophy of psychology, as well as having other philosophical aims. They were all developed through critical analyses of the empirical research available at the time and conceptual integration of what seemed to these existentialist philosophers to be the most robust empirical information. They were intended neither as applications of the science of the mind, nor as an alternative to it, but as unifying that science into an overarching framework that accommodates the robust findings and shapes agendas for further empirical research. This feature of existentialism has not been very influential, because psychology has since developed a range of empirical methodologies that are generally considered more reliable than those employed in the work that Beauvoir, Fanon, and Sartre drew upon. But this proliferation has produced psychology's current state of fragmentation, which isolates leading theories from one another in a way that mitigates against their mutual enrichment. Existentialism could contribute to overcoming this problem by providing an integrative perspective developed from its existing conceptualization of the mind through revisions required for accommodating more recent robust empirical findings.

If it is to play this role, however, then philosophers of mind who draw on existentialism should not take the theory elaborated in Sartre's *Being and Nothingness* as the paradigm existentialist account of the mind, but turn instead to the canonical form of existentialism common to Beauvoir's *The Second Sex*, Fanon's *Black Skin, White Masks*, and Sartre's *Saint Genet*. At least, we should consider carefully whether Sartre was right to replace his initial variety of existentialism, which incorporated his idea that projects have no inertia of their own but are sustained only by the individual's continuing endorsement of them, with the idea of sedimentation employed by Beauvoir and Fanon. As we have seen in the course of this book, Sartre's initial variety of existentialism does not provide clear accounts of what it is to undertake a project, of how a project influences experience and cognition, or of how values are transmitted culturally. It seems, moreover, that these gaps in his theory cannot be filled except by replacing his idea of radical freedom with the idea of sedimentation. If this is right, then philosophical positions that employ the problematic aspect of Sartre's initial form of existentialism are likely to face problems of their own as a result.

We can see this difficulty in Richard Moran's influential theory of self-knowledge, which focuses on the fact that one can answer a question about one's own mental state through the deliberative process that forms that mental state. If asked whether you think it will snow tomorrow, you need not introspect your existing beliefs or make an inference from your behaviour. You can simply consider whether it will snow tomorrow. Your conclusion will both form your belief on this matter and announce that belief. If asked whether you would like to go to the cinema this evening, you can consider whether to go to the cinema this evening and announce your conclusion. It is because we have this authority to make up our own minds, argues Moran, that we have epistemic authority over our own minds. Only I can have this kind of insight into my beliefs and desires, because only I can form my beliefs and desires through deliberation. This conception of first-person authority is partly inspired by Sartre's theory in *Being and Nothingness* that our mental states persist only because we endorse them (Moran 2001: 77–83, 139–42, 164, 172–3, 192).

Moran's theory is challenged, however, by cases where a belief or desire has been reinforced through cognition and behaviour employing it repeatedly over time. For if this leads to the sedimentation of that mental state, as current social psychology suggests is the case, then that mental state will not simply be displaced by deliberation that leads to a contrary mental state. If my thought and behaviour have been shaped for many years by the goal of becoming an academic philosopher, for example, then deliberation resulting in the conclusion that I should instead become a lawyer will not simply displace the desire to be an academic philosopher. Instead, I will now have two desires: the newly decided upon desire to become a lawyer, and the sedimented desire to become an academic philosopher. Moran's theory therefore cannot account for knowledge of one's own sedimented mental states. Perhaps it could be supplemented by a further theory to deal with these cases, but that further theory might instead displace Moran's by accommodating the cases his theory covers as well as those his does not (Webber 2016b, 2017).

11.4 Stereotypes and Implicit Bias

These problems faced by Moran's account of self-knowledge are emblematic of the general problem faced by any theory of mind that endorses the idea found in *Being and Nothingness* that mental states have no inertia of their own but rely on the individual's continuing endorsement of them. This idea is not only challenged by our own experience of beliefs and desires persisting despite our rejection of them and having unwanted influence over our thought and behaviour, which might be explained as an experience of malfunction. It is more deeply challenged by the convergence of distinct research programmes in social psychology on the idea that the normal function of a mental state is to exert a degree of influence over cognition proportionate to its previous deployment in cognition. This closely resembles the idea of sedimentation found in the canonical works of existentialism. But there are important differences between existentialism and social psychology in the use to which this idea is put, differences that could themselves ground important contributions that existentialism could make to the science of the mind. We can see these differences clearly in current empirical research into implicit bias and stereotype threat.

An 'implicit bias' is a behavioural bias that indicates an attitude or association that the agent explicitly disagrees with. The term 'implicit' refers to the detection of cognitive items or processes through their effects on behaviour, including speech behaviour. Experiments have found, for example, that people will correctly identify a handgun more quickly if it is held by a black man than if it is held by a white man, and will be more likely to misidentify another object as a handgun if it is held by a black man than if it is held by a white man. This bias was found in both black people and white people playing a videogame in which they were to shoot the characters carrying handguns but not shoot the characters carrying other objects. The implicit measures here are the reliability of shooting only those people with handguns and the speed of making these identifications. Subjects were then asked explicitly about their views on the relation between ethnicity and violence, these questions being embedded in a large, anonymized, and confidential questionnaire. The bias detected by the implicit measures does not correlate with whether the subject explicitly associated black men with violence (Correll et al. 2002).

But it does correlate with whether the subject knew that society's stereotype of black men associates them with violence (Correll et al. 2002: 1323). The bias correlates, that is to say, with knowledge of the social stereotype but not with endorsement of that stereotype as accurate. Implicit bias experiments more generally tend to focus in this way on the effects that society's stereotypes of a particular group of people have on an individual's behaviour towards that group, where the individual knows of the stereotype but does not agree that it is accurate. In contrast, the term 'stereotype threat' has been developed to name the influence that society's stereotypes of a particular group of people have over the behaviour of members of that group when the stereotype is made salient. One classic experiment found that women performed less well than men on a mathematics test that had been described to them as producing gender differences, but equally well when it had been described as not producing gender differences (Spencer, Steele, and Quinn 1999). Another found that women taking a mathematics test performed less well when they took it alongside men taking it in the same room (Inzlicht and Ben-Zeev 2000).

Stereotype threat research might thus seem to support Beauvoir's theory of the role of social stereotyping in the construction of gender. But this would be threatened by three separate analyses of experiments into this idea of gender disparities in mathematics test scores, which have concluded that any effect of stereotype threat is at best very weak and perhaps non-existent (Stoet and Geary 2012; Ganley et al. 2013; Flore and Wicherts 2015). Beauvoir's theory, however, does not entail that a reminder of this stereotype will impede women's performance in mathematics tests. For her theory is rather that being stereotyped as inferior at mathematics influences an individual's choices across their development, so the stereotyped group are likely to become less adept at mathematics than if they had not been stereotyped in this way. This theory is consistent with the analyses of stereotype threat experiments. For there is indeed a gender disparity at the highest levels of performance on mathematics tests, though it is unclear how this emerges across childhood or whether there are gender disparities at lower levels of performance

(Stoet and Geary 2012: 93–4; Ganley et al. 2013: 1886–7). Beauvoir's theory might explain the disparity at high levels of achievement and could model the development of this disparity through social conditioning across childhood and adolescence. It could be used to ground specific hypotheses concerning the development of mathematical abilities and to design experiments testing these hypotheses.

The idea of implicit bias has proved to be more robust than the initial findings of stereotype threat. But the canonical form of existentialism has an important perspective to offer here too. Like implicit bias, Fanon's 'negrophobia' is a socially pervasive classification transmitted through cultural media, which then influences the thought and behaviour of people who repudiate it as well as of those who agree with it, including people negatively classified by it. Fanon's conception, however, is psychiatric rather than social psychological. His central concern is with effects of this classification on people who fall under it. Research into effects of perceived racial discrimination supports his view that being the victim of bias causes psychiatric problems (Pascoe and Richman 2009). But his further point that psychiatric problems stem from the internalization of this stereotype by its victims seems not yet to have been subjected to rigorous empirical research. This is perhaps because experimental psychology of stereotypes has been concerned primarily with the effects of their misrepresentation of people. Existentialism, by contrast, emphasizes their role in shaping the people they classify, a conceptual perspective that would significantly enrich current empirical research into stereotypes and implicit bias.

11.5 Existentialist Psychotherapy

Existentialism was developed as a psychoanalytic theory that traces an individual's behaviour to their projects, particularly to the values they have adopted at the heart of those projects. Sartre's initial form of existentialism held that the individual is free to alter these projects at any time, but as we have seen he soon found this idea to be unsatisfactory and embraced instead Beauvoir's idea that social meanings become sedimented in someone's outlook through the projects that person pursues in response to them. This theory of the sedimentation of social meanings, central to Fanon's *Black Skin, White Masks* as well as Beauvoir's *The Second Sex* and Sartre's *Saint Genet*, could ground important new contributions to psychotherapy as well as to social psychology. Richard Pearce has recently argued that the existentialist psychotherapy movement should shift its emphasis away from developing distinctively existentialist therapeutic techniques to the deeper aim of developing an existentialist understanding of the origins of the problems that psychotherapists help to address. This understanding, he argues, should embody Sartre's view that behaviour 'is grounded in human agency and reflective of conscious choice', in contrast to viewing behaviour as 'mechanically determined and therefore subject to "correction"' (2016: 86).

Given the shortcomings of Sartre's theory of radical freedom, this conception of human agency and conscious choice should reflect the role of sedimentation in the canonical works of existentialism. It should be grounded, that is to say, in the idea that the individual's projects and values are undertaken in a context not only of social structures and restrictions, but also of the individual's internalization of social meanings that they might not endorse. This internalization, according to existentialism, then shapes the individual's outlook and desires in ways that they might not notice. Sedimented social meanings can cause distress directly or can do so indirectly through their effects on behaviour. This is not to say that existentialist psychotherapy should not draw on Sartre's first existentialist treatise, *Being and Nothingness*, which includes a conception of freedom that is inconsistent with this idea of sedimentation. That book nevertheless contains a wealth of insights valuable for the development of existentialism. We should read Sartre's *Saint Genet* not simply as a rejection of this earlier book, but as a transformation of its central themes. Not every detail of the earlier theory that survives this transformation is explicitly repeated in the later book.

One important feature of existentialism across these works is the identification of the individual with their body. Indeed, this is central to the development of existentialism within the Freudian psychoanalytic tradition. 'Freudianism's value derives from the fact that the existent is a body', Beauvoir argues, in that 'the way he experiences himself as a body in the presence of other bodies correctly translates his situation' (SS: 69). It is this identification that underpins, for example, the centrality of sexuality to the psychoanalytic understanding of the individual. Because of this identification, moreover, phenomenological analyses of 'the lived body', particularly those of Heidegger and Merleau-Ponty, continue to inform the theory and practice of psychotherapy. But these analyses tend to cast the body solely as a site of trained habitual behaviours, inherited through upbringing and shaped by physical needs and social expectations. Existentialism, by contrast, explores how embodiment is shaped by the individual's projects and the social meanings these projects incorporate. In the canonical form of existentialism, this internalization of a social meaning becomes sedimented over time, but the influence of social meanings on perception and behaviour through projects is already a central concern of Sartre's first existentialist treatise.

Because social meanings are internalized through projects, according to existentialism, individuals are fundamentally gendered and racialized. Social groups are distinguished not only by habitual behaviours, but more deeply by the social meanings that shape each individual's experience of their own bodies and of the social and physical world. Beauvoir argues, for example, that being gendered as a woman involves living with a sense of shame caused by the sedimented internalization of the social meaning of femininity, which emphasizes beauty and purity beyond the reality of the female body (SS: 331, 347). In a reference to the feeling of physical contingency and limitation that Sartre describes in his first novel, Fanon describes his sense of inferiority triggered by being called a *'nègre'* as a bodily 'nausea' (BSWM: 92; see Sartre N: 143-6). If psychotherapy is to be renewed by the existentialist conception of embodiment, it should not focus solely on bodily habits. Although socialization as a member of a social group involves training in habitual practices characteristic of that group, it also entails the internalization of specific social meanings, which then shape one's experience of one's own behaviour and of the appearance and functions of one's body.

The classic existentialist works of Beauvoir, Sartre, and Fanon from 1943 to 1952 are rich in insights into this internalization of social meanings and its effect on one's experience of oneself and the world, ideas that might usefully inform the full range of therapeutic work. Since internalized social meanings shape the individual's perspective on the world, their understanding of their position in relation to other people, and the possibilities open to them, according to existentialism, they shape the projects the individual pursues, their experience of their own behaviour, their experience of their body, and their self-image. Because social meanings can have this effect without the individual realizing it, experiences of anxiety, depression, trauma, and other forms of distress can be deeply imbued with such social meanings even if the distressed person does not endorse them. It follows that subtle social influences can pervade the therapist's practice just as they can pervade the distress the therapist aims to alleviate. Attention to this social dimension of existentialism could therefore inform the procedures of psychotherapy as well as illuminating the causes of distress and suggesting ways of overcoming it.

11.6 Refining Existentialism

Just as attention to these aspects of existentialism could inform psychotherapy, this practical application could help to develop existentialism itself. The existentialist subordination of the family's influence on the individual to society's influence, for example, is challenged by therapeutic findings. Sartre represents Genet's family as simply the immediate instrument of their wider society (SG: 6, 18–19, 21–2, 34–5). Beauvoir considers the family too weak to counteract social pressure on the child to conform to gender roles (SS: 305–6). Fanon replaces the Freudian focus on the family with an emphasis on shared cultural media (BSWM: 121–4, 130–2, 165–9). By contrast, Lennox Thomas provides case studies from his psychotherapeutic practice to argue that colonial images of superiority and inferiority survive by 'generational transmission' through a family's stories, rituals, expectations, and behavioural styles, remaining today 'as ubiquitous as great grandma's recipe for apple pie' (2013: 126).[2] We should see this idea of generational transmission as complementary to, rather than a rival to, the existentialist theory of the interiorization of

---

[2] In a pair of books grounded in her own psychotherapeutic practice, Barbara Fletchman Smith develops a theory of the generational transmission through black families of imagery that is damaging to the lives of black people. Her theory might seem at odds with Fanon's theory of racialization, but on closer analysis might be compatible with it. Fletchman Smith is concerned with the effects of slavery rather than colonialism, arguing that the forced destruction of families continues to have negative effects on attitudes towards love and parenting among descendants of enslaved people. But there is no obvious tension between these different historical foci. The tension arises because Fletchman Smith grounds her analyses in a Freudian theoretical framework of Oedipal infant development (2000: ch. 2; 2011: ch. 4) and Fanon rejects the relevance of that framework, specifically claiming that the idea of the Oedipus complex does not apply in the French Antilles (BSWM: 130). This tension is merely superficial, however, since Fanon's knowledge of Freud was very limited when he wrote that book (see 8.4 above). Therefore, it remains an open question whether Fletchman Smith's analysis is compatible with a Fanonian analysis of racialization despite this apparent disagreement.

social meanings. This raises the question of how social and familial influences interact.

Similarly, classical existentialism lacks any consideration of the interdependence of gender and racial categorization. Beauvoir briefly compares gender with race in *The Second Sex*, but does not consider how gender may be constructed differently according to ethnic group (SS: 322, 670). Fanon does analyse the novels of Mayotte Capécia as examples of black women's experience under colonialism (BSWM: 25–35). This analysis has been widely criticized, not least for its assumption that these novels accurately represent the author's own outlook and experiences (Wiedorn 2017). His book as a whole, however, focuses on the experience of black men. What is missing from existentialism is thus any analysis of what Kimberlé Crenshaw has called 'intersectionality': the fact that some aspects of one's experience are unique to one's particular combination of race and gender, and perhaps other social features too (1989: 149). As with generational transmission, however, this oversight does not warrant the rejection of existentialism. It shows only that existentialism needs to be refined.

Alongside such refinements to the existentialist conception of the kinds of meanings that become sedimented in an individual's outlook, refinements might also need to be made to this existentialist idea of sedimentation itself. Engagement with empirical research and theory construction in social psychology could develop the existentialist idea that the individual's repeated deployment of evaluative commitments shapes their cognitive system. It might be, for example, that repetition of particular kinds of deployment or in particular contexts is required, or at least is more effective. People often report that their outlook on life has been transformed by becoming parents for the first time, for example. This could be an effect of the emotional impact of becoming a parent, of the intense workload of caring for an infant, or the combination of the two. More broadly, it remains an open question how much a change in environment or other circumstances influences the process of sedimentation. The empirical focus in this area has been on the strengthening of mental states, but the existentialist concern with ethics raises the question of how they can be weakened. Does a value become less sedimented the longer it is not explicitly deployed in reasoning or action, or is its influence reduced only by the sedimentation of a contrary value?

More substantial alterations to existentialism might be demanded by features of human cognition that challenge the core existentialist idea that all motivation is ultimately grounded in the individual's chosen projects. Sexual orientation might seem a clear example. Sartre views homosexuality, in both *Being and Nothingness* and *Saint Genet*, as a manifestation of the individual's projects (B&N: 86–7; SG: 72). This is part of a general theory of sexual desire, and indeed of all affectivity (B&N: 634–6). But no significant challenge to existentialism is presented by the view that sexual orientation is an innate and fixed feature of the individual. The idea that existence precedes essence entails only that sexual desires, fantasies, and actions are grounded in projects. These are expressions of one's sexual potential, which itself is a feature of one's physiology (Pearce 2014: 102–3). Existentialism holds only that the expression of potential is mediated by the holism of projects. It is the hiker's physiology, their bodily potential, that generates the feeling of tiredness, in Sartre's example, but the hiker's projects determine whether this tiredness is experienced as a reason to stop, as the feeling of appropriation and mastery of the natural environment, or in some other way (B&N: 476–7). Existentialism thus leaves open whether one's sexual preference for men, for women, or for both is a feature of one's sexual potential or of the expression of that potential. It even leaves open whether the same answer to this question applies to all individuals.

A stronger challenge is presented by the idea that some problematic abnormalities of motivation and behaviour manifest fixed cognitive features that can also be present in weaker forms. If someone's social interactions exhibit a lack of reciprocity, an intense preoccupation with a narrow range of interests, a lack of engagement with other people's interests, and an inflexible adherence to rituals, that person might be diagnosed with autistic spectrum disorder, but only if these characteristics impair their functioning enough that they need support in navigating ordinary life.[3] The term 'spectrum' indicates that these features can exist independently of one another and in varying strengths. These features

---

[3] This example describes symptoms sufficient for a diagnosis of Autistic Spectrum Disorder according to the fifth edition of the American Psychiatric Association's *Diagnostic and Statistical Manual* (DSM-5), but also sufficient for a diagnosis of Asperger's Disorder according to the fourth edition (DSM-IV) and Asperger Syndrome according to the tenth revision of the World Health Organization's *International Statistical Classification* (ICD-10), a diagnosis subsumed into the broader category of Autistic Spectrum Disorder in DSM-5.

are currently thought to result from a combination of genetic inheritance and childhood development. It follows that an individual's character, particularly in relation to social interaction, might result partly from such fixed qualities even if these do not warrant diagnosis as a disorder. Must existentialism classify these features as departures from normal human existence, even if they turn out to be fairly common? Or could such structural features of an individual's cognition be accommodated within the theory that existence precedes essence?

11.7 Existentialist Reading and Writing

These challenges and refinements concern the form of existentialism, the basic theory that an individual's motivations are ultimately grounded in the projects they have adopted and can change. Works that draw on and develop this theory could also extend its content beyond the specific social meanings analysed by Beauvoir, Fanon, and Sartre. The existentialist focus on the interaction of the individual's specific embodiment and their social context in shaping their outlook and self-image may provide useful insights into a wide range of issues raised by racial and gender stereotypes, class structures, bodily and cognitive differences, and illnesses, across cultural contexts. These applications of existentialism stand at the intersection of the social sciences, empirical psychology, psychiatry, and psychotherapy, to be informed by research in each of these domains and reciprocally to influence the conceptualization and design of that research. As the classical existentialists themselves emphasize, however, there is an important source of insights into these domains in addition to the empirical and the clinical. This source is literature, both fictional and theoretical, in both its content and its style.

For according to existentialism, all of an individual's undertakings manifest their values and the social meanings internalized in pursuit of these values. There is no reason why writing should be an exception. Beauvoir's theory that literary fiction articulates its author's metaphysical vision, which we considered in Chapter 4, is therefore part of her existentialism. For the metaphysical vision she has in mind here is an understanding of the nature of human existence itself. In her own case, this is an existentialist conception arrived at through careful philosophical analysis. If it is true, as Sartre claims, that the denial of human freedom in bad faith is a widespread social phenomenon, then other authors may have internalized this alternative conception of human existence without careful scrutiny. The existentialist theory of sedimentation explains how a vision of human existence can be synthesized and then expressed without the author explicitly thinking about it. But the same theory predicts that even carefully formulated views of human existence can incorporate unexamined assumptions that reflect the ideas prevalent in the author's social context.

Texts that express a vision of human existence, whether explicitly or implicitly, are thus not simply sites of the coalescence of social meanings that had surrounded their authors, according to existentialism, but are rather driven by the values that their authors have chosen to pursue in the context of those social meanings, values whose own contours or expression might incorporate such meanings in ways that the author is unaware of and might even disavow. A text may well embody genuine original insights reflecting the author's pursuit of their particular values, but also have aspects that have been silently shaped by the author's social context. Beauvoir's analysis of motherhood in *The Second Sex* provides a nice example. Women have largely been confined to raising their children, she notes, which leaves no time for paid employment. 'In a properly organised society', Beauvoir argues, 'the child would in great part be taken care of by the group', allowing mothers to work outside the home (SS: 582). The idea that the fathers should take an equal share of childcare and domestic duties does not appear in Beauvoir's argument. She assumes implicitly that men belong in full-time employment, which is why she can only gesture vaguely at 'the group' as a potential provider of childcare.

Fanon's existentialist analyses of texts focus on claims they make and imply about people living in colonial conditions. Sartre extends this kind of analysis to the literary surface of the text itself. He describes Negritude poetry as an explicitly chosen effort to explore the internalized collective memory of the violence of slavery through the destruction and reconstitution of the French language (BO: 280–7). His analysis of Genet's poetry aims to explain not only the poet's conscious decisions, but also his aesthetic taste in words, images, metaphors, and other literary devices (SG: 584). This develops a point Sartre has made since his first philosophical publications, that 'there is not a taste, a mannerism, or a human act that is not revealing' of the individual's projects (B&N: 589; see also STE: 11). In his initial form of existentialism, this was the claim that a person's tastes all reflect their values. But once he had accepted the idea of sedimentation, he held that tastes can also manifest social meanings incorporated into the individual's projects.

To take an existentialist approach to reading a theoretical or literary text, therefore, is to understand that text neither as expressing only its author's ideas nor as embodying only a set of cultural influences, but as resulting from the author's pursuit of their chosen values, where this pursuit is more or less tempered by social influences. It is to accept Beauvoir's claim that both theoretical and literary texts are explorations of the author's outlook, originating in explicit thought and research and in background cultural influences. It is to ask, as Fanon and Sartre ask, why this author with these particular goals and this particular cultural background wrote this particular work. If the existentialists are right, this kind of analysis can be applied to both the content and the form of a text and offers insight not only into that specific text, but more broadly into the ways in which one's cultural context interacts with one's chosen values to shape one's outlook. Indeed, if the existentialists are right, then reading a text in this way thus provides insight into nothing less than the basic human condition itself.

Bibliography

Works by Simone de Beauvoir, Albert Camus, Frantz Fanon, Sigmund Freud, Martin Heidegger, Maurice Merleau-Ponty, and Jean-Paul Sartre are indicated by the abbreviations used in the text and are listed in order of first publication. All other items are listed in the usual way.

American Psychiatric Association. 1994. DSM-IV. *Diagnostic and Statistical Manual of Mental Disorders*. Fourth edition. Washington DC: American Psychiatric Publishing.

American Psychiatric Association. 2013. DSM-5. *Diagnostic and Statistical Manual of Mental Disorders*. Fifth edition. Washington DC: American Psychiatric Publishing.

Aronson, Ronald. 2004. *Camus and Sartre: The Story of a Friendship and the Quarrel That Ended It*. Chicago: University of Chicago Press.

Arp, Kristana. 2001. *The Bonds of Freedom: Simone de Beauvoir's Existentialist Ethics*. Chicago: Open Court.

Azzi, Marie-Denise Boros. 1981. Representation of Character in Sartre's Drama, Fiction, and Biography. In *The Philosophy of Jean-Paul Sartre*, edited by Paul Arthur Schilpp, 438–76. La Salle IL: Open Court, The Library of Living Philosophers.

Baert, Patrick. 2015. *The Existentialist Moment: The Rise of Sartre as a Public Intellectual*. Cambridge: Polity.

Bakewell, Sarah. 2016. *At The Existentialist Café: Freedom, Being, and Apricot Cocktails with Jean-Paul Sartre, Simone de Beauvoir, Albert Camus, Martin Heidegger, Maurice Merleau-Ponty and Others*. London: Chatto and Windus.

Barnes, Hazel. 1998. Self-Encounter in *She Came To Stay*. In *Simone de Beauvoir: A Critical Reader*, edited by Elizabeth Fallaize, 158–70. London: Routledge.

Barrett, William. 1958. *Irrational Man: A Study in Existential Philosophy*. New York: Doubleday.

Beauvoir, Simone de. SCS. *She Came To Stay*. Translated by Yvonne Moyse and Roger Senhouse. London: Harper, 2006. First published as *L'Invitée* (Paris: Gallimard, 1943).

Beauvoir, Simone de. P&C. *Pyrrhus and Cineas*. Translated by Marybeth Timmerman. In *Philosophical Writings*, by Simone de Beauvoir, edited by Margaret A. Simons, Marybeth Timmerman, and Mary Beth Mader, 89–149. Chicago: University of Illinois Press, 2004. First published as *Pyrrhus et Cinéas* (Paris: Gallimard, 1944).

Beauvoir, Simone de. MIPR. Moral Idealism and Political Realism. Translated by Anne Deing Cordero. In *Philosophical Writings*, by Simone de Beauvoir, edited by Margaret A. Simons, Marybeth Timmerman, and Mary Beth Mader, 175–93. Urbana IL: University of Illinois Press, 2004. First published in *Les Temps Modernes* 1, no. 2 (1945): 248–68.

Beauvoir, Simone de. RPP. A Review of *The Phenomenology of Perception* by Maurice Merleau-Ponty. Translated by Marybeth Timmerman. In *Philosophical Writings*, by Simone de Beauvoir, edited by Margaret A. Simons, Marybeth Timmerman, and Mary Beth Mader, 159–64. Urbana: University of Illinois Press, 2004. First published in *Les Temps Modernes* 1, no. 2 (1945): 363–7.

Beauvoir, Simone de. EPW. Existentialism and Popular Wisdom. Translated by Marybeth Timmerman. In *Philosophical Writings*, by Simone de Beauvoir, edited by Margaret A. Simons, Marybeth Timmerman, and Mary Beth Mader, 203–20. Urbana IL: University of Illinois Press, 2004. First published in *Les Temps Modernes* 1, no. 3 (1945): 385–404.

Beauvoir, Simone de. JPS. Jean-Paul Sartre. Translated by Marybeth Timmerman. In *Philosophical Writings*, by Simone de Beauvoir, edited by Margaret A. Simons, Marybeth Timmerman, and Mary Beth Mader, 229–35. Urbana IL: University of Chicago Press, 2004. Originally published in *Harper's Bazaar*, January 1946: 113, 158, 160.

Beauvoir, Simone de. LM. Literature and Metaphysics. Translated by Veronique Zaytzeff. In *Philosophical Writings*, by Simone de Beauvoir, edited by Margaret A. Simons, Marybeth Timmerman, and Mary Beth Mader, 269–76. Urbana IL: University of Illinois Press, 2004. First published in *Les Temps Modernes* 1, no. 7 (1946): 1153–63.

Beauvoir, Simone de. EA. *The Ethics of Ambiguity*. Translated by Bernard Frechtman. New York: Citadel Press, 1948. First published in *Les Temps Modernes* 2, nos. 14–17 (1946–7): 193–211, 385–408, 638–64, 846–74.

Beauvoir, Simone de. SS. *The Second Sex*. Translated by Constance Borde and Sheila Malovany-Chevalier. London: Jonathan Cape, 2009. First published as *Le Deuxieme Sexe* in two volumes (Paris: Gallimard, 1949).

Beauvoir, Simone de. MPPS. Merleau-Ponty and Pseudo-Sartreanism. Translated by Véronique Zaytzeff and Frederick M. Morrison. In *Political Writings*, by Simone de Beauvoir, edited by Margaret A. Simons, Marybeth Timmerman, and Mary Beth Mader, 206–57. Urbana: University of Illinois Press, 2012. First published in *Les Temps Modernes* 114–15 (1955): 201–72.

Beauvoir, Simone de. PL. *The Prime of Life*. Translated by Peter Green. Harmondsworth: Penguin, 1965. First published as *La Force de l'Âge* (Paris: Gallimard, 1960).

Beauvoir, Simone de. FC. *Force of Circumstance*. Translated by Richard Howard. Harmondsworth: Penguin, 1968. First published as *La Force des Choses* (Paris: Gallimard, 1963).

Bergoffen, Debra. 2009. Getting the Beauvoir We Deserve. In *Beauvoir and Sartre: The Riddle of Influence*, edited by Christine Daigle and Jacob Golomb, 13–29. Bloomington IN: Indiana University Press.

Bernasconi, Robert. 2005. The European Knows and Does Not Know: Fanon's Response to Sartre. In *Frantz Fanon's Black Skin, White Masks: New Interdisciplinary Essays*, edited by Max Silverman, 100–11. Manchester: University of Manchester Press.

Bernasconi, Robert. 2006. *How to Read Sartre*. London: Granta.

Bhabha, Homi. 1986. Foreword: Remembering Fanon: Self, Psyche and the Colonial Condition. In *Black Skin, White Masks*, translated by Charles Lam Markmann, vii–xxvi. London: Pluto Press.

Blackham, H. J. 1952. *Six Existentialist Thinkers*. London: Routledge and Kegan Paul.

Brown, Lee and Alan Hausman. 1981. Mechanism, Intentionality, and the Unconscious: A Comparison of Sartre and Freud. In *The Philosophy of Jean-Paul Sartre*, edited by Paul Arthur Schilpp, 539–81. La Salle IL: Open Court, The Library of Living Philosophers.

Butler, Judith. 1998. Sex and Gender in *The Second Sex*. In *Simone de Beauvoir: A Critical Reader*, edited by Elizabeth Fallaize, 30–42. London: Routledge.

Camus, Albert. SN. On Jean-Paul Sartre's *La Nausée*. Translated by Ellen Conroy Kennedy. In Albert Camus, *Lyrical and Critical Essays*, 199–202. New York: Alfred A. Knopf, 1968. First published in *Alger Républicain*, 20 October 1938.

Camus, Albert. TO. *The Outsider*. Translated by Sandra Smith. London: Penguin, 2012. First published as *L'Étranger* (Paris: Gallimard, 1942).

Camus, Albert. MS. *The Myth of Sisyphus*. Translated by Justin O'Brien. London: Penguin, 1975. First published as *Le Myth de Sisyphe* (Paris: Gallimard, 1942).

Camus, Albert. LGF. Letters to a German Friend. Translated by Justin O'Brien. In Albert Camus, *Resistance, Rebellion, and Death*, 1–32. New York: Alfred A. Knopf, 1960. First published as *Lettres à un Ami Allemande* (Paris: Gallimard, 1945).

Camus, Albert. IJD. An Interview with Jeanine Delpech. Translated by Ellen Conroy Kennedy. In Albert Camus, *Lyrical and Critical Essays*, 345–8. New York: Alfred A. Knopf, 1968. First published in *Les Nouvelles Littéraires*, 15 November 1945.

Camus, Albert. TR. *The Rebel*. Translated by Anthony Bower. Harmondsworth: Penguin, 2000. First published as *L'Homme Révolté* (Paris: Gallimard, 1951).

Camus, Albert. PS. Preface to *The Stranger*. Translated by Ellen Conroy Kennedy. In Albert Camus, *Lyrical and Critical Essays*, 335–7. New York: Alfred A. Knopf, 1968. First published as a preface in *L'Étranger* by Albert Camus, edited by Germaine Brée and Carlos Lynes (New York: Appleton-Century-Crofts, American University edition, 1955).

Camus, Albert. CN. *Notebooks 1942–1951*. Translated by Justin O'Brien. Chicago: Ivan R. Dee, 2010. First published as *Carnets II: Janvier 1942–Mars 1951* (Paris: Gallimard, 1964).

Caute, David. 1970. *Fanon*. London: Fontana.

Chapman, Graham, John Cleese, Terry Gilliam, Eric Idle, Terry Jones, and Michael Palin. 1989. *Monty Python's Flying Circus: Just The Words*, edited by Roger Wilmut, volume 2. London: Methuen.

Chisholm, Dianne. 2008. Climbing Like A Girl: An Exemplary Adventure in Feminist Phenomenology. *Hypatia* 23: 9–40.

Cooper, David E. 1990. *Existentialism: A Reconstruction*. Oxford: Blackwell.

Cooper, David E. 2012. Existentialism as Philosophical Movement. In *The Cambridge Companion to Existentialism*, edited by Steven Crowell, 27–49. Cambridge: Cambridge University Press.

Correll, Joshua, Bernadette Park, Charles Judd, and Bernd Wittenbrink. 2002. The Police Officer's Dilemma: Using Ethnicity to Disambiguate Potentially Threatening Individuals. *Journal of Personality and Social Psychology* 83: 1314–29.

Cox, Gary. 2009. *Sartre and Fiction*. London: Continuum.

Crenshaw, Kimberlé. 1989. Demarginalizing the Intersection of Race and Sex: A Black Feminist Critique of Antidiscrimination Doctrine, Feminist Theory and Antiracist Politics. *The University of Chicago Legal Forum* 1989: 139–67.

Crowell, Steven. 2012. Existentialism and its Legacy. In *The Cambridge Companion to Existentialism*, edited by Steven Crowell, 3–24. Cambridge: Cambridge University Press.

Descartes, René. 1984. *The Philosophical Writings of Descartes* volume II. Translated by John Cottingham, Robert Stoothoff, and Dugald Murdoch. Cambridge: Cambridge University Press.

Detmer, David. 2008. *Sartre Explained: From Bad Faith to Authenticity*. La Salle IL: Open Court.

Deutscher, Penelope. 2008. *The Philosophy of Simone de Beauvoir: Ambiguity, Conversion, Resistance*. Cambridge: Cambridge University Press.

Dreyfus, Hubert. 2006. The Roots of Existentialism. In *A Companion to Phenomenology and Existentialism*, edited by Hubert L. Dreyfus and Mark A. Wrathall, 137–61. Oxford: Blackwell.

Earnshaw, Steven. 2006. *Existentialism: A Guide for the Perplexed*. London and New York: Continuum.

Eshleman, Matthew. 2009. Beauvoir and Sartre on Freedom, Intersubjectivity, and Normative Justification. In *Beauvoir and Sartre: The Riddle of Influence*, edited by Christine Daigle and Jacob Golomb, 65–89. Bloomington IN: Indiana University Press.

Eshleman, Matthew. 2011. What Is It Like To Be Free? In *Reading Sartre: On Phenomenology and Existentialism*, edited by Jonathan Webber, 31–47. Abingdon: Routledge.

Fanon, Frantz. NAS. The 'North African Syndrome'. In *Toward the African Revolution: Political Essays*, by Frantz Fanon, translated by Haakon Chevalier, 3–16. New York: Grove Press, 1969. First published in *L'Esprit* February 1952.

Fanon, Frantz. BSWM. *Black Skin, White Masks*. Translated by Richard Philcox. New York: Grove Press, 2008. First published as *Peau noire, masques blancs* (Paris: Éditions du Seuil, 1952).

Fletchman Smith, Barbara. 2000. *Mental Slavery: Psychoanalytic Studies of Caribbean People*. London: Karnac Books.

Fletchman Smith, Barbara. 2011. *Transcending the Legacies of Slavery: A Psychoanalytic View*. London: Karnac Books.

Flore, Paulette C., and Jelte M. Wicherts. 2015. Does Stereotype Threat Influence Performance of Girls in Stereotyped Domains? A Meta-Analysis. *Journal of School Psychology* 53: 25–44.

Flynn, Thomas. 2006. *Existentialism: A Very Short Introduction*. Oxford and New York: Oxford University Press.

Foley, John. 2008. *Albert Camus: From the Absurd to Revolt*. Stocksfield: Acumen.

Føllesdal, Dagfinn. 1981. Sartre on Freedom. In *The Philosophy of Jean-Paul Sartre*, edited by Paul Arthur Schilpp, 392–407. La Salle IL: Open Court, The Library of Living Philosophers.

Freud, Sigmund. TU. The Unconscious. Translated by James Strachey, Anna Freud, Alix Strachey, and Alan Tyson. In *The Standard Edition of the Complete Psychological Works of Sigmund Freud* volume 14, edited by James Strachey and Anna Freud, 159–204. London: The Hogarth Press and the Institute of Psycho-Analysis, 1957. First published in *Internationale Zeitschrift für Psychoanalyse* 3, nos. 4–5 (1915): 189–203, 257–69.

Freud, Sigmund. EI. *The Ego and the Id*. Translated by James Strachey, Anna Freud, Alix Strachey, and Alan Tyson. In *The Standard Edition of the Complete Psychological Works of Sigmund Freud* volume 19, edited by James Strachey and Anna Freud, 12–59. London: The Hogarth Press and the Institute of Psycho-Analysis, 1961. First published as *Das Ich Und Das Es* (Leipzig: Internationaler Psycho-analytischer Verlag, 1923).

Fullbrook, Edward. 2004. Introduction to Two Unpublished Chapters from *She Came To Stay*. In Simone de Beauvoir, *Philosophical Writings*, edited by Margaret A. Simons, 33–40. Urbana IL: University of Illinois Press.

Fullbrook, Kate, and Edward Fullbrook. 1995. Sartre's Secret Key. In *Feminist Interpretations of Simone de Beauvoir*, edited by Margaret A. Simons, 97–111. University Park PA: Pennsylvania State University Press.

Ganley, Colleen M., Leigh A. Mingle, Allison M. Ryan, Katherine Ryan, Marina Vasilyeva, and Michelle Perry. 2013. An Examination of Stereotype Threat Effects on Girls' Mathematics Performance. *Developmental Psychology* 49: 1886–97.

Gardner, Sebastian. 2000. Psychoanalysis and the Personal/Subpersonal Distinction. *Philosophical Explorations* 3: 96–119.

Gardner, Sebastian. 2005. Sartre, Intersubjectivity, and German Idealism. *Journal of the History of Philosophy* 43: 325–51.

Gilbert, Margaret. 2006. Character, Essence, Action: Considerations on Character Traits after Sartre. *The Pluralist* 1: 40–52.

Gordon, Lewis. 2015. *What Fanon Said*. London: Hurst.

Grimsley, Ronald. 1960. *Existentialist Thought*. Second edition. Cardiff: University of Wales Press.

Haddour, Azzedine. 2005. Sartre and Fanon: On Negritude and Political Participation. In *Sartre Today: A Centenary Celebration*, edited by Adrian van den Hoven and Andrew Leak, 286–301. New York: Berghahn.

Haddour, Azzedine. 2011. Being Colonized. In *Reading Sartre: On Phenomenology and Existentialism*, edited by Jonathan Webber, 73–89. London: Routledge.

Hall, Stuart. 1996. The After-life of Frantz Fanon: Why Fanon? Why Now? Why *Black Skin White Masks*? In *The Fact of Blackness: Frantz Fanon and Visual Representation*, edited by Alan Read, 12–37. London: Institute of Contemporary Arts.

Harman, Gilbert. 2009. Skepticism about Character Traits. *The Journal of Ethics* 13: 235–42.

Heath, Jane. 1998. *She Came To Stay*: The Phallus Strikes Back. In *Simone de Beauvoir: A Critical Reader*, edited by Elizabeth Fallaize, 172–82. London: Routledge.

Heidegger, Martin. B&T. *Being and Time*. Translated by John Macquarrie and Edward Robinson. Oxford: Blackwell, 1962. First published as *Sein und Zeit: Erste Hälfte* (Halle: Max Niemeyer, 1927).

Heidegger, Martin. LH. Letter on Humanism. In *Basic Writings*, by Martin Heidegger, edited by David Farrell Krell. London: Routledge, 2011. First published as *Über den Humanismus* (Frankfurt am Main: Vittorio Klostermann, 1947).

Howells, Christina. 1988. *Sartre: The Necessity of Freedom*. Cambridge: Cambridge University Press.

Howells, Christina. 2011. *Mortal Subjects: Passions of the Soul in Late Twentieth-Century Thought*. Cambridge: Polity Press.

Hudis, Peter. 2015. *Frantz Fanon: Philosopher of the Barricades*. London: Pluto Press.

Hume, David. 1739. *A Treatise of Human Nature*. London: John Noon.

Inzlicht, Michael and Talia Ben-Zeev 2000. A Threatening Intellectual Environment: Why Females Are Susceptible to Experiencing Problem-Solving Deficits in the Presence of Males. *Psychological Science* 11: 365–71.

James, Susan. 2003. Complicity and Slavery in The Second Sex. In *The Cambridge Companion to Simone de Beauvoir*, edited by Claudia Card, 149–67. Cambridge: Cambridge University Press.

Jeanson, Francis. 1952. Préface. In *Peau noire, masques blancs*, by Frantz Fanon. Paris: Éditions du Seuil.

Joseph, Felicity, Jack Reynolds, and Ashley Woodward. 2011. Introduction. In *The Continuum Companion to Existentialism*, edited by Felicity Joseph, Jack Reynolds, and Ashley Woodward, 1–14. London: Continuum.

Judy, Ronald. 1996. Fanon's Body of Black Experience. In *Fanon: A Critical Reader*, edited by Lewis R. Gordon, T. Denean Sharpley-Whiting, and Renée T. White, 53–73. Oxford: Blackwell.

Kant, Immanuel. 1997. *Groundwork for the Metaphysics of Morals*. Translated by Mary Gregor. Cambridge: Cambridge University Press.

King, Adele. 1964. *Camus*. Edinburgh: Oliver and Boyd.

Kirkpatrick, Kate. 2017. *Sartre and Theology*. London: Bloomsbury.

Korsgaard, Christine. 1986. Kant's Formula of Humanity. *Kant-Studien* 77: 183–202.

Korsgaard, Christine. 1996. *The Sources of Normativity*. Cambridge: Cambridge University Press.

Korsgaard, Christine. 1997. Introduction. In Immanuel Kant, *Groundwork for the Metaphysics of Morals*, translated by Mary Gregor. Cambridge: Cambridge University Press.

Korsgaard, Christine. Forthcoming. Valuing Our Humanity. In *Respect for Persons*, edited by Oliver Sensen and Richard Dean. Available at: http://www.people.fas.harvard.edu/~korsgaar/CMK.Valuing.Our.Humanity.pdf (last accessed 16 February 2018).

Kripke, Saul. 1980. *Naming and Necessity*. Cambridge: Harvard University Press.

Kruks, Sonia. 1995. Simone de Beauvoir: Teaching Sartre About Freedom. In *Feminist Interpretations of Simone de Beauvoir*, edited by Margaret A. Simons, 79–95. University Park PA: Pennsylvania State University Press.

Kruks, Sonia. 1996. Fanon, Sartre, and Identity Politics. In *Fanon: A Critical Reader*, edited by Lewis R. Gordon, T. Denean Sharpley-Whiting, and Renée T. White, 122–33. Oxford: Blackwell.

Kruks, Sonia. 1998. The Weight of Situation. In *Simone de Beauvoir: A Critical Reader*, edited by Elizabeth Fallaize, 45–71. London: Routledge.

Landau, Iddo. 2012. Foundationless Freedom and Meaninglessness of Life in Sartre's *Being and Nothingness*. *Sartre Studies International* 18: 1–8.

Langer, Monika. 2003. Beauvoir and Merleau-Ponty on Ambiguity. In *The Cambridge Companion to Simone de Beauvoir*, edited by Claudia Card, 87–106. Cambridge: Cambridge University Press.

Le Doeuff, Michèle. 1987. Operative Philosophy: Simone de Beauvoir and Existentialism. In *Critical Essays on Simone de Beauvoir*, edited by Elaine Marks, 144–54. Boston MA: GK Hall and Co.

Le Doeuff, Michèle. 1995. Simone de Beauvoir: Falling into (Ambiguous) Line. Translated by Margaret A. Simons. In *Feminist Interpretations of Simone de Beauvoir*, edited by Margaret A. Simons, 59–65. University Park PA: Pennsylvania State University Press.

Lee, Christopher. 2015. *Frantz Fanon: Toward a Revolutionary Humanism*. Athens: Ohio University Press.

Macey, David. 2000. *Frantz Fanon: A Biography*. London: Verso.

Macey, David. 2005. Adieu Foulard. Adieu Madras. In *Frantz Fanon's Black Skin, White Masks: New Interdisciplinary Essays*, edited by Max Silverman, 12–31. Manchester: University of Manchester Press.

Macquarrie, John. 1972. *Existentialism: An Introduction, Guide, and Assessment*. Harmondsworth: Penguin.

Malpas, Jeff. 2012. Existentialism as Literature. In *The Cambridge Companion to Existentialism*, edited by Steven Crowell, 291–321. Cambridge and New York: Cambridge University Press.

Martin, Andy. 2012. *The Boxer and the Goalkeeper: Sartre vs Camus*. London: Simon & Schuster.

Masters, Brian. 1974. *Camus: A Study*. London: Heinemann.

McBride, William. 2012. Existentialism as a Cultural Movement. In *The Cambridge Companion to Existentialism*, edited by Steven Crowell, 50–69. Cambridge: Cambridge University Press.

McInerney, Peter. 1979. Self-determination and the Project. *The Journal of Philosophy* 76: 663–77.

Merleau-Ponty, Maurice. MN. Metaphysics and the Novel. In Maurice Merleau-Ponty, *Sense and Non-Sense*, translated by Hubert L. Dreyfus and Patricia Allen Dreyfus, 26–40. Evanston IL: Northwestern University Press, 1964. First published in *Cahiers du Sud* 22, no. 270 (1945) 194–207.

Merleau-Ponty, Maurice. PP. *Phenomenology of Perception*. Translated by Donald A. Landes. London: Routledge, 2012. First published as *Phénoménologie de la Perception* (Paris: Gallimard, 1945).

Merleau-Ponty, Maurice. BE. The Battle over Existentialism. In Maurice Merleau-Ponty, *Sense and Non-Sense*, translated by Hubert L. Dreyfus and Patricia Allen Dreyfus, 71–82. Chicago: Northwestern University Press, 1992. First published in *Les Temps Modernes* 1, no. 2 (1945): 344–56.

Merleau-Ponty, Maurice. AD. *Adventures of the Dialectic*. Translated by Joseph Bien. Evanston IL: Northwestern University Press, 1973. First published as *Les Aventures de la Dialectique* (Paris: Gallimard, 1955).

Mill, John Stuart. 1869. *The Subjection of Women*. London: Longmans, Green, Reader, and Dyer.

Mischel, Walter and Yuichi Shoda. 1995. A Cognitive-Affective System Theory of Personality: Reconceptualizing Situations, Dispositions, Dynamics, and Invariance in Personality Structure. *Psychological Review* 102: 246–68.

Moi, Toril. 2008. *Simone de Beauvoir: The Making of an Intellectual Woman*. Oxford: Oxford University Press.

Moran, Richard. 2001. *Authority and Estrangement: An Essay on Self-Knowledge*. Princeton: Princeton University Press.

Morris, Phyllis Sutton. 1976. *Sartre's Concept of a Person: An Analytic Approach*. Amherst: University of Massachusetts Press.

Moser, Susanne. 2008. *Freedom and Recognition in the Work of Simone de Beauvoir*. Frankfurt: Peter Lang.

Murdoch, Iris. 1950. Review of *The Ethics of Ambiguity* by Simone de Beauvoir. *Mind* 54: 127–8.

Murdoch, Iris. 1957. Hegel in Modern Dress. *The New Statesman and Nation* 53, 1367 (25 May): 675–6.

Nagel, Thomas. 1971. The Absurd. *The Journal of Philosophy* 68: 716–27.

Nayar, Pramod. 2013. *Frantz Fanon*. London: Routledge.

Neiman, Paul George. 2017. Camus on Authenticity in Political Violence. *European Journal of Philosophy*. Online publication. DOI: 10.1111/ejop.12241

Neu, Jerome. 1988. Divided Minds: Sartre's 'Bad Faith' Critique of Freud. *The Review of Metaphysics* 42: 79–101.

Nietzsche, Freidrich. 1998. *Beyond Good and Evil: Prelude to a Philosophy of the Future*. Translated by Marion Faber. Oxford: Oxford University Press.

O'Brien, Conor Cruise. 1970. *Camus*. London: Fontana.

O'Donohoe, Benedict. 2005. *Sartre's Theatre: Acts for Life*. Bern: Peter Lang.

Orwell, George. 1948. Problem Picture: review of *Portrait of the Anti-Semite* by Jean-Paul Sartre. *The Observer*. 7 November: 5.

Parry, Benita. 1999. Resistance Theory/Theorizing Resistance or Two Cheers for Nativism. In *Rethinking Fanon: The Continuing Dialogue*, edited by Nigel C. Gibson, 215–50. Amherst NY: Humanity Books.

Pascoe, Elizabeth A. and Laura Smart Richman. 2009. Perceived Discrimination and Health: A Meta-Analytic Review. *Psychological Bulletin* 135: 531–54.

Pearce, Richard. 2014. Sexual Expression, Authenticity, and Bad Faith. In *Sexuality: Existential Perspectives*, edited by Martin Milton, 92–115. Monmouth: PCCS Books.

Pearce, Richard. 2016. The Liberation Psychologist: A Tribute to Jean-Paul Sartre. In *Therapy and the Counter-tradition: The Edge of Philosophy*, edited by Manu Bazzano and Julie Webb, 76–89. London: Routledge.

Pettersen, Tove. 2015. Existential Humanism and Moral Freedom in Simone de Beauvoir's Ethics. In *Simone de Beauvoir: A Humanist Thinker*, edited by Tove Pettersen and Annlaug Bjørsnøs, 69–91. Leiden: Koninklijke Brill.

Pitt, Rebecca. 2013. Play and Being in Jean-Paul Sartre's *Being and Nothingness*. In *The Philosophy of Play*, edited by Emily Ryall, Wendy Russell, and Malcolm Maclean, 109–19. New York: Routledge.

Poellner, Peter. 2015. Early Sartre on Freedom and Ethics. *European Journal of Philosophy* 23: 221–47.

Reath, Andrews. 1994. Legislating the Moral Law. *Noûs* 28: 435–64.

Reynolds, Jack. 2006. *Understanding Existentialism*. Durham: Acumen.

Rybalka, Michel. 1999. Publication and Reception of *Anti-Semite and Jew*. *October* 87: 161–82.

Sandford, Stella. 2006. *How To Read Beauvoir*. London: Granta.

Sartre, Jean-Paul. N. *Nausea*. Translated by Robert Baldick. Harmondsworth: Penguin, 1963. First published as *La Nausée* (Paris: Gallimard, 1938).

Sartre, Jean-Paul. STE. *Sketch for a Theory of the Emotions*. Translated by Philip Mairet. Second edition. London and New York: Routledge, 2002. First published as *Esquisse d'une Théorie des Emotions* (Paris: Hermann, 1939).

Sartre, Jean-Paul. IPPI. *The Imaginary: A Phenomenological Psychology of the Imagination*. Translated by Jonathan Webber. London: Routledge, 2004. Translation of *L'Imaginaire: Psychologie Phénoménologique de l'Imagination*, revised by Arlette Elkaïm-Sartre. Paris: Gallimard, 1986. Original edition published in 1940.

Sartre, Jean-Paul. OE. *The Outsider* Explained. In Jean-Paul Sartre, *Critical Essays (Situations I)*, translated by Chris Turner, 148–84. New York: Seagull Books, 2010. First published in *Cahiers du Sud* 19, no. 253 (1943): 189–206.

Sartre, Jean-Paul. B&N. *Being and Nothingness: An Essay on Phenomenological Ontology*. Translated by Hazel E. Barnes. Edited by Arlette Elkaïm-Sartre. London: Routledge, 2003. First published as *L'Être et le Néant: Essai d'Ontologie Phenomenologique* (Paris: Gallimard, 1943).

Sartre, Jean-Paul. HC. *Huis Clos*. Translated by Stuart Gilbert. In Jean-Paul Sartre, *Huis Clos and Other Plays*, 177–223. London: Penguin, 2000. First published as *Huis Clos* (Paris: Gallimard, 1944).

Sartre, Jean-Paul. AR. *The Age of Reason*. Translated by Eric Sutton. Harmondsworth: Penguin, 1986. First published as *L'Âge de Raison* (Paris: Gallimard, 1945).

Sartre, Jean-Paul. EH. *Existentialism Is A Humanism*. Translated by Carol Macomber. New Haven: Yale University Press, 2007. First published as *L'Existentialisme est une Humanisme* (Paris: Gallimard, 1946).

Sartre, Jean-Paul. A&J. *Anti-Semite and Jew*. Translated by George J. Becker. New York: Schocken Books, 1948. First published as *Réflections sur le Question Juive* (Paris: Gallimard, 1946).

Sartre, Jean-Paul. B. *Baudelaire*. Translated by Martin Turnell. New York: New Directions, 1950. First published as *Baudelaire* (Paris: Gallimard, 1946).

Sartre, Jean-Paul. BO. Black Orpheus. In *The Aftermath of War (Situations III)*, translated by Chris Turner, 259–329. Oxford: Seagull Books, 2008. First published as the introduction to Léopold Sédar Senghor, *Anthologies de la Nouvelle Poésie Nègre et Malgache* (Paris: Presses Universitaires de France, 1948).

Sartre, Jean-Paul. SG. *Saint Genet: Actor and Martyr*. Translated by Bernard Frechtman. Minneapolis: University of Minnesota Press, 2012. First published as *Saint Genet, comédien et martyr* (Paris: Gallimard, 1952).

Sartre, Jean-Paul. NE. No Exit. Transcript of a spoken preface that Sartre provided for a recording of the play published by the Deutsche Gramophone Company in 1965. Translated by Frank Jellinek. In *Sartre on Theatre*, edited by Michel Contat and Michel Rybalka, 198–201. London: Quartet Books, 1976.

Sherman, David. 2009. *Camus*. Chichester: Wiley-Blackwell.

Silverman, David. 2005. Reflections on the Human Question. In *Frantz Fanon's Black Skin, White Masks: New Interdisciplinary Essays*, edited by Max Silverman, 112–27. Manchester: University of Manchester Press.

Simons, Margaret. 1999. *Beauvoir and The Second Sex: Feminism, Race, and the Origins of Existentialism*. Lanham MD: Rowman and Littlefield.

Sirridge, Mary. 2003. Philosophy in Beauvoir's Fiction. In *The Cambridge Companion to Simone de Beauvoir*, edited by Claudia Card, 129–48. Cambridge: Cambridge University Press.

Smith, Colin. 1970. Sartre and Merleau-Ponty: The Case for a Modified Essentialism. *Journal of the British Society for Phenomenology* 1: 73–9.

Soll, Ivan. 1981. Sartre's Rejection of the Freudian Unconscious. In *The Philosophy of Jean-Paul Sartre*, edited by Paul Arthur Schilpp, 582–684. La Salle IL: Open Court, The Library of Living Philosophers.

Solomon, Robert C. 2006. *Dark Feelings, Grim Thoughts: Experience and Reflection in Camus and Sartre*. Oxford: Oxford University Press.

Spencer, Steven J., Claude M. Steele and Diane M. Quinn. 1999. Stereotype Threat and Women's Math Performance. *Journal of Experimental Social Psychology* 35: 4–28.

Stack, George and Robert Plant. 1982. The Phenomenon of 'The Look'. *Philosophy and Phenomenological Research* 42: 359–73.

Stewart, Jon. 1995. Merleau-Ponty's Criticisms of Sartre's Theory of Freedom. *Philosophy Today* 39: 311–24.

Stoet, Gijsbert and David C. Geary. 2012. Can Stereotype Threat Explain the Gender Gap in Mathematics Performance and Achievement? *Review of General Psychology* 16: 93–102.

Stone, Alison. 2017. Beauvoir and the Ambiguities of Motherhood. In *A Companion to Simone de Beauvoir*, edited by Laura Hengehold and Nancy Bauer, 122–33. Chichester: Wiley-Blackwell.
Taylor, Charles. 1976. Responsibility for Self. In *The Identities of Persons*, edited by Amelie Oksenberg Rorty, 281–99. Berkeley: University of California Press.
Thody, Philip. 1964. *Albert Camus, 1913–1960*. London: Hamish Hamilton.
Thody, Philip. 1981. Sartre and the Concept of Moral Action: The Example of his Novels and Plays. In *The Philosophy of Jean-Paul Sartre*, edited by Paul Arthur Schilpp, 422–37. La Salle IL: Open Court, The Library of Living Philosophers.
Thomas, Lennox. 2013. Empires of Mind: Colonial History and its Implications for Counselling and Psychotherapy. *Psychodynamic Practice* 19: 117–28.
Tidd, Ursula. 1999. *Simone de Beauvoir: Gender and Testimony*. Cambridge: Cambridge University Press.
Tidd, Ursula. 2004. *Simone de Beauvoir*. London: Routledge.
Tognieri, Ralf. 2013. Director's Notes. In *No Way Out (Huis Clos)*, production programme, 1–2. Bristol: Kelvin Players.
Vergès, Françoise. 2005. Where To Begin? 'Le commencement' in *Peau noire, masques blancs* and in Creolisation. In *Frantz Fanon's Black Skin, White Masks: New Interdisciplinary Essays*, edited by Max Silverman, 32–45. Manchester: University of Manchester Press.
Warnock, Mary. 1967. *Existentialist Ethics*. London: Macmillan.
Webber, Jonathan. 2009. *The Existentialism of Jean-Paul Sartre*. New York: Routledge.
Webber, Jonathan. 2011. Bad Faith and the Other. In *Reading Sartre: On Phenomenology and Existentialism*, edited by Jonathan Webber, 180–94. Abingdon: Routledge.
Webber, Jonathan. 2015. Character, Attitude and Disposition. *European Journal of Philosophy* 23: 1082–96.
Webber, Jonathan. 2016a. Instilling Virtue. In *From Personality to Virtue: Essays on the Philosophy of Character*, edited by Alberto Masala and Jonathan Webber, 134–54. Oxford: Oxford University Press.
Webber, Jonathan. 2016b. Knowing One's Own Desires. In *Philosophy of Mind and Phenomenology: Conceptual and Empirical Approaches*, edited by Daniel Dahlstrom, Andreas Elpidorou, and Walter Hopp, 165–79. New York: Routledge.
Webber, Jonathan. 2017. Habituation and First-Person Authority. In *Time and the Philosophy of Action*, edited by Roman Altshuler and Michael Sigrist, 189–204. New York: Routledge.
Webber, Jonathan. 2018. Sartre's Transcendental Phenomenology. In *The Oxford Handbook of the History of Phenomenology*, edited by Dan Zahavi, 286–301. Oxford: Oxford University Press.
Webber, Jonathan. Forthcoming. Sartre's Critique of Husserl. Under review.

Whitford, Margaret. 1979. Merleau-Ponty's Critique of Sartre's Philosophy: An Interpretive Account. *French Studies* 33: 305–18.

Wider, Kathleen. 1999. The Self and Others: Imitation in Infants and Sartre's Analysis of The Look. *Continental Philosophy Review* 32: 195–210.

Wiedorn, Michael. 2017. On Rereading Mayotte Capécia Today. *Women in French Studies* 25: 29–40.

Wilkerson, William. 2010. Time and Ambiguity: Reassessing Merleau-Ponty on Sartrean Freedom. *Journal of the History of Philosophy* 48: 207–34.

Witt, Charlotte. 2013. Gender Essentialism: Aristotle or Locke? In *Powers and Capacities in Philosophy: The New Aristotelianism*, edited by Ruth Groff and John Greco, 308–18. London and New York: Routledge.

Wollstonecraft, Mary. 1792. *A Vindication of the Rights of Woman: With Strictures on Political and Moral Subjects*. London: Joseph Johnson.

World Health Organization. ICD-10. *International Statistical Classification of Diseases and Related Health Problems*. Tenth revision. Geneva: World Health Organization, 1992.

Young, Iris Marion. 1980. Throwing like a Girl: A Phenomenology of Feminine Body Comportment Motility and Spatiality. *Human Studies* 3: 137–56.

Index

All works by Sartre and Beauvoir and the works of Camus, Fanon, and Merleau-Ponty that receive extended discussion are indexed by title. Other works are indexed under the author's name. *n* = footnote.

absurdity
　origins 152–4
　in *The Outsider* 24–9, 32, 38, 153
　problem(s) of 152, 154–6, 157, 158, 163–4, 165, 167, 176, 179
accessibility, of mental items 193–4
Adler, Alfred 85*n*
Adventures of the Dialectic (Merleau-Ponty) 55
　critique of Sartre 39–40, 42–3, 44, 56
The Age of Reason (Sartre) 42, 53
　compared with *She Came to Stay* 66–7
agency, human/rational
　Kantian analysis 173–5
　objective value 185–6
alienation 12–13
Anti-Semite and Jew (Sartre) 10–11, 116–18, 121, 124–5, 128, 130, 138, 166
　arguments for authenticity 11–13, 19, 163–4, 165, 166–8
　in Beauvoir's work 170–2, 175–87
　conditional 179–80
　restrictions on 178–9
　weaknesses 189–90
Aristotle 3, 8, 11, 12, 71, 165, 192–3
Aronson, Ronald 20, 37
Arp, Kristana 183
Asperger syndrome 204*n*
attitudes 193
authenticity viii, 169–87
　vs. bad faith (inauthenticity) 119–22, 164, 165
　defined 152
　moral component 166
　and race 119–20, 130
　and social conditioning 189–92
　see also arguments for authenticity
autism 204–5, 204*n*

bad faith vii, 34–5*n*, 48–9, 84–7, 205–6
　centrality to Sartrean existentialism 123–5
　dramatic treatments 107–12
　effect on self-image 10, 12
　and other people 10, 109–12
　as project 121–3
　racial/cultural sources 118–22, 124–5
　reasons for adoption 122–5
　vs. sedimentation 114–16
Baert, Patrick 116
Bakewell, Sarah 5, 75
Barnes, Hazel 59, 74
Barrett, William 15
Baudelaire, Charles 89, 129*n*
Baudelaire (Sartre) 89, 129*n*
Beauvoir, Simone de 2*n*
　argument for authenticity 170–2, 175–87
　autobiographical elements of work 57, 65–6
　psychological theory 7–9, 195, 198–9
　relationship with Merleau-Ponty 39, 44, 75 (*see also under* Merleau-Ponty, Maurice)
　see also differences between Sartre and Beauvoir; *titles of works*
Being and Nothingness (Sartre) vii, 5, 6–7*n*, 8, 57, 71, 78, 89, 95, 140*n*, 192, 204
　on absurdity 153–4
　on bad faith 122
　critique of Freudian theory 82, 84, 85–9, 95, 128
　on freedom 40–2, 48–9, 51, 55–6, 65–6, 68, 200
　on inter-personal relations 109–10, 111, 148*n*
　on mental states 196, 197
　on physical objects/reasons 43–4, 45–6, 48, 51–2

Being and Nothingness (Sartre) (*cont.*)
  terminology 45–6
Ben-Zeev, Talia 198
Bergoffen, Debra 74
Bernasconi, Robert 97, 139*n*, 143, 158
Bhabha, Homi 132–3, 134, 135, 148–9
bias, implicit 197–9
'Black Orpheus' (Sartre) 129–30, 138–9, 140*n*
Black Skin, White Masks (Fanon) viii, 11, 14, 131–50, 188, 195, 201, 202
  common themes with Beauvoir 146–7
  critical analyses 132–4, 148*n*
  existentialist elements 132, 135–6, 145–50, 151–2, 199–200
  genesis/publication 131
  (lack of) structure 132–4
  open-endedness 144–5, 148–9
  prose style 132
  psychiatric content/objectives 132–3, 140–1, 148–9, 150, 199
  terminology 134–5, 136
  treatment of 'mask' motif 135–7
Blackham, H. J. 15*n*
body, identification of individual with 200–1
Brown, Lee 84
Butler, Judith 92

Camus, Albert vii, 2*n*, 19, 95, 154
  differences with Sartre 20–1, 37–8, 131
  ethical theory 36–7
  'On Jean-Paul Sartre's *La Nausée*' 30, 65
  opposition to existentialism 4, 6, 14, 33–5
  Sartre's/Beauvoir's comments on 14
  The Myth of Sisyphus 24–6, 29, 30, 34, 35*n*, 153
  The Rebel 32, 36–7, 131–2
  see also *The Outsider*
Capécia, Mayotte 132, 203
Caute, David 135
Césaire, Aimé 132
childhood, role in formation of individual 89–90, 91, 123, 124–6, 128–9, 129*n*, 188, 194
'The Childhood of a Leader' (Sartre) 129*n*

Chisholm, Diane 114
Christianity, compatibility with existentialism 2–3
collective unconscious 140–1
colonialism 33, 132
  indigenous peoples' responses to 134–42
Communism 39
The Communists and Peace (Sartre) 39, 56
conflict, role in human relations 110–12
Cooper, David E. 15, 78, 110
Cox, Gary 97
Crenshaw, Kimberlé 203
Crowell, Steven 9

definition of existentialism 1–19
  canonical features 2, 6, 14, 40, 151, 188
  evolution 1–2
  first expression 2–3
  historical divergences 1–2, 4–5, 9, 188–9
  need for reappraisal 16–18
  (perceived) difficulty/diversity of 15, 15*n*
  see also differences between Sartre and Beauvoir
'degradation', use of term 69, 190, 191–2
Descartes, René/Cartesianism 79–81, 84, 87
  'cogito' argument 32–3, 171–2
  critiqued by/compared with Beauvoir 92, 171–2, 175
despair 159–62
Detmer, David 97
Deutscher, Penelope 74
differences between Sartre and Beauvoir vii, 2, 17–18, 34, 74
  on form of existentialism 71–3, 78–9, 95, 113–14, 123–4, 125*n*
  on freedom 4–5, 9–10, 56, 65–70, 93
  on projects/commitment 65–7
  on psychoanalysis 77
  resolution viii, 113, 114, 116, 125, 127
Dostoevsky, Fyodor 89
dreams, symbolic meaning 93–4
Dreyfus, Hubert 15*n*

Earnshaw, Steven 15*n*
ends, value of 175–82
  arguments establishing 175–7, 181–2
  need for extensiveness 183–5

incompatibility with suppression of
  objective values 178
 as potential means 178-9, 181-3
Eshleman, Matthew 48, 68-9
essence
 preceded by existence 4-6, 7, 33-4,
  188
 (problems of) definition 3
 teleological definition 3-4
The Ethics of Ambiguity
  (Beauvoir) 170-1, 183, 187
L'Étranger (Camus) see *The Outsider*
eudaimonism viii, 12-13, 156-68
 and arguments for
  authenticity 11-13, 19, 163-4,
  165-8
 and despair 159-62
 limitations 163-5, 189-90
 and other people 162-3
 and racial theory 156-9
'exigency', in Sartrean terminology 45-6
existentialism
 Anglophone studies 15, 15*n*, 17*n*
 as basis of literary analysis 205-7
 coinage of term vii
 future directions 202-5
 and humanism 11-14
 and other people 9-11
 and psychoanalysis 8-9, 17, 194-202
 and social meanings 199-202
 see also definition of existentialism
'Existentialism and Popular Wisdom'
  (Beauvoir) 2-3, 60
'Existentialism Is A Humanism'
  (Sartre) 2, 3-4, 18, 35, 41, 53,
  166-8, 173*n*
'existentialist', label affixed to
  thinkers 14, 16

The Family Idiot (Sartre) 89
Fanon, Frantz vii, 2*n*, 12, 195, 199, 207
 biographical background 131
 commonalities with Beauvoir 146-8
 critique of/differences with
  Sartre 138-40, 139*n*, 140*n*, 144*n*,
  146, 147-8
 'Essai sur la désalienation du
  Noir' 131
 'The North African Syndrome' 135
 The Wretched of the Earth 132, 145
 see also *Black Skin, White Masks*

fiction, as vehicle for existentialist
 thought 57-8, 205-6
Flaubert, Gustave 89
Fletchman Smith, Barbara 202*n*
Flore, Paulette C. 198
Flynn, Thomas 15*n*
Foley, John 29, 33
The Force of Circumstance
  (Beauvoir) 179-80*n*, 187
freedom
 centrality to existentialist theory 6, 40
 disagreements over 4-5, 9-10
 influence of other people 9-10
 interpretations of Sartrean view 51
 Merleau-Ponty's critiques of Sartrean
  view 39-40, 42-4, 49-51, 53,
  70-1
 metaphysical (ontological) 6, 6-7*n*,
  190-2
 objective value 51-2
 oversimplification of Sartrean view 40
 'radical' 4-5, 49, 66-7, 87-9, 125*n*,
  200
 and reasons 48-9
 relationship with voluntary
  action 40-2
 Sartre's *vs.* Beauvoir's views 4-5,
  9-10, 56, 65-7
 without reasons 50-2
Freud, Sigmund/Freudian theory 8-9,
  17, 19, 76-94, 200-1, 202*n*
 Beauvoir's commentary/
  similarities 89-90, 91, 93-4
 compared with Descartes 79-81, 87
 compared with existentialism 80-1,
  86-9, 134
 and development of sexuality 89-90
 Fanon's critique of 140-1
 and repression 77-8
 resistance to diagnosis/
  treatment 86-8
 Sartre's critique of 82-4, 85-9, 128
 superego, theory of 83, 85, 126
 terminology 82-3
 The Ego and the Id 77-8, 82-4
 'The Unconscious' 77-8
Fullbrook, Edward/Kate 74

Ganley, Colleen M. 198-9
Gardner, Sebastian 77, 167
Geary, David C. 198-9

gender theory 9, 11, 89–94, 198–9
  linked with race 146–7, 203
  and stereotyping 198
Genet, Jean 11, 18, 125–9
  'conversion' to criminality 126–7
  early life/upbringing 125–6, 129n, 202
  as exemplar of sedimentation 126–7, 128–9
Gilbert, Margaret 42
God, 'desire to be' 34–5n
Gordon, Lewis 133–4, 137, 147, 149
Grimsley, Ronald 15n

Haddour, Azzedine 120, 129, 137, 144n
Hall, Stuart 133, 149
Harman, Gilbert 42
Hausman, Alan 84
Heath, Jane 58, 59, 64
Heidegger, Martin 2n, 201
  as 'existentialist' 14
  Being and Time 7, 8, 16
  'Letter on Humanism' 8
  terminology 16
Howells, Christina 5, 66–7n, 110
Hudis, Peter 148n
Huis Clos (Sartre) vii, 10, 95–112, 148n
  character development 103–5, 103–9, 107–8
  characterization 96–8, 100–2, 108–9
  eschatological setting 98–100, 105–6, 109
  existentialist message 106–7, 108–9, 112
  genesis 95
  as political allegory 95–6
  production history 95–6
  Sartre's comments on 105–6, 112
  title 98–9
  treatment of bad faith 107–12
  treatment of self-image 96–8
human nature
  Camus' theory of 4, 6, 34–5, 36n
  denial of (as absolute) 4, 12–13, 151
  and morality/solidarity 36–7
humanism 11–14, 166–8
Hume, David 50, 51, 53–4
Husserl, Edmund 47

The Imaginary: A Phenomenological Psychology of the Imagination (Sartre) 7

immanence 69, 190–1, 191n
inauthenticity *see under* authenticity
inferiority complex 50, 76, 85–6, 85n
  differing conceptions 114–15
  and gender 90–1, 93
  and race 135, 136, 139–42, 144–5, 158, 201
interiorization 71, 88, 202–3
Inzlicht, Michael 198

James, Susan 17n, 93n, 162n
Jaspers, Karl 16n
Jeanson, Francis 37, 131–2
Jewish people/culture 10–11, 116–18, 121, 124, 130
  cultural identity 117–18
Joseph, Felicity 15n
Judy, Ronald 144n, 147, 157
Jung, Carl Gustav 140–1

Kafka, Franz, *The Trial* 105n
Kant, Immanuel 12, 13–14, 18, 166, 169, 170–2, 185–7, 193
  arguments compared with Beauvoir's 172, 175, 186
  Groundwork for the Metaphysics of Morals 13, 173–5, 175n
Kaufman, Walter 15, 16, 17
Kierkegaard, Søren 16, 16n, 17n
King, Adele 23
Kirkpatrick, Kate 17n
knowledge, sedimentation of 6, 62, 71
Korsgaard, Christine 173–4, 175, 181, 184
Kripke, Saul 3
Kruks, Sonia 67–70, 72, 74, 93, 144n, 146

Landau, Iddo 163
Langer, Monika 74
Laredo, Joseph 23n
Le Doeuff, Michèle 74, 93
Lee, Christopher 133, 137
L'Étranger (Camus) see *The Outsider*
'Literature and Metaphysics' (Beauvoir) 57–8, 60, 69, 73

Macey, David 140, 149
Macquarrie, John 15n
Malpas, Jeff 17n
Martin, Andy 20

Masters, Brian 31*n*
McBride, William 15
McInerney, Peter 53
means *see under* ends
Merleau-Ponty, Maurice vii, 2*n*, 5–6, 19, 39–56, 91, 147, 201
 Beauvoir's critiques of 39, 44, 55–6, 67, 128
 commentary on *She Came to Stay* 57, 58–62, 75
 critiques of Sartre 6, 39–40, 42–4, 49–51, 53, 54–5, 62, 66, 70–1, 125*n*, 190
 friendship with Beauvoir/Sartre 39, 44, 56
 'Metaphysics and the Novel' 57, 58–60
 political stance 39
 theory of reasons 46–7
 see also *Adventures of the Dialectic*; *The Phenomenology of Perception*
'Merleau-Ponty and Pseudo-Sartreanism' (Beauvoir) 44, 55–6, 67, 128
'metamorphosis', use of term 126
Mischel, Walter 194
Moi, Toril 64–5
Montaigne, Michel de 171
Monty Python's Flying Circus (TV) 178
Moran, Richard 196–7
Morris, Phyllis Sutton 42
Moser, Susanne 183
motherhood 206
motivation 193
 abnormalities 204–5
 sedimentation of 6, 61–2
Murdoch, Iris 18, 170

Nagel, Thomas 24, 154–6, 163
Nausea (Sartre) 20, 45*n*, 152–3
 Camus' review of 30, 65
 compared with *Being and Nothingness* 44, 45, 153
 compared with *The Outsider* 30, 31
Nayar, Pramod 135
Negritude movement 137–9, 141–2, 144
 Fanon's critique of 137–8, 139, 143, 144*n*
 objectives 137
 Sartre's analysis of 138–40, 139*n*, 144*n*, 206–7

Neiman, Paul George 36*n*
Neu, Jerome 80
Nietzsche, Friedrich 171
nihilism
 in *The Outsider* 26
 rejection of 28, 29, 32–3

O'Brien, Conor Cruise 33
O'Donohue, Benedict 97
Orwell, George 124, 130
other people 9–11, 162–3
 individual's responses to views held by 9–10
The Outsider (Camus) vii, 20–38, 54–5
 absurdist elements 24–9, 38, 153
 anti-existentialist elements 33–5
 Beauvoir's commentary 29, 30
 Camus' commentary 22, 33
 Cartesian elements 32–3
 character development 26–9, 31*n*, 32–3
 characterization 21–4, 31
 Sartre's review/comments 20, 37–8
 translations 23*n*
 treatment of colonialism 33
 treatment of human nature 33–5

Paris, Nazi occupation of 95–6
Parry, Benita 144*n*
Pascoe, Elizabeth A. 199
Pearce, Richard 200, 204
Pettersen, Tove 170*n*
phenomenology 6
The Phenomenology of Perception (Merleau-Ponty) 46–7, 60–2
 Beauvoir's review of 55, 63, 67, 71
 critique of Sartre 6, 43–4, 54–6, 190
Pitt, Rebecca 164
Plant, Robert 110–12
Poellner, Peter 48, 51–2, 54, 167, 173
'point of departure', concept of 175–6
power, distinguished from freedom 192
The Prime of Life (Beauvoir) 179–80*n*
projects 6, 7–8
 commitment to 52–4, 63–4, 65–7, 113–14, 127
 (difficulty of) alteration/abandonment 41–2, 50, 52–3, 55
 freedom (not) to pursue 49
 influence on perceptions 43–4
 orientation to specific end 41–2

projects (cont.)
  origins of 60
  and potential 204
  role in formation of character/
    experience 12, 29–31, 85
  sedimentation of 9, 11, 60–2, 71–2,
    125n
psychoanalysis see Freudian theory
psychology 7–9, 192–7
  and accessibility 193–4
  and attitudes 193
  centrality to existentialist thought 195
  cognitive–affective system
    model 194–5
  and motivation 193
  and self-knowledge 196–7
  social 192–4
  see also Freudian theory
psychotherapy 199–202, 202n
Pyrrhus and Cineas (Beauvoir) 13, 18,
    60, 78, 168
  on absurdity 154
  on authenticity 170–2, 175, 183–4,
    185–7, 189
  commentary on Camus 29, 30, 35–6
  compared with *She Came to
    Stay* 73–4
  on freedom/power 68–9, 70, 192

Quinn, Diane M. 198

racial theory viii, 11, 12, 131–50, 201,
    206–7
  and bad faith 118–20
  linked with gender 146–7, 203
  and sedimentation 129–30
  and stereotyping 197–9
  see also *Black Skin, White Masks*;
    Jewish people/culture
rational meaning, search for 34, 34–5n
reasons 45–7
  Merleau-Ponty's account of 46–7
  phenomenology of 47–8, 55
  Sartre's account of 45–6
Reath, Andrews 186
reflection, pure vs. impure 47–8
'A Review of *The Phenomenology of
    Perception*' (Beauvoir) 55, 63, 67,
    68, 71
revolution see violence, political
Reynolds, Jack 15n

Richman, Laura Smart 199
Rybalka, Michel 116

Saint Genet (Sartre) viii, 11, 14, 18, 56,
    125–9, 146, 151, 188, 195, 199–200,
    202, 204, 206
Sandford, Stella 171, 179, 183
Sartre, Jean-Paul 1–2, 2n
  definition of 'essence' 3–4
  on 'desire to be God' 34–5n
  fictionalized representations 65–7
  political theory 37–8
  psychological theory 7–9, 195
  realignment of existentialist
    outlook viii, 2, 113, 114, 116, 125,
    127, 128–9, 195–6, 200–1, 206–7
  relationship with Camus 20–1, 37–8
  see also differences between Sartre and
    Beauvoir; titles of works
The Second Sex (Beauvoir) vii, 5, 9, 11,
    60, 78–9, 126, 128, 129n, 130, 147,
    151, 188, 199–200, 206
  on freedom 69, 190–2
  psychological theory 77, 89–94, 95,
    195, 200–1, 202–3
  terminology 69, 190–2
sedimentation 5–6, 113–30, 199–200,
    203, 205–6
  vs. bad faith 114–16, 123–4
  as character formation 192–4
  and gender 91–2, 93–4, 127
  of knowledge 6, 62, 71
  of motives 6, 61–2
  of projects 9, 11, 60–2, 71–2, 125n
  and racial/cultural values 129
  Sartre's acceptance of 114, 125, 127,
    130, 195–6, 199–200, 206–7
self-knowledge, theory of 196–7
Senghor, Leopold 132, 138
sexuality 204
She Came to Stay (Beauvoir) vii, 5,
    57–75, 95, 128, 151
  autobiographical elements 65–6
  characterization 58–60, 63–5
  critique of Sartre 65–7
  Merleau-Ponty's commentary
    57–62, 75
  metaphysical elements 58–60, 64–5
  relationship with theoretical
    works 73–5
  studies 67–70

Sherman, David 22–3, 32, 35*n*
Shoda, Yuichi 194
Silverman, Max 120, 139*n*, 144*n*
Simons, Margaret 129*n*
Sirridge, Mary 65
situation(s), impact on individual freedom 43–4, 50–2, 54–6, 67–70
Sketch for a Theory of Emotions (Sartre) 45*n*
slavery 178, 190, 202*n*
  role in black consciousness 129–30
Smith, Colin 40
Smith, Sandra 23*n*
solidarity, theory of 36–7
Soll, Ivan 80
Solomon, Robert C. 15, 16, 17, 22–3, 35*n*, 97, 103
Spencer, Steven J. 198
Stack, George 110–12
Steele, Claude M. 198
stereotypes 197–9
Stewart, Jon 43
Stoet, Gijsbert 198–9
Stoic philosophy 17*n*
Stone, Alison 191*n*
superego, theory of 83, 85, 126
symbolism 93–4

Taylor, Charles 53
teleology 3–4
Les Temps Modernes (periodical) 20, 39, 43*n*, 116
Thody, Philip 31*n*, 105, 167–8

Thomas, Lennox 202
Tidd, Ursula 74, 183
Tognieri, Ralf 102
'transcendence', use of term 69, 190–2

Vergès, Françoise 144*n*, 146
violence, political 35–8
  Camus' views on 36–7
  Sartre's views on 37–8

The Wall (Sartre) 20
Warnock, Mary 15*n*
Whitford, Margaret 44, 62*n*
Wicherts, Jelte M. 198
Wider, Kathleen 110
Wiedorn, Michael 203
Wilkerson, William 43, 50
Witt, Charlotte 3
Wollstonecraft, Mary 96
women 89–94
  complicity in own oppression 92–3, 93*n*
  social/psychological conditioning 89–91, 114, 191–2, 191*n*, 206
  social stereotyping 198–9
World War Two *see* Paris, Nazi occupation of
Wright, Richard 118, 132

Young, Iris Marion 114, 190

Zeno of Elea 154

Printed and bound by CPI Group (UK) Ltd, Croydon, CR0 4YY